Items should be be returned to the library from which they were borrowed on or before the date stamped above, unless a renewal has been granted.

 **SWINDON** BOROUGH COUNCIL

SBC.LIB 02

The Mysterious

MISS MARIE CORELLI

For my father, Tom Ridsdill Smith

Fame is a vapour; popularity is an accident. The only earthly certainty is oblivion.
Mark Twain

Nearly all bookish people are snobs, and especially the more enlightened among them. They are apt to assume that if a writer has immense circulation, if he is enjoyed by plain persons, and if he can still fill several theatres at once, he cannot possibly be worth reading and merits only indifference and disdain.
Arnold Bennett, *Evening Standard*, 19 July 1928

Authorship is not so much a function of the brain as it is of the heart. And the heart is a universal organ.
Gilbert Frankau, *Daily Mail*, 1926

Remember that if you do persuade yourselves into thinking I am a Somebody, and if I turn out after all to be a Nobody, it is not my fault. Don't blame me; blame your own self-deception. Inasmuch as it is necessary in my case to bear in mind that the Name is not the Person.
Marie Corelli, *The Silver Domino*, 1892

The Mysterious

MISS MARIE CORELLI

*Queen of Victorian
Bestsellers*

Teresa Ransom

SUTTON PUBLISHING

First published in the United Kingdom in 1999 by
Sutton Publishing Limited · Phoenix Mill
Thrupp · Stroud · Gloucestershire · GL5 2BU

British Library Cataloguing in Publication Data
A catalogue record for this book is available from the British Library.

ISBN 0-7509-1570-6

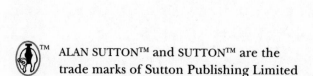 ALAN SUTTON™ and SUTTON™ are the
trade marks of Sutton Publishing Limited

Typeset in 10/13 pt New Baskerville.
Typesetting and origination by
Sutton Publishing Limited.
Printed in Great Britain by
MPG Books, Bodmin, Cornwall.

Contents

Plates

Acknowledgements

I would like to thank many people in Stratford-upon-Avon for their help and enthusiasm in this quest to unravel the mystery of Marie Corelli. Special thanks to Dr Robert Bearman, Mairi McDonald, Eileen Alberti and all at the Shakespeare Birthplace Trust Record Office for their encouragement and help in unearthing documents, suggesting sources and providing photographs. I would like to thank Annie Davis's great-nephew, John Wells, for allowing me to read the Annie Davis Collection, giving me permission to use her photograph and to quote from her poems, and to thank Annie Davis's niece, Miss M.A. Brown, for giving me much useful background information on the family. Daphne Ingram kindly showed me around Mason Croft, which helped me to place Marie in her own setting. She also allowed me to take photographs.

Mrs Mary Turner at the Dorking and District Museum was very helpful with cuttings and early records of life in and around Fern Dell, and the Guildford Record Office helped me to try and track down Marie Corelli's origins. The British Library in London has kindly given me permission to quote from the Bentley Papers, and in Scotland I wish to thank the Trustees of the National Library of Scotland for permission to quote from books and manuscripts in their care.

In Los Angeles, I must thank the Department of Special Collections, Charles E. Young Research Library, at UCLA, for allowing me to quote from letters in their archives. Also Diana and Peter Moriarty for their help and hospitality. In New York I was given generous access to and permission to quote from manuscripts in the Marie Corelli archives in the Berg Collection of English and American Literature at the New York Public Library, Astor, Lenox and Tilden Foundations. I also wish to thank Laurie Guilfoyle for her encouragement and generosity.

In Australia I would like to thank Jessica Adams for an illuminating horoscope of Marie Corelli based on her given birth date. And of course a very special thank you to my three children, without whose help and support this book would never have been finished.

Sydney and Cambridge, 1999

The Enigma of Marie Corelli

Marie Corelli, the author, a household name in 1900, was not the person her adoring public believed her to be. She lived under a false name and gave a false date of birth; she invented her past and declared her parents to be variously Italian, American or Scottish, and she had a single burning ambition. Early in her life she had written 'I have made up my mind to be "somebody" and I'll be as unlike anybody else as I can.' In this she was entirely successful. Her first book, published in 1886, *A Romance of Two Worlds*, was written when she was thirty-one years old and it set a pattern for all subsequent publications when it was condemned by the critics but devoured by an appreciative public. Her heroines stayed eternally young (as did Marie who told her publisher she was seventeen) and were beautiful, pure and good. During the next thirty-eight years she wrote a further thirty books and, with the publication of *The Sorrows of Satan* in 1895, became the top-selling author in Britain. She was the acknowledged 'Queen of the Victorian Bestsellers', but her readers never suspected that her greatest work of fiction was her own life. What the public didn't know was that hiding behind the posing and the arrogance was a woman who had a shameful and unmentionable past. Marie Corelli was in reality Mary Mills or Minnie Mackay, illegitimate, exceptionally short, opinionated and with memories of an impoverished and miserable childhood. Marie Corelli, the beautiful and popular novelist, was entirely self-created and she fought savagely to protect her image, reacting fiercely when it was threatened.

Marie's fans were legion and ranged from Queen Victoria, who insisted that she be sent a copy of every new book, down to the poorest of shop girls. She created a unique field of pseudo-Christian fantasy for an age which was obsessed by table rapping and spiritualism, and became the leading exponent of the uplifting novel, which denounced corruption and pointed the way to an idealised world. She wrote with such fierce passion about real and imagined wrongs, about heaven and hell, about joy and despair, that she swept her readers along in a torrent of emotion. Unlike earlier 'literary' writers who wrote for a more intellectual public,

Marie wrote, as she said, 'directly from her heart to the hearts of the people'. She wrote herself out of the misery of her childhood into the glorious freedom of make-believe, and carried along with her not only the romantics of all ages and every class, but the masses of ordinary people who only became literate when compulsory education was introduced in 1876. She transported her readers to utopian planets where the good were rewarded and the evil punished, all so unlike the grim reality of Victorian England.

In the rapidly changing times of the late nineteenth century, Marie Corelli's books reflected the concerns of her readers. She preached against corruption in the Church and deplored the worldliness and lack of faith of the priests. In 'Society and Sunday', she declared that Sunday was being ignored. Cards and gambling or motoring were much to blame, and it was largely the fault of the clergy, who were out of touch with modern thought and science. 'They fail to seize the problems of the time. They forget, or wilfully ignore the discoveries of the age, yet in these could be found endless subject matter for the divinist arguments. Religion and Science viewed broadly do not clash so much as they combine. To the devout and deeply studious mind, the marvels of science are the truths of religion made manifest. Society sees for itself that too many clerics are either blatant or timorous. Some of them bully; others crawl. None of them seems to be able to cope with the great dark wave of infidelity and atheism which has swept over the modern world, stealthily, but overwhelmingly, sucking many a struggling soul down into the depths of suicidal despair.'[1]

Marie was also a strong feminist, believing that women should have more power and recognition and should be considered the equals of men, yet at the same time she felt that woman's place was in the home and strongly disapproved of the suffragettes, calling them 'Ladies who scream'. In 'The Advance of Women' she admonishes, 'There is one thing that women generally, in the struggle for intellectual free life, should always remember – one thing they are too often and too apt to forget – namely, that the laws, as they at present exist, are made *by* men, *for* men. There are no really stringent laws on the protection of women's interests except the Married Women's Property Act, which is a great and needful boon.' Women should be in medicine, law and education, said Marie: 'One welcomes heartily the idea of women lawyers, in the hope that when their keen, quick brains learn to grasp the huge, unwieldy and complex machinery in the middle called Justice, they may, perhaps, be able to effect some reforms on behalf of their own sex.'[2] She derided the power of the press; the indiscriminate way in which reporters used stories for their own ends, and the intrusive harassment of press photographers. She had a tilt at journalism. 'Is not Journalism free? Not so . . . it is not the "voice of the people" at all; it is simply the voice of a few editors. Were the most gifted man that ever held pen to write a letter to any of the papers on a crying subject of national shame, he would be refused a hearing unless he were a friend of the proprietors of whatever journal he elected to write to. And men of genius seldom are friends of editors – a curious fact, but true.'[3]

She was bitter about the exclusiveness of London society, repressively controlled by a few peeresses who restricted entrance into the hallowed circle to a chosen few. 'The balance of things is becoming alarmingly unequal; the "aristocratic" set are a scandal to the world with their divorce cases, their bankruptcies, their laxity of principle, their listless indifference to consequences; they never read, they never learn, they never appear to see anything beyond themselves. Whereas the "bas-peuple" *are* reading, and reading the books that have helped to make national destinies – they *are* learning, and they are not afraid to express opinions. They do not think a Duke who seduces his friend's wife merely "unfortunate" – they call him in plain language a low blackguard.'[4] She deplored the vulgarity of wealth, epitomised by Andrew Carnegie: 'Millionaires are for the most part ill-mannered and illiterate, and singularly uninteresting in their conversation.' A staunch conservationist, she disliked the American bounder who 'comes to Great Britain with the fixed impression that everything in the "doomed old place" can be bought for money. Unfortunately he is often right. . . . Famous estates are knocked down to him – manuscripts and pictures, which should be the preciously guarded property of the nation, are easily purchased by him, – and laughing in his sleeve at the purblind apathy of the British Government, which calmly looks on while he pockets such relics of national greatness as unborn generations will vainly and indignantly ask for, – he congratulates himself on possessing, as he says, "the only few things that the old country has got left worth having".'[5]

Not only were manuscripts and pictures for sale, but, it seems, titles: 'there is always a British title going a-begging, always some decayed or degenerate semi-drunken peer, whose fortunes are on the verge of black ruin, ready and willing to devour, monster-like, the holocaust of an American virgin, provided bags of bullion are flung with her, into his capacious maw. . . . New blood – fresh sap, is sorely needed to invigorate the grand old tree of the British aristocracy, which has of late been looking sadly as though dry rot were setting in, – as though the woodlice were at work in its heart, and the rats burrowing in its root.'[6] She railed against the dangers of Demon Drink, the harmful effects of adulterated liquor, and the subsequent ruination and degradation of the addict. More and more Marie began to see herself as a moral crusader – a veiled prophetess – a preserver of the past.

As Marie's fame increased the 'sweet young girl' became more opinionated and autocratic. Hungry for recognition she wrote her own publicity notices and sent them to the newspapers, insisting that they be published without any alteration. In this she was not alone; books could be 'boomed' (promoted) for money, as she showed later in her novels. And yet, while seeking publicity in the newspapers, she hid from photographers and refused to have her picture taken, fearful of being seen as she was. Her eccentricities became legendary. She argued with critics; refused to send them copies of her latest book and trained her Yorkshire terrier to tear up their reviews. For though she wanted critical acclaim, she insisted it be on her own terms. When she lived in Stratford-upon-Avon, to the astonishment of the locals, she imported a Venetian gondola, complete with Venetian gondolier in full regalia, to transport her on the River Avon. She always hid the secret of her shameful birth by so confusing the facts of her early life that it was impossible for any prying journalist to expose her as a bastard. In later life she always dropped at least ten years from her age, probably as much to cover the immorality of her birth as for reasons of vanity, and dressed in clothes which were unsuitably young.

To disguise her lack of inches she always wore a dress with a long train and stood on a raised dais to greet her guests. For these affectations she became the butt of ill-natured jokes and sometimes an object of ridicule. She is acknowledged to be the model for Lucia, her friend E.F. Benson's character in the *Mapp and Lucia* books. Marie never married, but shared her house and her life with Bertha van der Vyver, her devoted companion, who provided stability and love and managed the household while Marie wrote.

Her novels reflect the vast changes from Victorian rigidity to Edwardian opulence. In her lifetime education became universal, the Church lost much of its power, and science produced Charles Darwin, electricity, telephones, x-rays and the motor car. In Marie Corelli's novels these changes, many of which she deplored, are the driving force for her characters. Viewed in the context of her time her books assume a new importance. They cover the changes from George Eliot, Charles Dickens and Anthony Trollope to H.G. Wells, Rider Haggard and Ethel M. Dell, and she has her own impassioned message for her readers. 'The power of the pen remains, even in these days, the greatest power for good and evil in the world. With the little instrument which rests so lightly in the hand, whole nations can be moved. It is nothing to look at; generally speaking it is a mere bit of wood with a nib at the end of it – but when it is poised between thumb and finger, it becomes a living thing – it moves with the pulsations of the loving heart and thinking brain, and writes down, almost unconsciously, the thoughts that live – the words that burn. This is a phase of the power of the pen – to make the beautiful, the quaint, the terrible, or the wonderful things of the imagination seem an absolute reality.'[7]

'WHO WAS MARIE CORELLI?' shrieked the news headlines after she died in 1924, but her past was obscured by such a fog of lies and deceit that it was impossible to discover. After her death her obituaries reflected the controversial attitudes the press held about her, but even the least charitable conceded that she had been immensely popular.

Daily Telegraph, 22 April 1924

What were the qualities with which Marie Corelli was endowed? The first was an extremely powerful imagination; the second an inventive faculty, occasionally melodramatic, but always fertile and suggestive; and the third was a style rich and prodigal in colour, not always chastened, but everywhere vivid and alert. It would be easy enough to pick holes in Miss Corelli's work, as wanting in the higher graces of literature. Meanwhile it remains an incontestable fact that she had an enormous public of admirers and that her novels enjoyed a sale larger probably than fell to the lot of nearly all her contemporaries. For this many reasons may be assigned. She wielded a most vigorous pen. She never was afraid to utter her opinions with extreme and sometimes disconcerting frankness. She was endowed with an imagination of unbounded scope. Above all, her novels were always readable. But the main cause of her popularity was that she aimed directly at the heart of the people, and gave them as much sentiment and pathos and melodrama – couched in an equally descriptive and exuberant style – as they could possibly desire. Whatever was in her mind came forth with all the turbulence of a river in spate. And the public adored her.

Manchester Guardian, 1924

She never saw shades, but dealt only in black and gold. . . . She had a great many gifts, a tremendous energy and a desire to astonish people. In some ways she made me think of a moral feminine Lord Byron. The date of Marie Corelli's birth is, we believe, one of the secrets of the Registrar General.

Morning Post, 22 April 1924

She was never restrained from attacking either institutions or human types by the slightest consciousness of insufficient knowledge. Her full-blooded Turkey-carpet style of writing with its half dozen words where one would do, is, however, not peculiar to her but is equally characteristic of numerous writers who never succeed in reaching the great heart of the public. Where, then, lay her secret? It will probably be found in her extraordinary power of telling a story, of dramatic, vivid narration, which atoned for all her lack of perspective, of sympathy, and of humour.

Review of Reviews, May 1924

Miss Corelli was the type 'best-seller', and in her day the most widely read of them all. . . .[She] was read by the entire middle-class, who bought in all many hundreds of thousands of her works at six shillings the volume . . . . Miss Corelli's novels were not only novels but manifestos, and at her zenith their advent was blared forth like the opening of the Wembley Exhibition. She considered herself, and millions of people took her to be, a social critic, a woman with a mission, a prophetess. She spoke to the suburbs and the country towns as a kind of popular equivalent of Carlyle and Mr Bernard Shaw, a rigid moralist denouncing the shams and follies of Society, a daring theologian who was prepared to give the devil more than his due. . . . She was a Veiled Prophetess too, which added to her impressiveness. . . . She appeared little in public, seldom condescended to an interview, disliked her portrait appearing in the papers, and, after a certain stage, forbade various copies of her books to be sent to the critics. The voice spoke from behind the curtain, voluminously and violently about marriage or the Church of England. Then there would be a year's silence and then the oracle would utter concerning Roman Catholicism or smoking by women, and a swarm of red volumes would settle like locusts on the drawing-room tables of the United Kingdom. Her views though passionately held were negligible; she knew little; she wrote, often, very ungrammatically; her stories and her people were like nothing on earth. But nobody succeeds as a novelist with any public without some positive qualities.

Manchester Guardian, 22 April 1924
Miss Marie Corelli's writings, like so many other popular institutions of the last generation, are only names – if they are that – to the post war public. It is doubtful if any young woman nowadays reads Marie Corelli. Her admirers did not belong to any social strata, Queen Victoria, Queen Alexandra, the Empress Frederick of Germany, the late King of Italy all expressed their admiration of her writings, and Mr Gladstone called on her, Sir Frederick Leighton praised her and Tennyson gave her a tribute. She was famous in her twenties, and earned as much money in a few years as many of the modern masters of literature made in a lifetime. . . .Yet, despite all her success and her closeness to the mind and temper of so large a part of her generation, one cannot help thinking now that she was born before her time, and that her gifts might have found an even more appropriate expression and wider appeal through the mammoth productions of the modern kinema.

The Sphere, 26 April 1924
Her fame in America was so great that Corelli City, in Colorado, was named after her – a unique distinction.

Evening Standard, 21 April 1924
Whatever may be the verdict of posterity, Marie Corelli was certainly a literary phenomenon. Her success was achieved in spite of the hostility of critics and the sneers of 'superior persons.' Her faults as a writer were unconcealed. She was emotional and well-informed, but lacking humour. Perhaps she was at her best when aroused to indignation or describing placid scenes of rural life. She failed when she pilloried society. She judged the many by the few. She attacked all women for the sins of the 'smart set.' She was in her time the greatest literary 'protester.'

In 'Wormwood,' she protested against absinthe drinking in Paris; in 'The Mighty Atom' she raised her voice against the over-education of the child and the folly of bringing it up without any definite religious belief, and in 'The Master Christian' she pleaded that the Church should reform itself on scientific lines. She rarely showed mercy to the masculine victim of her pen. . . . Her charity was great and frequently, if quietly, expressed. In the passing of Miss Marie Corelli a great figure in the fiction of the last 30 years is lost, to the regret of many friends and a world wide public.

Evening Standard, 22 April 1924
EDITORIAL: Best Sellers.
The work of Miss Marie Corelli and of some equally popular novelists of later generations may have much in it that by strict literary standards is bad – so much, perhaps, as to deprive it of any hope of immortality. But the great public admires these authors not for what is bad in them but for what is good, for qualities which better authors would be better for possessing. To succeed on this scale, to please so many people, a novelist must have, whatever else is lacking, a gift of fluent and abundant narrative, a certain generosity of the imagination. These qualities often lead to strange results when they are not controlled by strict taste; but in some authors more highly approved by the critics, strict taste occasionally controls them out of existence altogether.

So wrote the critics.

This woman, who came from nowhere, had a meteoric rise in a blaze of literary fame; dined with princes, fought fierce battles of conscience, split the town of Stratford-upon-Avon into warring factions, and became the most famous author in Britain in the early 1900s, has now virtually vanished from public memory. Decried and dismissed by many critics, she was adored by her readers who surrounded and mobbed her whenever she appeared in public. She was a phenomenon of her time, who like all shooting stars burnt itself out before vanishing. But the plot of her passing through the heavens must be charted because for a time she illuminated late Victorian England in a way which still has echoes for us today.

CHAPTER 1

Minnie Mackay

Where can clues be found for a life so beset with evasion and subterfuge that to find the truth is like looking for a single grain of sand along miles of golden beach? Reality and illusion. A magic show – a conjuror's sleight of hand. The lady vanishes and reappears on the other side of the stage. So successful was Marie in disguising her past, that it was not until after her death in 1924, that newspapers, searching for her origins to write their obituaries, discovered that her history was shrouded in an impenetrable fog. Fact and fiction had become indistinguishable and journalists, determined to titillate their readers' curiosity, invented wilder and wilder stories. After a few months of intense speculation the matter was allowed to drop.

It was known that she had been brought up by the poet and journalist Charles Mackay who was believed to be her stepfather, but who may have been something more. In an unpublished manuscript found after her death Marie Corelli wrote:

My father had been all in all to me, for of my mother I had no remembrance save the general impression I had gathered from a picture of her which always hung in my father's study; an oil painting of a slender fair girl with large earnest grey eyes and a plaintive, sweet face on which there was an expression that was appealing and noble. I am told that she was a Venetian and that I resembled her greatly, but for my part I saw no likeness, unless perhaps in the dreamy look of the eyes which was partly caused by the unusual length of the eyelashes. My father . . . was a profound scholar, deeply versed in the study of languages. . . . Books upon books he had written in English, in French, in German, in Italian – some of them had been moderately successful, – many had failed, but more had won for him sufficient fortune to enable him to keep the wolf from the door in his latter days. He hid his troubles from me for the most part, though I knew his means were very limited and that our little household had to be managed with the strictest economy, but only Anita, an old servant who had been with mother as maid and my nurse, was acquainted with the real state of his pecuniary affairs.[1]

Is this tale just the invention of a fertile, lonely mind prone to day-dreaming and make-believe, or is it autobiographical? What were the origins of this woman known variously as Mary Mills, Minnie Mackay, or Marie Corelli? We know of her public face, or as much as she permits us to see, but so much is hidden.

In a letter to a Mrs Cudlip on 23 December 1889 Marie wrote: 'My name is *not* Mackay, nor am I related to the Mackays at all. I was *adopted* by the late Charles Mackay LLD, LSA who lost his own daughter by fever in Italy – but my name is Corelli, and though my mother was Scotch, I am much more Italian than British! I know you will be kind enough to always remember this.'[2] And again in 1904 writing to Alex Rae Brown, Marie declared: 'I see by your allusions to my "mother" that you have not been made aware of my legal position with regard to the Mackay family . . . I was Dr Mackay's *adopted* daughter – *not* his own, – and dearly as I loved him, I cannot claim the slightest relationship with either himself or any of his people. *I know who my own father and mother were quite well, –* and *I have relations living of my own.* I think this ought to be made quite clear to you.'[3]

To be illegitimate in Victorian society was a sin past forgiving, as Marie Corelli wrote in *Innocent*: 'There's many a piece of wicked injustice in the world, but nothing more wicked than to set shame or blame on a child that's born without permit of law, or blessing of priest. For it's not the child's fault, – it's brought into the world without its own consent, – and yet the world fastens a slur on it! That's downright brutal and senseless! – for if there is any blame attached to the matter it should be fastened on the parents, and not on the child.'[4]

It is important to consider this mystery of Marie's past because it had such an influence on her whole life and her attitude to her 'stepfather'; on the way she fought against injustice, either real or imagined; on her over-reaction to perceived slights; her immense generosity, especially to children; her need to idealise her own image and yet, at the same time, her fear of intrusion into her private life.

Charles Mackay was Scottish, born in 1814, and educated in London and Brussels. He was a journalist and worked first on the *Morning Chronicle* with Charles Dickens, and then briefly on the *Glasgow Argus*. In 1847 he joined the new *Daily Telegraph*, and in 1848 became political and literary editor on the *Illustrated London News* under Charles Ingram. He was also the author of many popular songs and, in collaboration with Henry Russell, the composer, wrote 'Cheer Boys Cheer', 'To the West to the West', 'There's a Good Time Coming', and many other songs much loved by the Victorians. He was married to Rosa Henrietta by whom he had four children, three sons and one daughter, but Rosa left him in 1853 after Mackay was reputed to have had an affair with 'an imperfectly educated young woman', Elizabeth Mary Mills.

A child was born on 1 May 1855, and named Mary. She was thought to be the daughter of Elizabeth Mary – also known as Ellen – and Charles Mackay. There is no record of this, but it was not then compulsory to record a birth and if, as is believed, she was illegitimate, there were good reasons for not doing so. It seems that she was brought up in London, living with her mother for the first six years of her life. When his wife died in 1860, Mackay waited for a year of official mourning before he married Ellen/Elizabeth Mary Mills in February 1861. After the wedding they lived at 18 Avenue Road with six-year-old Mary Mills, who, for the next phase of her life was known as Minnie Mackay. It was on 14 December 1861 that Prince Albert died of typhoid fever and the Queen went into perpetual mourning.

Mackay began to have serious financial problems with a new wife to support and with no permanent employment, and in 1861 was granted a literary pension of £100 a year by Lord Palmerston. He had been writing numerous letters to acquaintances in search of a job and received a letter from an American friend, William H. Seward, dated 7 November 1861. 'Will you not make another visit to this country? . . . Come, I pray you, with your wife, and take shelter in my home here.'[5]

In February 1862 Mackay found a posting with *The Times* in New York. He reported on the American Civil War, and wrote in his recollections: 'I engaged a passage to Boston on the 22nd February [1862]. The prospect being one of a long-continued residence in New York, I took my faithful and dearly-beloved wife and infant daughter along with me.'[6] (Young Mary/Minnie would have been six.) In the early part of their visit the family visited Three Rivers in Canada where 'Mr Rousseau had been apprised of our coming and canoes and a scow were in readiness. My wife and daughter did not like the fragile look of the canoes, so the scow, in deference to their timidity, was chosen for our transit.'[7]

It seems strange that young Minnie, who was with Mackay and Ellen in America for nearly two years from early 1862 to the end of 1863, denied that she had ever visited the country, for it now seems certain that she was there. At the end of 1863 Mackay returned to London for three months to take his wife and eight-year-old Minnie back to their home at 18 Avenue Road. The house has now been demolished to make way for a large block of flats, but judging by the remaining houses around it, it was an imposing residence. Mackay then returned to New York where he remained until December 1865, but his commission as war correspondent was not a success. Mackay, an opinionated and embittered journalist, felt that the South had a right to secede even though he deplored slavery, and his attitude was understandably resented by the Northerners in New York. He was perceived to be sympathising with the enemy and a traitor to the cause.

What was Minnie's place in Mackay's world? If Minnie was accepted as the daughter of Ellen Mills and adopted by Charles Mackay on his marriage, then the conventions were observed. It is certain that Minnie usually referred to Mackay as her stepfather, but, strangely enough, seldom mentioned Ellen or referred to her as her mother. If Ellen Mills took over the care of Minnie following the death of Minnie's natural mother, and if Mackay then married Ellen to give the child a stable home, we have another scenario. This is supported by a letter which Marie wrote to the editor of the *Financial News* who made the comment that she had 'taken refuge under a Franco-Italian name'. 'Will you permit me to say that my name is my legal appellation – my own in every way – and that if you have any doubt of the fact I am sure that my solicitor will be quite willing to supply you with proof of it! *I was adopted by Dr Charles Mackay's second wife* but, so far as any legality goes, I am no other than I now sign myself – Very faithfully yours, Marie Corelli.'

There is another somewhat melodramatic story of Marie's origins 'discovered' after her death by the *Daily Mail*, and told to them by a Leatherhead resident. 'About sixty years ago, about 9 o'clock, on a snowy winter's night, a knock was heard on the cottage door, which the servant answered. No one was there, but she observed a basket on the doorstep, and took it inside and, on uncovering it, there was found a baby girl, and at the bottom of the basket a ten pound note. There was no clue as to who the child was, and the old doctor decided that it would have to be taken the next day to the Dorking Union. However, they kept the child longer, thinking someone might come for it, and in the meantime they got fond of it and ultimately adopted it. This child was afterwards known as Marie Corelli.'[8]

Until now, the more generally accepted story is that Minnie was Mackay and Ellen's natural daughter. Once she had become famous she buried the secret of her birth in such a conflicting maze of fact and fiction it is hard to know where truth ends and make-believe begins.

Until the end of 1865 Mackay lived at 18 Avenue Road, Regents Park, and according to the *Post Office Directories* he did not move to Fern Dell, Box Hill, Surrey, until 1870 when Minnie was fifteen. Between 1866 and 1870 there is no permanent address given for Mackay, and yet, in a poem he wrote in 1865, Fern Dell was where he met Minnie's mother in 1853. This is supported by his marriage certificate on which Elizabeth Mary Mills gave her address as Croydon in Surrey, not far from Box Hill.

'The Swing on the Apple Tree at Fern Dell'

Twelve summers down the gulf of Time –
It seems but yesterday –
I made a swing from its sturdiest boughs
In the morn of merry May;
And from it swung my love, my life,
In the flush of her sunny youth.
And woo'd and won her to be my bride,
With all her love and truth.

And now I swing another as fair,
Her years are nearly ten;
And she laughs and sings and shouts, 'Papa!
Swing me again! again!'
And I swing her again and kiss her.
'Don't kick at the stars!' I cry.
And she chuckles with laughter, and says, 'I will,
If you swing me up as high!'[9]

Bertha van der Vyver, who later became Minnie's lifetime companion, mentioned in her *Memoirs of Marie Corelli* an elderly governess who came from Dorking three times a week to teach Minnie and who gave up the job because of her age. Bertha also found in one of Minnie's later unpublished manuscripts a description of another weekend governess, Miss Knox, who came from London and who, according to Minnie's account, found her eleven-year-old charge more than a handful. Minnie wrote, 'I managed to develop into a curiously determined independent little personality, with ideas and opinions more suited to some clever young man. . . . I instinctively did all I could to make myself a personality to be reckoned with. For this reason I devoured books whatever their qualities, and fed my brains with the thoughts of dead men. . . . Many books did I pore over with untiring patience, learning all I could, and craving to be taught more. I was indeed a very lonely child. . . . I had to play by myself and invent my own sports and games – and for this reason I had found my best pleasure in books and music. These talked to me – the books spoke to my mind, the music to my ear and mind as well, and so I came under influences which were destined to work unexpected results hereafter. . . . I'll be something more than pretty! – I'll be clever! . . . Full of healthy vitality, young and audacious enough, she was to believe that she – even she – might evolve for herself a nobler, higher, less servile and dependent way of existence than is found by the majority of men and women.'[10] 'Papa' adored his adopted daughter, as can be seen from several poems he wrote when she was young. He was proud of her looks and delighted in her company, and she did all she could to please him. It seems she may have had less pleasure from the company of Papa's friends, for she wrote in a later book:

> Pampered, petted and spoilt, told I must 'look pretty' and take pleasure in my clothes, I was even at the age of ten, capable of a certain amount of coquetry. Old roués, smelling of wine and tobacco, were eager to take me on their knees and pinch my soft flesh; they would press my innocent lips with their withered ones – withered and contaminated by the kisses of *cocottes* and 'soiled doves' of the town! – I have often wondered how it is these men can dare to touch a young child's mouth, knowing in themselves what beasts they are![11]

When the situation became too much for Miss Knox to handle, Minnie was sent to a Paris convent to be educated from 1866 to 1870. In a letter she wrote in 1904 to a young actor friend, Herbert Halliwell Hobbes, she described those years. 'I used to go with him [Mackay] every year to Scotland when I got my midsummer holidays from the Convent in Paris where I was educated from the ages of 11–15 – so I know every inch of the country'; and in 1909 she wrote again to Hobbes, 'I am taking up my singing again, having the music-room – and I am once more revelling in the lovely things I used to sing at the Paris Conservatoires.'[12]

A further verification of Minnie's whereabouts comes from Charles Cooper, the editor of the *Table* many years later, in 1924. The newspapers were desperate to solve the mystery of her birth and he was interviewed, as a personal friend of both Charles Mackay and Henry Russell. 'My close connection with the Russell family led to my often meeting Charles Mackay at their house in Kensington Gardens Square in 1868–69. His step-daughter Minnie was less frequently to be met as she was most of that time at school. The youngest daughter of the Russell family, Emma, was then 14, she and her chum Minnie were about of an age.'[13] Minnie often stayed with Henry Russell's family in London during that time and also with the van der Vyvers who lived nearby.

Countess van der Vyver, a beautiful woman who had been a lady-in-waiting to Queen Eugénie at the Court of Napoleon III in Paris, was an old friend of Charles Mackay, and had known him since his days in Belgium. Her first husband, Alphonso Peter Francisco Adrian van der Vyver, was a merchant from Belgium with Spanish connections. The Van der Vyver's eldest daughter, Pauline, was born in 1853; a second, Bertha Amelia Adriana Francisca, was born on 11 June 1854, and a third, Ada, followed in 1855. The van der Vyvers, and particularly Bertha, were to play an important part in Marie Corelli's life. The Countess had left her Belgian husband in 1860 and now lived with her three young daughters at 7 Cleveland Terrace, just north of Hyde Park, only three streets east of the Russells' house. Bertha van der Vyver was a year older than Minnie and they became firm friends. At the Countess's first meeting with Minnie, when Mackay had taken her to Brighton, she had tossed her up in her arms and Minnie had reached for a small gold gondola sewn on to a band of red velvet in her hair. The brooch was given to her as a memento and it remained one of her most cherished possessions.

Dr Mackay wrote to thank the Countess for allowing Minnie to play with her family, and she had replied: 'It is I, dear friend, who must thank you for allowing the Star of your Home to come here and brighten our own. She is a delightful child, steeped in poetry and tenderness. She breathes and inspires the beautiful and ideal.' Charles Mackay had introduced an American, Colonel Hiram Fuller, to the beautiful Countess, and these two were openly living together. In 1866 a boy, Orlando Fuller, was born, and later became known as Frank Orlando Vyver who, in a later census, was listed as 'adopted son', a general euphemism for illegitimate children. Minnie spent her holidays either staying with these friends in London, or visiting Scotland with her stepfather. During Minnie's convent years there is a record of Mackay, in autumn 1868, escorting Jefferson Davies, the President of the Southern Confederacy, on an extensive tour first to Edinburgh, then on to Glasgow, Oban, the Hebrides and Inverness, and Minnie was one of the party.

Minnie gave her 1901 biographer, Kent Carr, her version of her life in the convent school. 'I became for a time so absorbed in the mysteries of the religious life, that I had some vague ideas of founding a "New Order" and of being the leader of an entirely original community of Christian workers, who should indeed follow Christ in spirit and in truth. Fond of solitude and meditation, I was what my school companions called *devotée*, and was given to much reading and thought. I passed most of the hours of relaxation in the convent chapel, playing and improvising melodies on the great organ near the altar, preferring this mode of occupying myself to the games of croquet, tennis and archery in which all were permitted to engage.'[14] Her convent experiences were used as material for part of her early books, *A Romance of Two Worlds* and *Vendetta*. Bertha Vyver, Minnie's lifelong friend, quoted an undated letter from Minnie to her mother written from the convent school:

I am very content here, but of course I *can't* be happy away from home. But I cannot be positively *un*happy because everyone is so kind. . . . I do not find it at all hard getting up at half-past five; it is quite a refreshing novelty! And there is no solemn, cold immovable gravity here; in fact, we are all so easily amused, the least thing sets us into a laugh; but I have never once heard ill-natured merriment at another's expense, which you know often happens in large schools. A good many droll things happen among us, and we are not afraid to laugh. L——, I believe, thinks that a convent is the most *sad* place in the universe – so, if she comes to see you, tell her that a fashionable boarding-school is like sitting on the ice, and this convent is like sitting in the sun. You will see from this, dearest Mother, that I am very content. I am grateful for all the kindness and care shown me, so, though I cannot be exactly myself away from home – still, I will be brave and work hard to please you.[15]

This is the only time Minnie is recorded as having any direct communication with Ellen Mackay. In Minnie's own version of her childhood she talks of being a five- or six-year-old girl living at Fern Dell, at Box Hill near Mickleham, of living in a world of books and fairies and angels, and of shocking her governess by her precocious behaviour. She makes no mention of America or London, and is vague about when or where she was at the convent school. She was so successful a dissimulator that this version of her childhood came to be accepted as her true history. The verified facts are different, as she seems to have lived in London until she was eleven, during which time she passed two years in America; she spent the next four years at school in Paris and then went to live at Fern Dell. The false clues and blind alleys lead us deeper and deeper into the maze.

Certainly one of the things which allowed Minnie to claim that she was younger than her actual age was that, by all reports, she was extremely short. Even when adult Minnie was not much over 4 feet, and when young and slim she must often have been taken for a child. There are three photographs of her taken when she was very young, but her height and her given age is at variance with a surprisingly much older face. Later in life, in all her photographs, she is either partly concealed by furniture, or shown standing on a staircase or at the top of a flight of steps with a long train sweeping downwards, making it impossible to see where she ends and the stairs begin. When she was younger she enjoyed the protection created by her supposedly child status, and took advantage of it when asking for favours. Minnie writes to Papa from her Paris convent:

> Could you give me *a plot* for a *drama* to write and work out for our private theatricals, a dreadful plot of Love and Murder?
> *Mackay:* 'Don't know. Try me – with the offer of a thousand guineas! or, say, £1000 for the Love, and £3000 for the Murder!
> *Minnie:* You mercenary individual! No, Papa, without any nonsense, *do* help me to concoct a drama – *the plot,* at any rate.

The result of this collaboration was an evening entertainment on Wednesday 12 April 1871, consisting of a fairy extravaganza, 'The Three Wishes!' followed by 'the amusing Farce of *Ici on Parle Français*!!! To be followed by a succession of most Brilliant and Startling *Tableaux Vivants*!! . . . It is hoped that none of the spectators will make audible remarks of a character likely to disturb the self-command of those who perform in the *Tableaux Vivants.* Any person so offending is liable to be instantly turned out.' All this was organised by sixteen-year-old Minnie in the Theatre Royal, Box Hill, otherwise known as the School Room at Fern Dell. There is a note at the bottom of the programme, 'NO CRITICS OR GREAT GENIUSES admitted.'[16]

In the census of 1871, Fern Dell Cottage, Box Hill, was the home of Charles Mackay, fifty-six, and his wife Ellen (born in Madrid, Spain), forty-one, Minnie, sixteen, a cook and a housemaid. Mackay was now working as a freelance journalist and writing novels and poems. Money was becoming even more scarce.

Minnie had left her Paris convent; she was sixteen, and had no prospects apart from piano and singing lessons and reading her way through Mackay's extensive library which 'was an "olla-podrida" of random things, good, bad and indifferent – there were "standard" histories and classics, poets, novelists, and dramatists; there were many volumes of old, forgotten essays and political "squibs." Voltaire jostled with Plutarch, and Shakespeare with *The Tatler* and *Rambler* – and a large number of dictionaries, old and new, lumbered the shelves.'[17] Minnie's formal education seems to have been slight and, as was usually the case for Victorian daughters, consisted mainly of music and literature and some languages. She was not expected to earn her living and lacked discipline in her learning. This was to bring her much censure from the critics when she began to write. She said later, 'I was kept very much at home, and, owing to the lack of companions of my own age, I found my chief delight in reading, though few modern books ever came my way and I was not allowed to look at a newspaper.' There were no other young people with whom she could mix, and in her memories of that time she talked of the loneliness of her life.

Fern Dell, which burnt to the ground in 1894, was a wooden house on the Mickleham to Dorking road, situated next to Flint Cottage where the author George Meredith lived. Bertha in her *Memoirs* describes the house. 'Fern Dell was a charming, old fashioned house, consisting of drawing-room, dining-room, library and eight bedrooms; and a long room over the coach-house and stables. This long room was approached by a creeper-covered porch in the garden adjoining the library, and was used as a schoolroom. . . . From the windows the view of the hill and the surrounding country was very beautiful; but to the child the most important room of all was her own little sitting room, a small attic opposite her bedroom. . . . At the back of Fern Dell was a lovely garden, a beautiful lawn surrounded with syringa, lilac, laburnum, roses and a shrubbery of nut trees and ferns.'[18] Box Hill is isolated even now, and behind Flint Cottage and the site of Fern Dell is a steep hillside covered with trees and bushes. Flint Cottage is surrounded by massive hedges of box, 10 feet deep and 10 feet high, and on the other side of the road, cut between two steep hills and winding its way up to a lookout point at the top, is a broad sweep of downland.

In a letter written in April 1905 to George Meredith's son, Marie wrote, 'I remember *you*, chiefly because you seemed to be a very happy boy, while I "on the other side of the hedge" was a most lonely and miserable girl! The days of my childhood were days of such intense and bitter suffering, that I never willingly look back on them, nor can I be reminded of them without indescribable pain. My position was in itself uncomfortable – for to learn that my own parents were dead, and that I was adopted by good Dr Mackay out of the sheer kindness of his heart, and his old association with those dead parents, and to have no brothers or sisters of my own, and no companions, and anything to look forward to in the world, was enough, so I thought, to make anyone miserable – and indeed I was so *very* unhappy that I never care to think of it now.'[19]

Years later, when she was in her sixties, in one of her books Marie described a situation which sounded much like that of her own childhood. She declared that a woman must learn to exercise her own power. She 'had failed to learn this lesson in the days of her girlhood – she had believed, with quite touching filial faith, in the pious and excessively hypocritical twaddle her father talked about! "the fascination of modest pretty girls who were unconscious of their beauty", – with the result that she had seen him, with other men, avoid such "modest, pretty girls" altogether, and pay devoted court to *im*modest, "loud" and impertinent women, who asserted their "made-up" good looks with a frank boldness which "drew" the men on like a shoal of herrings in a net, and left the "modest pretty girls" out in the cold.'[20] As a young woman she knew no young men. 'How could I have any lover – I who had lived all my life with my father in a country village twenty miles away from London where we had neither friends nor neighbours, and where the only break in the monotony of my life had been the weekly trips to town for my music lessons. I knew something about what was meant by the expression "falling in love" for I had seen lovers strolling together through the country lanes, hand in hand, or arm in arm, looking very foolish and uncomfortable.'[21]

The people from the little village of Mickleham later tried to recall what she was like. 'I remember Minnie Mackay, as she was called, as a girl,' said George Rose, 'I thought then that she was Mr Mackay's daughter. She was a slim girl with a mass of fair hair. She was trained as a singer, and I heard her sing at a concert myself. She had an attractive voice. I am almost sure that she used Rose Trevor as her professional name.'[22] Rose Trevor is the name Mackay gave to one of the main characters in his epic poem, *A Man's Heart*, written in 1860.

Minnie, with the example of Mackay to inspire her, and with much time on her hands, tried her hand at writing. On 21 January 1874 she submitted a poem, 'Sappho', to *Blackwood's Magazine* and invented not only her name but her achievements:

Dear Mr Blackwood,
I had an idea of asking our friend Lord Neaves to plead my case with you. Finally I came to the conclusion that it would be better to have no intercessor, but to trust to your kindness, and to let my pen speak for itself. I am a constant contributor to St James Magazine under my nom-de-plume of Vivian Erle Clifford which nom-de-plume *I desire to retain*. I am aware that I am a very young aspirant to your good graces being as yet only nineteen.

P.S. May I entreat your answer soon. Suspense to me is the most trying of all trying things.[23]

Finding that Lord Neaves's name carried no more weight than that of Vivian Erle Clifford she wrote again under her own name from the van der Vyvers' address:

Dear Mr Blackwood,   The Laurels, Belsize Park
I have written to both you and your uncle respecting my poem 'Sappho' and have received no answer. My father is surprised at the silence and so, I confess, am I. Please answer my request soon, it is so hard to be kept in suspense.

Faithfully yours, Minnie Mackay.[24]

This time she did get an answer – a rejection – and Minnie, more importunate than many novice writers, battled on with a series of letters.

May 4th 1874.   The Laurels
I cannot help feeling *very much* disappointed at your decision. . . .
May I ask you once more to consider your decision. You ask if I write prose? Yes – but I have lately contented myself with small satires against a few of the social absurdities that have appeared visible during my short experience. I meditate trying my hand at a novel, as many tell me that I could write a good one – but if I do it will not be one full of the sickly sentiment that seems so beloved by the public – Therefore I suppose it will be a failure.[25]

Three months later she tried again.

August 22nd 1874.   Box Hill
I write to ask you if a good article on 'Music and Song' would suit you. I am very well up in the subject, being perfectly at home with the classical composers as well as the modern 'show' ones and I am a most fervent admirer and student of Scottish music. My father encourages me to hope that such a subject well-handled would suit you, but advised me to ask you if it will before settling down to write about it in sober earnest.[26]

The reply must have been encouraging and the article was duly written.

Oct 10th 1874
I have been some time in writing 'Music and Song' which I now send – as I was anxious to do my *very best* for you. I have submitted it to Papa's criticism (which is always severe) and he is much pleased, and thinks you will also be pleased. I *do* hope you will! You can hardly imagine how very anxious I am and have been about it.[27]

The next letter was decidedly miffed.

October 20th 1875.   Fern Dell
It is now more than a year, since I wrote and sent for your approbation an article on 'Music', which has never been acknowledged by you in any way whatever. You must remember that when I proposed writing it, you heartily encouraged me and led me to hope that it might appear in your Magazine. I worked hard at it. . . . Why has it been disregarded – if it was unworthy of a place why not tell me so?[28]

And again:

Nov. 23rd 1875.
Dear Mr Blackwood,
I venture to write to you at my father's suggestion to enquire of you whether your uncle is ill? . . . I wrote to him more than three weeks ago respecting an article of mine which he himself encouraged me to write, and as I have received no answer, I am afraid that perhaps ill health is interfering with his attention to correspondence. I shall be obliged if you will answer this letter at your earliest convenience.'[29]

Mr Blackwood refused to be bullied and that correspondence ceases. It is interesting to note the 'little girl' approach of these letters, which is evident in most of her early correspondence. No doubt it worked with Papa and his friends, but most editors were less susceptible.

By 1875 Ellen Mackay was suffering from 'malignant disease of the intestines' and was very ill. She was no longer able to care for Mackay or to chaperone Minnie. It was then that Bertha's mother, the Countess van der Vyver, about to travel to America with Colonel Fuller, suggested that Bertha join the Mackay household, a suggestion which was immediately accepted. Ellen Mackay, who remains a shadowy figure in Minnie's life, died on 2 February 1876. In any reference to her she appears more in the guise of a housekeeper than that of a wife and mother. Mackay barely refers to her after the marriage in 1861, and Minnie in only one letter written from the convent. In the census of 1871 her birthplace is given as Madrid, Spain, which makes one wonder if Elizabeth Mary Mills and Ellen were in truth the same person. Madrid may indicate some connection with the Countess van der Vyver's time as lady-in-waiting to the Spanish wife of Napoleon III in Paris. It is conceivable that Minnie's reference in the unpublished work to 'Anita, who had been with my mother as maid and my nurse', may refer to Mackay's wife. On her death certificate this mysterious lady is called Ellen which is later crossed out and changed to Elizabeth Mary. She is buried in Mickleham churchyard. Bertha and Minnie together took over the running of the house, and stayed together for the rest of their lives.

The financial situation at Fern Dell became increasingly difficult. Mackay still had his pension of £100 a year, but his income from writing had greatly diminished. Neither Minnie nor Bertha was able to give any help. They were trained for nothing but music, and although Bertha had some independent means, Minnie was totally dependent upon her stepfather. She was very conscious of her obligations to him, and this feeling of helpless dependency, and a fierce resolve to become independent, coloured many of her later actions. On 26 July 1881 Minnie was writing to *Blackwood's Magazine* once more. 'I have often tried to win sufficient of your approbation to obtain occasional admission into the magazine, – but though often defeated, I am never beaten.' She offers Mr Blackwood five sonnets translated – '*nearly* literally from the Italian of Giovanni Prati. You may not know that Italian is a second tongue with me, and that I am very conversant with Italian literature, but it is so.'[30] They were still not impressed.

Living at Fern Dell according to the census of 1881 were 67-year-old Charles Mackay and his middle son, George Eric Mackay. Eric had been summoned back to England because of his father's ill health, and he gave his age as forty (it should have been forty-six). Both Minnie and Bertha were listed, and gave their ages as twenty-two (they should have been twenty-six and twenty-seven respectively). Minnie was already beginning to shed her years!

George Eric Mackay, who was to play an important part in Minnie's life, was a miserable failure of a man. When he left school in Inverness his father tried to settle him in a career, first in business and then literature. He objected to what he called 'a beggarly profession', and demanded to go on the stage. As Kent Carr described it: 'Charles Kean tried his powers as an actor, but found him wanting in perseverance. Frank Mori then tried his voice, and thought it sufficiently good for him to try the career of an opera singer. His father sent him to Italy for training when he was about twenty-four years of age, and for five or six years paid ten pounds a month for his musical education. All this time, however, he never took any lessons at all, but merely passed his days in amusement. This fact coming to his father's knowledge, the money supplies were stopped.'[31] This pretentious ne'er-do-well then lived somewhat precariously, remaining in Italy to teach French and English, writing odd articles for the press and publishing a small book of poems which was not a success. He tried to start two newspapers, both failures, and got himself heavily into debt.

Bertha thought he should come back to England when Mackay became ill and admitted later: 'We discussed the matter and agreed to risk it – not very wisely – for it only added new difficulties and many troubles and responsibilities to our lives. Though I sent him an ample cheque, he arrived in England without any money.'[32] Eric then settled, like a cuckoo, into the comfortable nest of Fern Dell and happily allowed himself to be supported. Minnie was delighted to meet her half-brother and, believing his stories of bad luck, encouraged him in every way she could. Eric wrote to thank her. 'I am happier than I have been since boyhood, for I have a little sister again, and that little sister – the best and brightest in the world – does everything for me.'[33] Eric decided that he was tired of literature, and having attended a concert with Minnie to listen to the famous violinist Sarasate, thought he would become a violin player: would Minnie please find him a violin? 'His "little Sister" warned him that it was somewhat late to begin, but nothing would move him from his fancy, so she managed to get him an old "Guarnerius" violin from Chappell on the quarterly instalment system, which she paid until it was all cleared off; while she also, with the assistance of her ever sympathetic friend Miss Vyver, managed to pay for his lessons on the instrument. He never did, however, manage to play more than a simple tune in single note upon it.'[34] There is a revealing description of the two Mackays, father and son, from T.P. O'Connor: 'I remember Mackay well – a short, stoutish, red-faced man, with a certain bitterness in his talk. . . . Eric was a little like his father – short, stoutish, ruddy-faced. He had even more than the usual share of irritability and unaccountability of the race of poets to which he belonged.'[35]

In June 1883 Charles Mackay had a severe stroke and the household was advised to move to London as he needed to be close to good medical care, and it was not thought that he would live long. Jane, Minnie's personal maid, accompanied the family to their new home. Bertha and Minnie first found lodgings in Earls Court Road and after a few weeks a house at 47 Longridge Road, Kensington, on the border of Earls Court, into which they moved. The house was tall and thin with a basement and an attic, and must have seemed wonderfully central after the isolation of Box Hill.

Minnie decided it was time to change tack. The Mackay family name was proving unsuccessful with *Blackwood's Magazine*; she would try something new. She disguised her sprawling, rather childish writing into a neat, carefully practised copperplate, and changed her address and her name.

18 Marlborough Square, Chelsea, London SW.   May 25th 1883
Signorina Marie Corelli ventures to approach the learned editor of the renowned 'Blackwood's Magazine', sincerely trusting she may be pardoned for her temerity in hoping that the accompanying little poems may be deemed worthy of acceptance and insertion in those long celebrated pages. Signorina Corelli is a Venetian, and the direct descendant (through a long line of ancestry) of the great Michael Angelo Corelli [*sic*], the famous composer and also on another side of the family from one of the Doges of Venice – but she has been partly educated in France and partly in England.

She went on to say that she had already gained some recognition in French and English and on the Continent, that she contributed largely to many of the business journals, and to various London publications. She had published a small volume of English poems. She had been highly commended by the late Lord Neaves, who had advised her to contact Blackwoods, 'but travelling and residence abroad banished the idea for some time. However she hopes the editor of Blackwoods would look favourably upon her efforts.'[36] There was no signature – and no answer from Mr Blackwood. On 29 November 1883 Minnie tried out her nom-de-plume again and wrote to Clement Scott, the editor of *Theatre Magazine*.

Many thanks for the 'Annual' which is charmingly brought out; I like your story *immensely* . . . So my poem is put off till January. Never mind – I am not a conceited 'bas-blue' [*sic*] and I can endure the delay. You are very good to try and insert the paragraph about me –, if it does not appear in the Dec number, 'twill answer my purpose as well in January. I wish you had asked me to write something for the 'Annual' –!

Marie di Corelli.[37]

Lack of money was becoming a major worry. Mackay, once he had recovered enough to write again, was pleading with *Blackwood's Magazine* to publish a book of his on obscure and misinterpreted words in Shakespeare. On 21 December he wrote, 'your decision one way or the other is of importance', and again on 31 December with more urgency. 'Were not this a case of *urgent importance to me*, I would await your leisure . . . but I have no alternative.' As Minnie remembered: 'He was so much of a dreamer that he found it hard to get on in the world, and as he grew older he became less and less practical; and then dark times came. Instead of trying to write and produce those things by which he could earn an income, he devoted himself to studies which had very little interest for the majority. . . . He devoted himself to etymology. He had published one work on the Gaelic, and now he was possessed by the idea that he could do something great with Asian dialects. We could not wean him from it, and so, as he was approaching seventy years of age, this dear old man laboured away; and as for us, we began to dread the future, and sometimes we were nearly in want.'[38]

Minnie and Bertha decided that the former would give a concert to an invited audience, in the hope that this might lead to a career for Minnie as the pianist at social gatherings. This was recalled after her death.

In the year 1882 or 1883 I made the passing acquaintance of Miss Marie Corelli, then known as Miss Minnie Mackay. . . . It was in the evening, and there was a roomful of people, but the only distinct impression that survives is of a dark, curly haired young man who was introduced as Eric Mackay, and of a very small lady with pale blue eyes and fluffy fair hair, the adopted daughter of the house, Miss Minnie Mackay. Miss Mackay was very frank and friendly, and confided to me that she was in the throes of making a momentous decision. She had to earn her living, and the question was whether to take up literary work or to try and turn her musical powers to practical account. If the Signorina could not get an acceptance as an author, she would try her skills as a pianist. The particular direction in which she thought of exercising her musical gifts was, perhaps, rather characteristic in its daring. She proposed to sit at the piano at 'At Homes' and 'improvise'. Had she possessed a sense of humour she might have added, in view of the well known habit of such gatherings, 'for the stimulation of conversation', but I think the project was conceived in all seriousness. . . . From the calm way in which Miss Mackay spoke of improvising in public, an ordeal paralysing to the creative faculties of most of us, I gathered that she was not troubled with self consciousness, and certainly that trait was abundantly illustrated afterwards in the course of her somewhat stormy literary career.[39]

In her first book, *A Romance of Two Worlds*, Minnie discussed her idea of improvisation. 'In England, at least, people do not understand the art of improvising. They think it is to take a little theme and compose variations on it – the mere ABC of the art. But to sit down at the piano and plan a whole sonata or symphony in your head, and play it while planning it, it is a thing they do not and will not understand.'[40] The concert was to be held at the house of Dr and Mrs Tanner at 102 Harley Street. From reports, remembered and recorded by Bertha, the concert was a success.

A novelty in the musical line took place on the evening of December 4th. Signorina Marie Corelli gave an 'Improvisation' – that is, she undertook to compose, in the presence of her audience, no less than fifteen original pieces; and she most successfully carried out what she had promised. The uncharitable among the audience said she must have planned out her works beforehand, but those who know her are well aware that this is just what she cannot do. She thinks out her subject while at the piano. . . . Her touch is brilliant and her execution marvellous. Considering the physical exertion she went through, and the immense strain on the nerves that it must have been to absorb her whole being into her music as she undoubtedly did, her performance was certainly remarkable.[41]

There was a strong element of the theatrical in the presentation. Minnie wrote: 'I played – losing myself in mazes of melody, and travelling harmoniously in and out of the different keys with that sense of perfect joy known only to those who can improvise with ease, and catch the unwritten music of the nature, which always appeals most strongly to emotions that are unspoilt by contact with the world, and which are quick to respond to what is purely instinctive art.'[42] The concert before an invited audience was well received, but Minnie found it a considerable strain. Still pursuing the musical career for which she had been trained, she went on to sing at St James's Hall and she also gave a concert in Edinburgh to a mixed reception. This attempt was short-lived. Her voice, though pleasant enough for social occasions, was not strong enough for her to become a professional singer, and the stress she felt in playing the piano before an audience made her look for some other way of earning a living. She was still trying to encourage Eric into some sort of career and she was quite happy to play with the truth on his behalf if she thought it would help. In 1885 she wrote to George Bentley, the publisher, to ask him to look at some of Eric's poems. 'I can tell you that Eric Mackay is a man of perhaps thirty-six years of age [he was fifty] with a remarkably fine head and handsome features, – he is no relation of the author Dr Charles Mackay, nor of any other Mackays that I know. He is singularly reticent concerning his family affairs. . . . I am, as I think I told you half Italian, half American. But I am very young at present [she was thirty], and live principally in hope! I shall with your permission send you my novel when out, as it is rather a strange one and perhaps may merit a word of notice.'[43]

By bullying Eric and by dint of much hard work she eventually collected together twelve of his poems, and gave the book the title *Love Letters of a Violinist.* She corrected the proofs, selected the binding, and when George Bentley rejected the poems, found a publisher, Messrs Field & Teur, and made herself responsible for the costs, apparently selling some jewellery to pay for it. The book was published anonymously, but was not well reviewed, except by Minnie herself, who reviewed it in *London Society* under the pseudonym of W. Stanislas Leslie. It sold badly, and then Eric gave the copyright as a gift to the publishers of the 'Canterbury Poets' series. This, of course, earned him no money, and repaid none of his debts to Minnie. Why she went to such extraordinary lengths to help Eric is hard to fathom. It is apparent, however, that he could be very charming, especially to women, and no doubt it suited him well to be cared for and fussed over by Minnie and Bertha. In a letter to George Bentley, Minnie describes Eric as 'a self denying, modest, patient worker, a man who never had an unkind word to say of anybody, an exceptional character'. Later events were to prove her sadly deluded.

Minnie had had a few poems published by Clement Scott. Written in the style of Shakespearean sonnets they earned praise but no money. At last, in July 1885, she had an article accepted and published in *Temple Bar*. She was paid 10 guineas for 'One of the World's Wonders', a well-written description of a shell cave she visited while on holiday in Margate. This was exciting and encouraging, but it was not enough: she had to find a more consistent income.

> There was no hope that my step-father would change, and no hope of help from my step-brother. I was desperate, and it was then that I decided to write a romance. I had my own little room and my books, and I suppose I was full of imagination. . . . And so I wrote with all the speed I could, and one day I thrilled with great joy for the book was done. Yes, but then to find someone to publish it. That was the problem. I scarcely knew how to begin. It was a struggle, and I had some disappointments. Then I decided to try George Bentley. That was the turning point in my life. If it had not been for George Bentley I wonder what would have happened. What should I have been doing now?[44]

The publisher accepted Minnie's novel and a contract was drawn up on 5 September 1885 between George Bentley and Mlle Marie Corelli for a book in three volumes to be called *Lifted Up*. She was to get £40 upon signature, a further £30 on selling 450 copies and a further £30 upon selling 550 copies. When the book was published on 19 February 1886, it was renamed *A Romance of Two Worlds*, but turned out to be long enough for only two volumes. The payments stayed the same, but the number of copies needing to be sold went up to 750. 'There is a turning-point in every human life – or rather several turning-points – and at each one are gathered certain threads of destiny which may either be involved in a tangle or woven distinctly as a clue – but which in any case lead to change in the formerly accepted order of things.'[45]

For the first time in her life, little Minnie Mackay had been accepted. Accepted, however, not as a 31-year-old spinster, living in genteel poverty, but in her new guise as Signorina Marie Corelli, the young, beautiful, Italian writer, with a romantic and mysterious past.

'I must invent a name – and make it famous!' Involuntarily she clenched her small hand as though she held some prize within its soft grasp. 'Why not? Other people have done the same – I can but try! If I fail ——!'

Her delicate fingers relaxed, – in her imagination she saw some coveted splendour slip from her hold, and her little face grew set and serious as though she had already suffered a whole life's disillusion.

'I can but try,' she repeated – 'something urges me on – something tells me I may succeed. And then ——!'[46]

The play was about to begin.

CHAPTER 2

The Little Lady

All his readers had advised George Bentley not to publish *A Romance of Two Worlds*, and had done so in no uncertain terms. Intrigued by this, so the story goes, Bentley himself read it and decided to publish anyway. It was a brave move, and one which repaid him handsomely. He wrote to Marie: 'The book, as a story, is bold, clever, extravagant; it is an effort of wild imagination. Though I think it will provoke much adverse criticism, all must allow it to be the work of an accomplished mind, and its style of writing will commend it. I think it will be considered by some as the production of a visionary. Nothing now remains but to try and make a success of your first venture. The work has the merit of originality.'[1]

He wrote to her again after he had visited her for the first time. 'I am so glad to have seen you. I little expected to see so young a person as the authoress of works involving in their creation faculties which at your age are mostly not sufficiently developed for such works.' Marie was thirty-one, but happily took advantage of the situation. If the elderly gentleman who patronised her in such an avuncular way chose to think of her as a sweet young thing, well, why not let him? She was used to being her father's little girl, it was a role she had been brought up to play, and she looked the part. 'You like my looks – many people do. Yet after all there's nothing so deceptive as one's outward appearance. The reason of this is that as soon as childhood is past, we are always pretending to be what we are not – and thus, with constant practice from our youth up, we manage to make our physical frames complete disguises for our actual selves.'[2]

All descriptions of her at this time remark on her extreme youth, her vivacity and her lack of height. All her life she was known as 'the little lady' by her friends. There is one early photograph of her standing on the staircase at Longridge Road dressed in a simple white gown with a train flowing down the stairs. The photograph was taken by Bertha using the pseudonym of Adrian, and was taken in about 1888 when Marie was thirty-three. She looks about twenty. There is another early photograph taken in

1898 at the Royal Hotel, Woodhill Spa, when she was forty-three. It is a picture of a very petite woman, who from her image could again be taken for twenty-five, sitting beside Bertha on a seat in the Winter Garden.

In *A Romance of Two Worlds*, Zara, the beautiful and mysterious heroine, asks the author:

'Do you know how old I am?'
I guessed seventeen, or at any rate not more than twenty.
'I am thirty-eight,' said Zara.
Thirty-eight! Impossible! I would not believe it. I could not.[3]

In almost all her books Marie created a heroine who, like herself, was small, fair-haired, blue-eyed and looked much younger than her years. Her first book was published as a rank outsider in a sea of novels of adventure or social comment. Contemporary works were Mark Twain's *Huckleberry Finn* in 1884, Rider Haggard's *King Solomon's Mines* in 1885 and also in 1885, her old neighbour, George Meredith's, *Diana of the Crossways*. The latter book was based on the life of Caroline Norton. In 1886 Frances Hodgson Burnett wrote *Little Lord Fauntleroy*, and R.L. Stevenson, *Dr Jekyll and Mr Hyde*. Marie Corelli's *A Romance of Two Worlds* in 1886 set a pattern for what became her unique, mystical, style.

The *Whitehall Review* critic said on 4 March:

There is no question as to Marie Corelli's power as a writer, but her choice of subjects is open to question; doubt and mystery march hand in hand, not that *A Romance of Two Worlds* is a novel in the Johnsonian acceptance of the term, it is much of a treatise on electricity in its bearing on our life and actions. . . . Human electricity is the author's theme, and so thoroughly does she believe in this science herself that she waxes eloquent and impassioned and discourses so fluently that, in spite of himself, the reader is carried away from the world into the land of dreams.'[4]

Marie wrote this book at a time when spiritualism and hypnotism were both popular and fashionable. She did not entirely approve of either.

I find that the majority of persons who profess eagerness to know something of the higher forms of spiritual progress, would rather believe in anything but the too-familiar doctrine of Christianity. They will pin their faith on table-turning, magnetic slate-writing, and other illusive phenomena; but when it is suggested that, instead of all these things, they shall try to live such a careful, self-denying life as shall successfully foster the germ of Divinity within them, *thus making it capable of the highest clairvoyance and spiritual ability*, they are vaguely vexed and bewildered. . . . Hypnotism, which is merely animal magnetism called by a new name . . . has nothing whatever in common with what I may designate spiritual electric force.[5]

In the prologue she wrote:

In the present narration, which I have purposely called a 'romance', I do not expect to be believed, as I can only relate what I myself have experienced. I know that men and women of to-day must have proofs, or what they are willing to accept as proofs, before they will credit anything that purports to be of a spiritual tendency; – something startling – some miracle of a stupendous nature, such as according to prophecy they are all unfit to receive. Few will admit the subtle influence and incontestable, though mysterious authority exercised upon their lives by higher intelligences than their own – intelligences unseen, unknown, but felt. . . . Unbelief is nearly supreme in the world today. Were an angel to descend from heaven in the middle of a great square, the crowd would think he had got himself up on pulleys and wires, and would try to discover his apparatus.[6]

Marie writes about the supernatural as experienced by her heroine, young, fair-haired and debilitated by her attempts to earn a living as a musician, who, in order to cure her nervous exhaustion, is sent on a spiritual journey by her Physical Electrician to visit other planets. Marie's readers were more than ready to believe stories of mysterious elixirs which could be used as a cure, and of how they could be transported to another world by Physical Electricity. The book also promised a winning combination of immortality and eternal youth.

It opens with the heroine suffering from a series of nervous ailments. 'I became filled with the gloomiest anticipations of evil; and my system was strung up by slow degrees to such a high tension of physical and mental excitement, that the quietest and most soothing of friendly voices had no other effect on me than to jar and irritate.' She journeys to Paris to consult a Physical Electrician, Heliobas, and at her approach to his house the doors swing noiselessly open and she enters a spacious hall. There is a fountain playing and the delicate smell of exotic plants. Heliobas and his beautiful sister, Zara, welcome their young visitor. Heliobas cures her symptoms with elixirs and electricity and then offers to show her other worlds.

> At one time people mocked at the wild idea that a message could flash in a moment of time from one side of the Atlantic to the other by means of a cable laid under the sea; now that it is an established fact, the world has grown accustomed to it, and has ceased to regard it as a wonder. Granting human electricity to exist, why should not a communication be established, like a sort of spiritual Atlantic cable, between man and beings of other spheres and other solar systems? The more I reflected on the subject the more lost I became in daring speculations concerning the other world, to which I was soon to be lifted.[7]

When she agrees to space travel Heliobas sends her spirit away from her body and warns her, 'You will experience an *internal* electric shock, which, like a sword, will separate in twain body and spirit. The spiritual part of you will be lifted up above material forces; the bodily part will remain inert and useless till the life, which is actually *you*, returns to put its machinery in motion once more.' She describes what this space travel feels like. 'A dense darkness now grew thickly around me – I lost all power over my limbs – I felt myself being lifted up forcibly and rapidly, up, up, into some illimitable, terrible space of blackness and nothingness. I could not think, move, or cry out – I could only feel that I was rising, rising, steadily, swiftly, breathlessly . . . when suddenly a long quivering flash of radiance, like a fragment of a rainbow, struck dazzlingly across my sight. . . . I was only conscious of light.'[8]

She is lifted up by Azul, Heliobas's angel bride, to view life on the other planets. She visits world after world until at last her progress is stopped by the centre of the universe. 'What I beheld was a Circle, so huge that no mortal measurements could compass it – a wide Ring composed of seven colours, rainbow-like, but flashing with perpetual motion and brilliancy. But wonderful as the ring was, it encompassed a Sphere yet more marvellous and dazzling; a great Globe of opal-tinted light, revolving, as it were upon its own axis, and ever surrounded by that scintillating, jewel-like wreath of electricity, whose only motion was to shine and burn within itself for ever.' Her angel-guide tells her, 'That burning Ring thou seest is the result of the Creator's ever-working Intelligence; from it all the Universe has sprung.'[9] When the young heroine has viewed these mysteries she returns to earth and her own body, with a greater understanding of the meaning of life, the importance of electrical communication and the truth of Christianity. 'God's Cable is laid between us and His Heaven in the person of Christ. . . . By His re-ascension into Heaven He established that much-needed electric communication between us and the Central Sphere.'[10] As the unnamed heroine gets better, she realises that all is not well with Zara, who is pining for her Twin Soul: 'Nothing in the world is single . . . there is no soul on earth that is complete, *alone*. Like everything else it is dual. It is like half a flame that seeks the other half, and is dissatisfied and restless till it attains its object.'[11]

One evening, after an exotic dinner party given for some American friends of the heroine, when the guests are assembled in the drawing-room, there is a sudden thunderstorm. Zara wanders out on to the terrace and while there, a bolt of lightning strikes her and she falls dead to the ground. She has gone to join her Twin Soul. 'Thou shalt love and be beloved for ever by thine own Twin Soul; wherever that spirit may be now, it must join thee hereafter.'[12] The heroine is devastated, but realises that she must now get on with her own life, enriched by her experiences. She imparts her new beliefs to her readers.

> Belief – belief in God – belief in all things noble, unworldly, lofty, and beautiful, is rapidly being crushed under foot by – what? By mere lust of gain! Be sure, good people, be very sure that you are right in denying God for the sake of man – in abjuring the spiritual for the material – before you rush recklessly onward! . . . If you admit to yourselves the possibility of a future and eternal state of existence, would it not be well for you to inquire seriously how you are preparing for it in these wild days? Look at society around you, and ask yourselves: Whither is our 'Progress' tending – Forward or Backward – Upward or Downward? Which way? Fight the problem out! . . .We are the arbiters of our own fate, and that fact is the most important one of our lives.[13]

This call to her readers was rabble-rousing stuff, and to many, locked into poverty and a rigid class system, it must have seemed like an impossible dream. It was a call which Marie repeated again and again in her books.

She knew it was possible, for had not she, herself, escaped from her own dismal fate? What is interesting is to find, in Mackay's *Recollections*, transcriptions of conversations he held in about 1840 with Thomas De Quincey and Professor John Pringle Nichol, the author of *Architecture of the Heavens*. John Pringle Nichol believed in 'that dream of science – a dream here, that may be proved a reality hereafter – that all the orbs of heaven are habitable or inhabited worlds, fitted to be the abodes of happy or rational creatures.'

> *De Quincey*: The degradation of the body is a mistake. The body is as divine as the soul. The stars are bodies.
> *Mackay*: Yes, and as bodies, differing vastly as they do from our bodies, in which our souls dwell for a time, may they not have souls also that dwell in their bodies for myriads of years . . . and having souls, is it too wild a fancy to imagine, that they reason, that they think, that they may sorrow, and that they may rejoice, and that star may speak to star, planet to planet, as we three are speaking now.[14]

Marie had read the books in Mackay's study, and they became an endless source of material for her plots.

The world of 1886 was one of rigid social customs. Queen Victoria, Empress of India, was still in mourning for Prince Albert. Moody and Sankey, the American revivalists, brought a form of Evangelical religion to England which was strong on hell and eternal punishment. They combined fear, severity and threats with reassurance and sentimentality. The Methodists were for the working class and the Church of England was known as 'The Tory party at prayer'. The Church, which had been an immutable power in the community and the central focus of life, was beginning to be just one of a number of things which could be done with one's free time. Roller skating was popular and the penny-farthing bicycle had been replaced by Lawson's safety bicycle, which could be ridden by women. There were sweeping changes emerging in what people believed about themselves, their society and the natural world. Clergymen had until now been the moral authority, but the ever increasing discoveries of scientists began to challenge their infallibility. Education was no longer confined to Church schools, but with the passing of the Education Act of 1870 was widely available in the new Board Schools and became compulsory from 1876, thus creating a vast new army of readers avid for sensational and romantic novels.

Electricity was a recent discovery, and when *A Romance of Two Worlds* was published in 1886, was still something of a novelty. Electric light was produced by Edison in America in 1879, but in 1886 gas was still the most general form of lighting. It wasn't until 1887 that Edison and Swan produced an electric lamp for domestic use, but there was still no national system for producing and supplying electricity, and most people preferred gas. The telephone had been patented by Alexander Graham Bell in 1876, but was slow to be accepted. Even in 1882 *The Times* reported that there was only one telephone for every 3,000 people in London. The electric telegraph, however, had been in operation since 1837, and was widely patronised for getting messages to their destinations with speed; the Atlantic Cable was completed in 1865. Telegrams were almost as common as letters. Marconi did not arrive in London with his wireless until 1896.

It was for this changing, questioning world that Marie Corelli, with her strange, narrow, upbringing and her dubious origins, began to write passionate and mystical novels. She was just what the public had been waiting for.

Today her first book is interesting for its ideas, so many of which are now accepted as commonplace, but when released in 1886 must have seemed bizarre. She talks of inventions and concepts scarcely thought of, such as electrical communication, space travel, electric bell-pushes and door-openers, electric lighting, impenetrable force fields, immortality, and resurrection to some mystical after-life. This mysterious world of space and time travel was ripe for the novelist's picking. It is interesting to note that Rider Haggard's *She* was published in 1887, and H.G. Wells's *The Time Machine* a little later in 1895.

Oscar Wilde, a year older than Marie, and, like her, at the beginning of his writing career, read *A Romance of Two Worlds* and told her, 'I have read the book over again . . . you certainly tell of marvellous things in a marvellous way.'[15] The critics, however, were dismissive: 'Miss Corelli would have been better advised had she embodied her ridiculous ideas in a sixpenny pamphlet. The names Heliobas and Zara are alone sufficient indications of the dullness of this book.'[16] said one unnamed critic. The *Athenaeum* of 13 March 1886 was kinder: 'The prologue, well peppered with italics . . . is so serious and didactic in its tone that one is compelled to accept Marie Corelli and her story in good faith, as being not consciously deceptive or misleading. . . . The book will make no converts; but considered as a romance, pure and simple, it may entertain its readers not a little. The style, at any rate is unexceptional, and the ideas are for the most part elevated and refined.' But the critics, like Bentley's readers, had misjudged the public's need for romance and mystery. By 1896, ten years after it was first published, *A Romance of Two Worlds* was into its fourteenth edition and had been translated into many languages.

In Victorian England the unmarried daughter's role was to stay at home and look after her parents, and Marie took on the role of carer and provider. She became the main support for the household, and this included taking on to her own shoulders the financial burden of the parasitic Eric. She encouraged Mackay to keep on writing, and either she or Bertha were constantly with him to transcribe his letters, his poems or his novels – possibly, from evidence, even writing part of them for him. Charles Mackay's *The Twin Soul, The Strange Experiences of Mr Rameses*, was published in 1887, the year after *A Romance of Two Worlds*. It was published anonymously, in two volumes, and has some similarities in plot to a number of Marie's books. A mysterious and sinister doctor, an expert on Egyptian relics, returns from the East, and is asked to look at two Egyptian mummies in the care of his friend. By hypnotic powers he brings one of them, a beautiful young woman, back to life, falls in love with her and marries her. They honeymoon in Egypt and spend one evening, unwisely, in the shadow of the Sphinx, where she is visited by a lover from a previous incarnation. She loses her mortal being and disappears in an unearthly flash. There are echoes of this not only in *A Romance of Two Worlds*, which precedes it, but in Marie's later books, *Ardath, The Soul of Lilith, Ziska* and *The Life Everlasting*. Marie obtained much of the background for many of her more obscure novels from Mackay's library or from his own writing and researches, and she refused to show him her books before they were published. It is certain that in 1886 there was very little money in the Mackay ménage, and writing was the only source of their somewhat precarious income.

On 19 July 1886, Marie signed a contract with Bentley for her next book, an Italian melodrama called *Vendetta*, which was already written. For this she was paid £50 on the day of publication and £50 when the sales reached 550 copies. It was a similar arrangement to the first. *Vendetta*, however, is one of the most unexpected of her books. Written in the masculine voice, the opening page takes the reader straight into the melodrama. 'I, who write this, am a dead man. Dead legally – dead by absolute proofs – dead and buried! . . . Yet . . . I live! I feel the warm blood coursing through my veins – the blood of thirty summers; – the prime of early manhood invigorates me, and makes these eyes of mine keen and bright – these muscles strong as iron – this hand powerful of grip – this well knit form erect and proud of bearing.'[17]

It would be hard for the voice of the narrator, Fabio Romani, to sound more different than the voice of the gentle, ailing, unnamed female of *A Romance of Two Worlds*. In *Vendetta* the reader is immediately plunged into a world of betrayal, death and vengeance. No more the gentle dreams of twin souls and heavenly travel, but an awakening in a savage and frightening underground tomb where the hero has been buried alive, and where he finally takes a dreadful revenge on his unfaithful wife. 'Cremation is the best way – the only way. . . . For loathly things are hidden deep in the mould – things foul and unnameable – long worms – slimy creatures with blind eyes and useless wings – abortions and deformities of the insect tribe born of poisonous vapour – creatures the very sight of which would drive you, O delicate woman, into a fit of hysteria, and would provoke even you, O strong man, to a shudder of repulsion.'[18]

The *World* stated the general critical view. 'The book is pure and unadulterated melodrama; but it is cleverly constructed, well written and a decided thriller.' How much, one wonders, is the anger and passion that pours from every page of this book directed at Marie's own lack of power in a male-dominated world? 'What is the usual fate that falls even to the best woman? Sorrow, pain and petty worry, unsatisfied longings, incompleted aims, the disappointment of an imperfect and fettered life – for say what you will to the contrary, woman's inferiority to man, her physical weakness, her inability to accomplish any great thing for the welfare of the world in which she lives, will always make her more or less an object of pity.'[19] Marie did not want to be pitied, she wanted to be admired and loved. Even more than that, she wanted to be famous. 'Why I have longed, and do long for fame, for wealth, for the world's applause, for all the things that you seem to think so petty and mean. How can I help it? Is not fame power? Is not money a double power, strong to assist one's self and those one loves? Is not the world's fame a necessary means to gain these things?'[20]

After the publication of her first two books Marie wrote to Bentley with some exciting news. 'Today I have received a letter from the *Prince of Wales* desiring a copy of *Vendetta* and *A Romance of Two Worlds* – !! Will you give orders for the firm to send them to his Royal Highness at Marlborough House *at once. . . . If you can manage it* will you put a paragraph on this in some of the leading evening papers thus "His Royal Highness the Prince of Wales has accepted a copy of Miss Marie Corelli's new novel *Vendetta!* – .'" For little Minnie Mackay this was acceptance indeed and she wanted the whole of London to know.

One of the intriguing things about Marie Corelli particularly at this early stage of her career is the difference between her public and her private face. This small fluffy person whom elderly gentlemen wished to protect was the same person who wrote the blood-curdling *Vendetta*, and who demanded recognition as a woman in her own right. Minnie Mackay was the feminine child/woman, Marie Corelli the passionate feminist writer. This dual identity is borne out by a letter she wrote to Bentley early in her career when she told him that as the Mackays were not well off, she, Marie Corelli, was 'possessing herself of the upper part of the house'. Her income was supplied by her godfather and an old uncle in Italy. She told him that Miss Mackay was very distressed that her father may have written Bentley a rebuking letter. 'He is very crusty at times, I believe.' The implication of the letter was that Marie Corelli and Minnie Mackay were two separate people.

She went to Tichnabruaich, Argyllshire, in August, leaving Bertha to care for Mackay. She needed a holiday from her next book, *Thelma*, for she had been suffering from severe headaches caused by eyestrain. While she was in her beloved Scotland one of her favourite occupations was to row out on the loch to catch fish. She wrote to Bertha: 'On Saturday afternoon we went out fishing . . . we pulled out very softly to a deep place and let down the anchor, and we commenced operations. We baited the lines with mussels, it was quite exciting waiting for a nibble. I caught the first fish – he came up wriggling and shining; he was what they call a *gildie*, delicious to eat (for I ate him the next morning at breakfast). . . . I do not get tired here at all. I was climbing and rowing all day yesterday and was not a bit fatigued. I can pull the oars as well as ever, quite strongly and evenly, feathering the blade in true style. I wish you were here.' She handled the oars well and had taught Bertha how to row and fish.

She went on to Inverness and wrote to Papa: 'Walking along the High Street, a superb rainbow suddenly shone out high over my head – I do not remember ever to have seen such a peculiarly brilliant one. Of course I accept the omen – and visions of my "Victoria" and trotting ponies, with my little Papa inside it, covered with a splendid rug of black fox fur (nothing cheaper would suit us, then), came before my eyes. . . .

But who shall satisfy my far-reaching Monte Cristo land of ambition!!!'[21] In Scotland she was more easy-going and enjoyed fresh air and exercise, and it was to Scotland she went when she was suffering from nervous collapse. *A Romance of Two Worlds*, followed immediately by *Vendetta*, had exhausted her, and although she had started her next book, she needed rest. She wrote to Bertha, '*Cheer up*, I shall come back so jolly, plump and rosy, and ready to fight no end of battles. I will try to be such a loving tender little person. I feel very ready for work, and shall not be at home two days before going bravely on with *Thelma*, which in many ways I shall make still better – that is to be your book, and the world will know that Bertha is Marie Corelli's dearest friend. It is my opinion that it will be my best, as it will certainly be my most elaborate work. I mean the best of the three till I write a fourth. . . . Yes, bright days are coming for all. "Marie Corelli" will attain her highest ambition when she can make those she loves free from worry, and can surround them with proofs of her devotion.'[22]

After a month of recuperation she was back in Longridge Road and working hard on *Thelma*, her most ambitious book so far. The book was dedicated to 'My dearest friend, Bertha Vyver, in recognition of her sweet companionship, tender sympathy, and most faithful love.' One can only speculate on the relationship between Marie and Bertha. It would be easy to assume that they were lesbian lovers – possibly they were – and yet it was not uncommon for Victorian women to live in close female friendship with other women. Society insisted that no woman could live alone and unchaperoned and so, if she was not married, then she must find a companion. In *A Romance of Two Worlds*, Marie wrote:

> I had warmed to her from the very first moment I had touched her hand, and I was overjoyed that she was willing to elect me as a friend. I therefore replied to her words by putting my arm around her waist and kissing her. My beautiful tender Zara! How innocently happy she seemed to be thus embraced! and how gently her fragrant lips met mine in that sisterly caress! . . . Zara and I became inseparables; we worked together, read together, and together every morning gave those finishing touches to the ordering and arrangement of the household which are essentially feminine. . . . We grew to love each other dearly with that ungrudging, sympathising, confiding friendship that is very rarely found between two women.[23]

There is an ingenuousness in some of Marie's writing which often conceals passionate undertones. As Frances Power Cobbe wrote in 1878, marriage could be contrasted with 'the celibate lives possible for women of independent means. Unmarried women lost few of the pleasures of their married sisters. . . . All women inherited the blessed power of a woman to make true and tender friendships, such as not one man's heart in a hundred can even imagine. This capacity meant that unmarried women need neither be lonely nor emotionally deprived. She could share her life and her home with a companion who shared her interests, who understood her nature, who offered her affection and support – and who gave her what a woman could otherwise never have: the inestimable comfort which came from having a wife!'[24] Bertha was Marie's lifelong partner, and except for the few times when they went for separate holidays, they were seldom apart. There are few letters between them and Marie's references to Bertha in letters was usually no more than 'Miss Vyver sends her best wishes'. Marie and Bertha were inseparable but there is no evidence that they were anything other than dearest friends. In every record of Marie, Bertha remains in the background, the faithful sister/companion, the one who was there to smooth the way, to offer comfort, to sort out problems. Marie called her Mamasita, and she was the rock of safety to which Marie always returned when she had gone too far. She was the one person who had known Marie from her early childhood, and the one person from whom she had no secrets. Over the huge fireplace in the music room of the home where they lived in Stratford-upon-Avon is an ornate wreath of carved lilies. On a shield in the centre are two sets of entwined initials, M.C. over B.V., and under the initials on a scroll is carved *Amor Vincit*. Many of Marie's readers would have identified with Marie and Bertha's relationship when the only alternatives for most women were either marriage or the dreaded fate of becoming the poor relation.

Marie's first two books had already been reprinted, and her readers waited eagerly to see what she would do next. The agreement to print *Thelma* was signed with Bentley on 2 April 1887 and this time, in recognition of her increasing popularity, the terms were increased to payment of £100 on publication and a further £50 on the sale of 700 copies. The book was released in June.

Thelma, a name which Marie is believed to have invented, is a Norwegian maiden of great beauty and pure and simple character. She falls in love with an English lord who, with friends, is visiting Norway in his yacht. He first sees her as she emerges from a cave beside the sea, and when he explores further, he discovers a wondrous burial tomb lined with shell patterns. Here Marie used the grotto she had described in her first successful article, 'One of the World's Wonders'. Sir Philip Errington woos Thelma, they marry and he takes her back to London as his bride. 'A thrill of amazement, incredulity, disappointment, indignation, and horror, rushed like a violent electric shock through the upper circles of London society, arousing the deepest disgust in the breasts of match-making matrons, and seriously ruffling the pretty feathers of certain bird-like beauties.'[25] Because Thelma is unknown in society the matrons are very put out. 'Of course it was to be expected that Bruce-Errington would behave like a fool, – his father was a fool before him. But I say it was *not* to be expected that he would outrage society by bringing that common wife of his to London, and expecting us to receive her! The thing is perfectly scandalous.'[26] Society was rigid and entrance was permitted only through the hallowed portals controlled by certain peeresses. There were many reasons why people were 'not received'. A bad marriage, an unsuitable family, divorce and illegitimacy featured high on the list. Marie's background failed in most of these. When she first became famous for her books, society was very dismissive. She found herself received by some but rejected by others. She was hurt and angry, and naive enough to let it show. When she wrote in *Thelma* of the back-stabbing and the intrigues that greeted the arrival of the unknown Norwegian bride, she well knew about what she was writing. In the book most of Errington's social set snub his bride, but at last they are both invited to Lady Winsleigh's 'crush'. As an American visitor says – 'We're all here to see the fisher-woman from the wilds of Norway, – the creature Sir Philip Errington married last year. I conclude she'll give us fits, all round, don't yew?' (To be American was acceptable only if you were very rich.)

Lady Winsleigh confides to a friend: 'Sir Philip is all very well – he is by birth a gentleman, – but the person he has married is not a lady, and it is an exceedingly unpleasant duty for me to have to receive her.' However, when Thelma arrives on the arm of her husband, her beauty and intelligence sweep all prejudice away, and even the most sarcastic of the society matrons is forced to admit that she is acceptable. Marie recreates her own experiences:

After that evening great changes came into Thelma's peaceful life. She had conquered her enemies, or so it seemed, – society threw down its barricades and rushed to meet her with open arms. Invitations crowded upon her, – often she grew tired and bewildered in the multiplicity of them all. . . . She became the centre of a large and ever-widening social circle, – painters, poets, novelists, wits, *savants*, and celebrities of high distinction crowded her rooms, striving to entertain her as well as themselves with that inane small talk and gossip too often practised by the wisest among us – and thus surrounded, she began to learn many puzzling and painful things of which in her old Norwegian life she had been happily ignorant. . . . She found that novelists, professing to be in sympathy with the heart of humanity, were no sooner brought into contact one with another than they plainly showed by look, voice, and manner, the contempt they entertained for each other's work, – that men of science were never so happy as when trying to upset each other's theories; – that men of religious combativeness were always on the alert to destroy each other's creeds, – and that in short there was a very general tendency to mean jealousies, miserable heart-burnings, and utter weariness all round.[27]

As the season draws towards its close, Thelma finds herself strangely tired and dispirited. 'The life she was compelled to lead was all unsuited to her nature – it was artificial and constrained, – and she was often unhappy. Why? Why, indeed! She did her best, – but she made enemies everywhere. Again, Why? Because she had a most pernicious, – most unpleasant habit of telling the truth.' Thelma becomes enmeshed in the schemes of Lady Winsleigh, who, bored with her own marriage, sets her cap at Errington. By twisting the truth, she makes Thelma believe that Errington is in love with another woman, and then encourages her old flame, Sir Francis Lennox, to flirt with Thelma. Unable to cope with such unfamiliar behaviour, Thelma runs away and tries to return to her home in Norway. After a perilous sea crossing in the bitter winter weather, she has to make her way overland by sledge to her father's house, and almost dies during the journey. Sir Philip Errington, learning the truth, follows her, and after a dramatic dash across the frozen wastes, arrives just in time to save her life. Thelma tells him, 'It was all so dreadful – so desolate! I wanted – I prayed to die also! The world was so empty – it seemed as if there was nothing left!'

'My Thelma,' whispers Philip, 'there is nothing left – nothing at all worth living for, – save Love.'

'Ah! but that,' she softly answers, 'is Everything!'

Thelma was immensely popular and many Corelli fans named their baby daughters after the heroine. Bentley called Marie 'My dear Thelma' in his letters, and she used the same name in her replies. Thelma, the innocent and beautiful outsider who found society corrupt and unwelcoming, was, like Marie, passionate and full of romantic idealism.

For Marie, the fame that she craved was beginning to come her way. She now had money for the first time in her life and she used it to pay household bills, to help her father and Eric, and to pay for holidays for herself and Bertha. She wrote to Mackay: 'You must not allow yourself to be depressed about anything – we are going to fight for you, and in a very little time I feel that "Marie Corelli" will be quite rich, able to do all sorts of good things for her darlings. Bright days are coming, of that I am quite certain.'

The next book, *Ardath*, published in 1889, combined the themes of her first three and was the most ambitious to date. It is a Cecil B. de Mille of a book with 600 pages of love, mysticism and passionate betrayal. This time Marie vowed that she would show the critics that she could write. 'Why shouldn't a book get noticed on its own merits without any appeal to cliquism and influential wire-pulling on the press?' She hungered for critical approval. She was desperate to be accepted as a serious writer and so far they had either ignored or mocked her. She shut herself into the back drawing-room at 47 Longridge Road, a tall narrow room which looked out over a small garden, and submerged herself in the ancient civilisation of Al-Kyris. The story is convoluted and combines passion with sermons. A young poet, Theos Alwyn, finds refuge from a mountain storm in a Caucasian monastery, where the leader is the monk Heliobas, already known to readers of *A Romance of Two Worlds.* Theos has lost his ability to write poetry and he has come to ask for help, so his soul is sent on a journey into space. When Theos returns to his body he tells Heliobas of meeting an angel in the Field of Ardath; she is his twin soul and he must return to find her. He journeys to the ruins of Babylon where he falls senseless and, when he wakes, finds he has travelled back in time to the Babylonian city of Al-Kyris where he meets his alter ego, Sah-lûma, a famous poet, and becomes one of his entourage. As he accompanies Sah-lûma and learns the history of the city, the tale unfolds in huge, dramatic panoramas like an epic film. Sin and corruption cause the fall of the city of Babylon. There is a bacchanalian feast given by Lysia, the high priestess, to her entourage of beautiful young men.

Loosening the gorgeous mantle herself from its jewelled clasps, it fell slowly from her symmetrical form on the perfumed floor with a rustle as of falling leaves. A sigh quivered audibly through the room – whether of grief, joy, hope, relief or despair it was difficult to tell. The pride and peril of a matchless loveliness was revealed in all its fatal seductiveness and invincible strength – the irresistible perfection of a woman's beauty was displayed to bewilder the sight and rouse the reckless passions of man! Who could look on such dangerous witching charms unmoved? Who could gaze on the exquisite outlines of a form fairer than that of any sculptured Venus and refuse to acknowledge its powerfully sweet attraction?[28]

Theos is bewitched, as are all the young men in her thrall, who, if they displease her are forced to drink poison and die in slow agony before the indifferent stare of their companions. The sensual strength of the writing is powerful as scene after scene unrolls. Theos is lured into Lysia's silken pavilion where she waits for him on a couch of heaped-up stemless roses.

He moved nearer to her, – he entwined her warm waist with his arms, and stared upon her as though he drank her beauty in with his eyes. Up to the crowning masses of her dusky hair where the little serpents heads darted forth glisteningly, – over the dainty curve of her white shoulders and bosom where the Symbolic Eye seemed to regard him with sleepy weirdness, – down to the blue-veined small feet in the silvery sandals, and up again to the red witchery of her mouth and black splendour of those twin fire-jewels that flashed beneath her heavy lashes – his gaze wandered hungrily, searchingly, passionately, – his heart beat like a wild thing struggling in its cage, but though his lips moved, he said no word, – she too was silent.[29]

Eventually, with overtones of Sodom and Gomorrah, the city is destroyed by an earthquake. In a scene of frightening retribution, Nagâya, the Serpent God, takes Lysia, the high priestess, as his victim in place of the sacrificial maiden. 'The more she struggled to release herself from its deathful embrace, the tighter its body contracted and the more maddened with fright it became. Shriek upon shriek broke from her lips and pierced the suffocating air, – while with all his great muscular force Zephorânim the King strove in desperate agony to tear her from the awful clutch of the monster he had but lately knelt to as divine! In vain – in vain! – the strongest efforts were useless, – the cruel, beautiful, pitiless Priestess of Nagâya was condemned to suffer the same frightful death she had so often mercilessly decreed for others!'

Theos, shattered by his experiences, escapes the earthquake and fire, to find himself back in his own world. 'Steadying his thoughts for a moment of calm reflection, he remembered what he had in charge to do, – *to redeem his Past*. To use and expend whatever force was in him for the good, the help, the consolation, and the love of others, – *not* to benefit himself! This was his task.'[30] He returns to London a changed man, and admits he has become a Christian. 'The fact is, Christianity has never yet been rightly taught, grasped or comprehended, – moreover, as long as men seek through it their own worldly advantage, it never will be, – so that the majority of people are really as ignorant of its true spiritual meaning, thanks to the quarrels and differences of sects and preachers.'[31] His friend Villiers bemoans the vulgarity of modern society. 'What can you expect from a community which is chiefly ruled by moneyed *parvenus*, but vulgarity? . . . And society is not only vulgar but demoralized, – moreover, what is worse, is, that, aided by its preachers and teachers, it is sinking into deeper depths of demoralization, with every passing month and year of time.'[32]

Marie launched into her favourite themes, corruption in the Church, the press, society, morals, education and the law; nothing was safe from attack. She lectured and seduced, slashing fearlessly at everything which displeased her, and the public loved it. As a girl her ambition was 'to be "somebody"' and that, in the eyes of her contemporaries, was her problem. Real ladies were resigned to their fate; never ambitious – and always married. She was none of those and, as she admitted, 'If a man or woman elects to stand out of the common ruck and say: "I refuse to live in a chaos of uncertainty, I will endeavour to know why my particular atom of self is considered a necessary, if infinitesimal, part of the Universe" – such a one is looked upon with either distrust or derision.'[33] The years of poverty, of fighting for recognition, of pestering publishers, of half-truths and fear of losing all that she had achieved, seemed to make her fearless. What would she write about next?

CHAPTER 3

'The New George Sand'

With *Thelma* Marie achieved the fame for which she had hungered; with
Ardath 34-year-old Miss Corelli was becoming a household name. She told
Bertha she attributed her good fortune to the simple fact that she always
tried to write straight from her heart to the hearts of others, regardless of
opinions and indifferent to results. Bertha had become fascinated with
the new medium, photography, and it is from this time that we have her
early photograph of Marie on the stairs at Longridge Road. She
remained a keen photographer all her life, but sadly, few of her pictures
now remain.

While Mackay was alive, Bertha and Marie took separate holidays and
wrote to each other daily while apart. In September 1889 Bertha paid her
annual visit to her mother's sister Mlle Camille de Gobart, a religious and
rather bigoted old lady who lived in Liège. Aunt Camille, who talked of little
but religion and good works, insisted on going to at least three early Masses
every morning, and expected Bertha to go with her. In Marie's letter to
Bertha she teased: 'Write to me as often as you can, and do not ogle that big
clumsy "Herman" too much with those eyes of yours; it is naughty. Mind you
tell me all your flirtations.' Bertha stayed in Liège for three weeks and when
Aunt Camille suggested she postpone her departure, Bertha asked Marie if
she could manage without her. The reply came swiftly: 'I have just got your
letter saying you are not coming till October 5th. I confess this is a most
bitter disappointment to me, for I have been calculating the month from
Thursday to Thursday. . . . I do implore you to come home, though I do not
wish to appear selfish, but I feel that I should be really ill if this nervous
strain goes on much longer. I write this in great haste. Oh, I do pray that
you will come home next week; do not let me pass two more Sundays before
I see you. – Your sorrowful wee one. Do, do come to oblige me.' Bertha
promised to return to London at once, and Marie was delighted.

My own little Mamasita! how glad we shall be to see you. I cannot tell
you how I long for the day. *Take care of yourself, and mind nothing
happens to you on the way.* I shall be so glad to see my old Ber back, for

I feel as if I had been very useless for a month, not having done a stroke of original work. Housekeeping wouldn't suit me. I have one of my splitting headaches today and a very bad cold into the bargain – trotting after the housekeeping, feeling ill and ready to tumble each minute, with a huge batch of proofs at home awaiting 'immediate correction', is not very inspiring. Your little wee one embraces you fondly and sends you dozens of tender kisses, and wishes you were here to sing 'Il était un petit navire!' to soothe her poor head. I am very glad you feel that you have left 'home' behind you, and I hope that it will always be home in the truest sense of the word, that is, a place where there is always love and unity.[1]

With Bertha's return they fell again into their easy way of life. Marie wrote every day between 10 and 2 o'clock in the back drawing-room while Bertha saw to the duties of the house and made sure that Marie was not disturbed. When they first arrived in London Eric had shared their home, but it was an impossible arrangement. There was constant friction between Dr Mackay and Eric, and the latter did not understand that in order to write Marie needed complete solitude. As a child, Marie had been told that she must never complain of feeling unwell – 'God is never sick' – and so even though she suffered frequently from severe headaches and nervous exhaustion brought on by overwork, she believed that it was wrong to show any weakness; however, she couldn't cope with Eric's demands. The two women found him rooms at 154 Earl's Court Road, for which they paid, for Eric had no money and only occasionally wrote verse. He had an unorthodox way of composing his poems, often writing the last line first, and in little home-made scribbling-books he blocked out the number of verses and then wrote lines at random as he thought of them, which led to strange staccato poetry. Eric was bitterly jealous of Marie's success, although more than happy to live off her earnings. J. Cuming Walters, editor of the *Birmingham Gazette*, neatly expressed his opinion of Eric's poetic ability. 'He is said to have written or thought out all his poems while walking about the country in the morning, which makes us rather wish that he had been a late-riser during recent years.'[2] In an effort to help Eric, Marie had put some of his poems into *Ardath*, but the critics were not impressed. Marie hoped that with this book she would at last be accepted as a serious writer and she poured her heart and soul into the story. She sent a copy to Lord Tennyson who wrote in reply; 'I thank you heartily for your kind letter and your gift of *Ardath*.

You do well not to care for fame. Modern fame is too often a crown of thorns, and brings all the vulgarity of the world upon you. I sometimes wish I had never written a line.'[3]

In June Marie went to a dinner party where she was the guest of honour. She was presented with a splendid bouquet of lilies, orchids and roses with the inscription 'The nearest approach we can find to the flowers of the Field of Ardath.' Affectionately called *La Mascotte* by her friends, Marie was now eagerly sought after as a celebrity. She met many well-known writers and actors, including Robert Browning and Wilson Barrett, the actor to whom she had dedicated *Vendetta*. Barrett sent her tickets for the first night of his production of *Hamlet*, which she much enjoyed and was delighted at the unexpected arrival of the Prince and Princess of Wales. Marie met Oscar Wilde at a grand 'crush' in Upper Philimore Place, and told Bertha she found him most amusing. Lady Wilde, his mother, was present, 'looking very eccentric in a train-dress of silver grey satin, with a hat as large as a small parasol and long streamers of silver grey tulle all floating about her', and Mrs Oscar Wilde, whom Marie thought very pretty, was dressed in a Directoire costume, with a tall cavalier hat and plume. Marie also met Rider Haggard, who had just published *She*, a book very much after her heart. He wrote to her: 'As to reviews I get out of the difficulty by never reading them. What is the use – they tell you nothing you do not know and only put a writer out of heart with his worth.' At another party Mr Farjeon flattered Marie by telling her that she was the only *new* writer among women who had really made any positive sensation among literary judges, and that everyone spoke of her as the new George Sand.

R.D. Blumenfield, a journalist who later became news editor of the *Daily Mail*, and editor of the *Daily Express*, sat next to her at a luncheon party: 'She made many strong, controversial points in her conversation. She showed that she preferred argument to flattery. She contradicted; she expostulated and she said some preposterous things; so that when I left Mrs Postlethwaite's table I felt that I had received a great deal of stimulus besides mere meat and drink.' George Bentley, her publisher, thought she was a capital talker. 'In the first place, she says really what she means, and so you are dealing with a reality. In the next place she has strong likes and dislikes, and good reasons for either.'

Marie was becoming a celebrity, and what comes through all her letters from this time is a tremendous sense of joy. She is accepted by society, she is famous and she is loved. Now she can begin to ignore the critics. She wrote to Bertha:

You must not mind when you see any abuse of me in the papers. I have the courage to attack truthfully the cliques of criticism and the party spirit pervading all modern art and literature, and, of course, those who are stung retaliate. But it does not in the least matter while all the best literary men are rallying round me, and Bentley is not only satisfied but proud to be my publisher. I am not very much afraid now of my financial future, as Mr Bentley seems to consider that my next books will all increase in royalties, so, if I keep my health and my wits about me, I shall probably be able to do many a pleasant thing for my dear Bertha – and the day may after all come when we may winter in Egypt together and look on the great Sphinx face to face! No one is like you in sincere honesty and love. I know how to value a true friend beyond all the mere fashionable acquaintances. I do love peace and rest: I shall never be a follower of Society.[4]

Ellen Terry, who lived six doors further down Longridge Road, was much admired by Marie who wished to make her acquaintance. She wrote to Bertha: 'I had a splendid view of Irving and Ellen Terry today. The well-known hansom stopped at 33 Longridge Road, and down came Irving with his tragedy strut; he then turned and handed the fair Ellen out, as though she were an empress, and she, with her fair hair and delicate smile, looks as though she trod on air. She really is very sweet.' Marie carefully wrapped up one of her most precious possessions, a pair of turquoise earrings, and sent them with a note to no. 33 begging Miss Terry to accept them as a token of her admiration. Back came a note from Miss Terry graciously accepting the gift and asking if she could call to thank Miss Corelli in person. Marie immediately wrote another letter: 'Only favour me by letting me know the day and hour you will come, for *I would not miss you for the world*. Mrs Siddons gave the earrings you now have to my mother, and I have always guarded them as something precious but, when I saw you in Viola – after being fascinated by your Beatrice – and moved to tears by your Juliet and Ophelia – I knew these trinkets must be offered to you – the most gifted and *spirituelle* genius of the modern stage. I long for your coming that I may try to tell you what I feel for you, and, awaiting with anxiety one line from you as a preparation, believe me, sincerely your earnest admirer, Marie Corelli.'[5] Miss Terry called, and a lifelong friendship developed.

One wonders how the earrings came to be in the possession of Marie's mother. The mystery is intriguing, for the famous Mrs Sarah Siddons died in 1831, twenty-four years before Marie was born. It seems unlikely that

Mrs Mackay, a thin, sad lady, who always remained in the background, would have made her acquaintance. It adds to the mystery of the identity of Marie's real mother.

Mrs Skirrow, the society hostess, wrote to Wilson Barrett to urge him to produce a stage version of *Vendetta,* and Lillie Langtry talked to Marie about playing the wicked heroine, Nina Romani. Marie was excited by all the attention, but was still aware of the impassable gulf between writers and society. '"Swagger" folk can never get it out of their fuddled heads that Literature belongs to Grub Street. Great poets, great philosophers, great romanticists are always vaguely alluded to by "swagger" society as "those sort of people". Those sort of people are so "interesting" say the blue-blooded noodles deprecatingly, excusing themselves as it were for knowing any members of the class literary.'[6]

On 24 May 1889, Marie sent a copy of *Ardath* to Mr Gladstone, 'as dealing with the scientific and religious questions which agitate the minds of many in the present day'. He called at Longridge Road but finding Marie out, left a note. Jane, Marie's maid, assured them – 'It was Mr Gladstone; I knew him by his collar and Mother Gamp umbrella; there was no mistaking him; he seemed very disappointed not to see you.' Marie wrote to him, 'I can hardly express to you my deep disappointment and regret that I unfortunately happened to be out today when you so greatly honoured me by a personal call . . . had the fates been more propitious I might have had the proud privilege of reverently greeting the most profound thinker and sage of the century.'[7]

In July she wrote again asking him to call. 'The earliest hour I am able to receive is 3 in the afternoon. Any time between that and six o'clock. It will be such a great privilege to talk to you again.' The following day Gladstone called at about 4 o'clock, accompanied by his wife, who, he assured them, was accustomed to wait for him and enjoyed the fresh air. Leaving his wife to drive around in the carriage he then stayed at Longridge Road for over two hours talking to Marie who reported he was 'a wonderful conversationalist, so clear and eloquent, and loves Italy and speaks Italian fluently; he seemed to put all his subjects in compressed packets on the table and slid so easily from one to the other; but the strength of his hands struck me the most, the hands of a man in the full strength and vigour of youth. His voice was as clear as a bell. He ran downstairs as alert as a ferret, and reached the front door before the maid could answer the drawing-room bell giving her warning of his departure.' Marie was very flattered when he told her, '*Ardath* is a magnificent conception, and I recognise in you a great power to move the masses and sway the thoughts of the people: it is a wonderful gift, and mind you use it well; but I don't think for a moment you will abuse it. There is a magnetism in your pen which will influence many.' His parting words were, 'God bless you, my dear child. Be brave; don't lose heart on the way.'

When Marie told Mr Bentley about Gladstone's visit he warmly congratulated her. 'It is an event in your life, an event of which you may well be proud, because the interview arises from his interest in the product of your brain and heart. It does him honour that he should thus seek to form an acquaintance of one whom he believes to be possibly moulding public opinion in religious matters and the progress of thought. I do most heartily congratulate you, because in the history of your life such an interview becomes a bit of your career. You write so modestly of the interview, your head all unturned, that I feel that a substratum of good sense underlies the talent God has given you.'[8] There is another, less flattering, report of Marie's meeting with Gladstone, in her satirical book, *The Silver Domino*, published four years later. 'We talked – but no! twas thou did talk, thou noble old man! and I – as all poor mortals must needs do in thy company – listened. Listened intently; helpless to remove thee from the chair in which thou sattest; hopeless of putting a stop to thy eloquence; while on, on, on, still on, rolled the stream of thy fluent and wordy contradictions. . . . Twas but thy unctuous flattery that vexed my soul; for Gladstonian praise is but Art's rebuke.'[9]

Eric, needing money, instigated a scheme which caused Marie considerable trouble. Advertisement cards were privately circulated around the libraries, with Mudie's name and Marie's name printed in conjunction with that of her book *Ardath*. The all-powerful circulating libraries were most displeased, and on 25 July 1889 Marie wrote to Gladstone imploring him for his help. 'I am threatened with having my new book "Ardath" *struck off the Circulating Library lists through no fault of my own*, you will give me your sympathy. Why – because an enthusiastic admirer of the book . . . had some little cards printed for private circulation. My publishers have received an intimation that unless these cards (in which *I* have had *no* hand whatever) be instantly suppressed, *they will withdraw my book from their lists altogether.*' It seemed that her work was to be 'killed', as she put it, because of some over-zealous friend: she did not name Eric. Gladstone's influence calmed the situation and by 28 July the wrath of the libraries had melted into thin air.

Marie and Eric went to Switzerland in September with Mrs Dawson and her niece, Laura, old friends of the Mackays, who lived at Fredley Farm near Box Hill. Marie wrote a happy letter to Bertha: 'I am *very well,* very merry, and not at all tired – getting quite brown and rosy. . . . Hair out of curl, and I don't mind; hat blown off, and I don't care – I feel quite a gipsy! I am looking forward with great delight to the excursion from Montreux to Chamonix over the Tête Noir. I think I shall try to see the Mer de Glace, if I don't get too nervous.' They arrived in Chamonix where, 'the spell seizes you, the air inspires you, and you feel as though you could go anywhere and dare anything!' When they reached the Mer de Glace she wrote:

We had to draw woollen socks over our boots to prevent slipping, and the guide requested us not to move without his assistance. Now imagine an ocean in storm with high billows and fancy that God said 'Stop! Be frozen as you are for ever and ever!' You have then some faint idea of the scene. Billows of ice – some a thousand feet thick – the colour is a brilliant sapphire blue, tinged here and there with green; these large ice waves are split in all manner of shapes, making deep crevasses and precipices of ice, so steep that it makes some people dizzy.

Two *men* tourists had been on it just before we went there. They were stuck and would not move an inch forward or backwards. They had *la vértige* and could scarcely manage to walk back to the hotel. Well, 'nervous' little I walked right across the most difficult part, and the guide, judging I had no fear, called me to lean on his arm and look down a crevasse. I did so – oh! it was beautiful – a sheer precipice of dazzling blue ice, and below the rush and roar of an unseen torrent. I enjoyed it more than I can say, and was in a perfect ecstasy of delight, it was such a sublime scene. . . . The guides always have great hooks and ropes ready in case any one has vertigo and slips down a crevasse. After leaving the Mer de Glace we descended – it was almost worse than the climb. I began to feel as if my knees were broken. The walk was fifteen miles, but I was not overtired.'[10]

Like many small people Marie had enormous energy, and was a good walker as a result of all the summers she spent with Dr Mackay when she was a girl, tramping around the Scottish Highlands. She returned to England refreshed, and delighted to get back to work.

Her next publication is an extraordinary little book: *My Wonderful Wife. A Study in Smoke.* Published by F.V. White & Co. in 1889 and only 118 pages long, it is a sardonic look at 'a fair specimen of women of the future'. She may have written it as a diversion after the intensity of *Ardath,* and she based it on her abhorrence for smoking and her dislike for 'the tomboy tennis-players and giantesses of the era', whom she did not consider to be women at all. 'They are merely the unnatural and strutting embryos of a new sex which will be neither male nor female.'[11] Marie wrote it as a chronicle by William Harwell-Trebkin of his outlandish marriage to Honoria Maggs, a 'man-woman'. Honoria goes to Scotland for a holiday with her friend Mrs Stirling from Glen Ruach who 'dresses as nearly like a man as is compatible with the present *convenances*; cuts her hair quite short, wears shirt-fronts and men's ties, shoots; bags her game, goes after salmon, rides a tricycle, has a perfect mania for fox-hunting (always in at the death), and *smokes* – ye gods, how she *does* smoke!'[12]

When Honoria returns from her Scottish holiday she has become booming and hearty. She, too, has cut her hair, is wearing knickerbockers and over them a short loose blouse and a short frilled petticoat, 'like the "Bloomer" costume only several degrees more "mannish"'. Her husband refuses to live with her and she tells him they must part. She will earn her living lecturing on 'The Advisability of Men's Apparel for Women'. When William Harwell-Trebkin is invited to one of his wife's lectures he goes along out of curiosity, and sees what he believes to be a young man walk on to the stage; it is Honoria. She lectures on the inconvenience of women's dress; heavy skirts with too many petticoats, of corsets and of 'busks', 'bustles', 'pads', of 'cushions', of 'steels', of low necks and short sleeves. She talks of long hair pinned up in heavy brain-stupefying coils, bodices that button in all manner of places, at the side, at the back, under the arm and on the shoulder. She talks of court trains and their length and weight, of jewels, bouquets and fans, and of long gloves with innumerable tiny buttons. Modern fashion is so inconvenient it is impossible for any society lady to dress herself unaided. When she declares that men's dress is more comfortable, with pockets and a soft and supportive waistcoat, the predominantly male audience laughs, but Honoria reasons with them.

> All great ideas have been first laughed at ever since the world began. The notion of steam as a motive power was laughed at; the Atlantic cable-wire was laughed at; and naturally the proposition of men's clothing for women must, like all other reforming propositions, be at the onset laughed to scorn also. But nevertheless it will take root – it *is* taking root – and it will win its way in spite of all opposition. . . . It is true, I say, that women who are resolved to walk in the full light of liberty, should cast off the trammels of old barbaric custom and

prejudice, and adopt *every* right, *every* privilege, which the other sex wish to debar her from enjoying! . . . Be free, women – be free! Freedom never palls, Independence never satiates, Progress never tires! Be ashamed to allow men *one iota* of that 'superiority' they wrongfully claim to possess! Dispute with them for every inch of the ground in *every* profession that you are desirous of entering; and beware – beware of yielding one single point of your hardly gained independence![13]

This is a strange little book, written as a satire and unlike Marie's usual idealistic theme, although today the attitudes seem very modern. As Honoria says, 'I'm a fair specimen of the woman of the future.' A strong diatribe against smoking, it is an attempt to parody a certain type of woman of whom Marie disapproved. Her attitude towards women was ambivalent. On the one hand she wanted more freedom for women and the right to live an independent and productive life, and on the other she wanted them to remain subservient. 'When women voluntarily resign their position as the silent monitors and models of grace and purity, down will go the pillars of society.' This was the time when Victorian feminists were beginning to fight for freedom from male dominance. It was the time of the 'New Woman', who demanded the right to make her own decisions. It was also the time in which Florence Nightingale fought successfully to make nursing a respectable profession for women. As Marie wrote later in *Free Opinions*: 'One of the most remarkable changes, perhaps, that has taken place in the passing of the years is the different position assigned to Woman from that which she occupied when Dickens and Thackeray wrote their wonderful novels. . . . Woman was so rarely brilliant – or shall we put it, she so rarely had the chance of asserting the brilliant qualities that are her natural endowment – that man was content to acknowledge any unusual talent on her part as an abnormal quality, infrequent enough to be safely admired.'[14]

Charles Mackay was now partly paralysed and needed either Bertha or Marie with him at all times. He was established on the ground floor of Longridge Road and still continued to write a little, though he dictated most of his letters and his articles. By November 1889, Marie and Bertha were becoming increasingly concerned about him. He could scarcely leave his bed and was becoming daily more helpless. Sometimes he was clear in his thoughts and talked about his youthful days in London, of Benjamin Lumley and Her Majesty's Theatre, where he and Henry Russell presented 'The Way West', a pageant of songs and mime about settlers in the New

World, but most of the time he wandered. For five long weeks Charles Mackay became slowly weaker, with Marie constantly by him. She did her writing when he slept, but for the rest of the time stayed at his bedside.

On Christmas Eve, at noon, the end came peacefully. Bertha wrote in her memoirs that they 'saw such a radiant light pass from over his face heavenward that Marie exclaimed, "Darling, you now see it all!"'[15] The funeral was fixed for 29 December, but was postponed at the last minute because of a thick fog. Mackay was buried in Kensal Green on 2 January and at the gates of the cemetery the Caledonian pipers paid their last tribute. There were many telegrams of condolence, including one from Queen Victoria. After the death of Dr Mackay Marie was prostrate with grief, and kept to her bed for three weeks. Theirs had been a close and loving relationship, and for most of her life he had been the only family she had ever known. Three weeks after Dr Mackay's death Marie met his lawyers and discovered something about her past which upset her deeply. Bertha took her to Eastbourne for a few days for a change of scene, and in January 1890 Marie wrote to George Bentley:

> I may truly say I have been in ignorance of my own history up to lately. Anyway I think it but fair to tell you that, if you ever wish to know the history of my relationship to the dear old man who has gone, I will sincerely tell it to you, though to do so, will possibly seem to cast an aspersion on the memory of him and of my dear, sweet, beautiful Venetian mother; that is why I hold my peace, and let the papers and gossiping tongues say what they choose and what they will. Any question *you* choose to ask shall be frankly answered – there are 'romances' in every life, though not till ten days ago, did I know there was *such* a romance in mine.[16]

Many people wrote their condolences. There was a letter from Gladstone at the beginning of February and her reply indicates her sense of loss. 'I have been in the greatest sorrow, having lost my beloved step-father, who was more to me than my father or indeed anyone in the world. I am now most truly, most sadly *alone*, – Life has considerably darkened for me and looks more like a wilderness than a garden.'[17] Marie resolved that as a fitting tribute to Dr Mackay she would make one last effort to get his work published in *Blackwood's Magazine*. She was determined to use the name bestowed on her by her adoptive father and it is interesting to see how, with the resumption of her childhood name, her handwriting

56

changes from the script of Marie Corelli to the untidy scrawl of Minnie Mackay. On 3 January 1890, she offered Mr Blackwood the last poem her father wrote, the evening before he was taken with his last illness. 'Others have begged for the poem', she told him, but she would rather Blackwood had it as her father was so essentially Scottish, and added, 'I need hardly say that the poem if you take it must *not* be paid for – it would be inexpressibly painful to me to take money for the last lines his dear and honoured hand ever penned. Minnie Mackay.'

Mr Blackwood finally surrendered. Marie sent him the poem on 6 January with a short letter. 'Received telegram, and hasten to place the little poem in your hands. . . . I know you honoured my dearest father, – but apart from his literary value, you can hardly imagine what a *nature* was his, – what a straightforward simple mind, what a great tender heart; ah! – he has left in our home a most blank and awful desolation, which even now, we can hardly realise to its entire extent. Minnie Mackay.'[18] This was the last time Marie signed herself Minnie.

Charles Mackay left her his entire estate and appointed 'my said daughter Minnie sole Executrix of this my Will hereby revoking all other wills'. Probate was granted on 23 January 1890 and Marie received the sum of £2,718 6s 9d. Their money worries were now at an end, though Eric's were not. He was left nothing and it seemed that they would not be rid of him. Outwardly he remained charming, but his influence over Marie was later almost to destroy her.

Hardly had they begun to regain their normal lives when, in April, they received word that Bertha's mother was seriously unwell and it was thought that she might not live. From the time when Marie and Bertha, as little children, first met at the Norfolk Hotel in Brighton, the Countess had been almost as much a mother to Marie, as she was to Bertha. When in London, Marie spent much of her time with the van der Vyvers, and she always called Bertha's mother Motherbird. Now their shared mother was dying, and coming so soon after the loss of Dr Mackay, it was almost more than they could bear. They went to Kensington to the Countess's house and nursed her until the end.

After it was over, needing to get away from the sorrow and grief, Marie, Bertha and Eric left Longridge Road in May to spend two weeks in the quiet and peace of Stratford-upon-Avon. They stayed at the Falcon Hotel in Stratford for ten days and passed the time so happily that Marie hoped they would return for a longer stay, but as she wished to finish her book, they returned to Longridge Road.

Bertha's thirty-sixth birthday was 11 June 1890. Eric unexpectedly presented her with a parcel containing a letter-book in brown leather with a lock and key, and with an inscription on the first page: 'To Bertha with all good wishes on her birthday. From her affectionate friend "George". June 11th 1890.' He dedicated a poem on the first page 'To My Lady in Wrath'. The use of his first name 'George' and the tone of the poem, indicates a surprising degree of intimacy between Eric and Bertha. Part of the poem reads:

Oh, come to me, come O my Love! in the morrow that waits for us both,
And the Future will pardon the Past, for the seeming collapse of an oath;
And the hope that is centred in thee, when the right to invest it is won,
Will illumine and gladden the world with a glory surpassing the sun!

Aye, Lady! believe it of me: I would rather be slain in the night,
I would rather be thrown in the sea when the hurricane's ready to smite,
I would rather be hunted of wolves in a winter of havoc and dearth,
Than endure the disdain of an hour from the sweetest woman on earth.[19]

Possibly Eric was either trying to make trouble between Bertha and Marie, or asking pardon for something he had done or said. There is no answering message from Bertha.

Marie's next book was finished and is a dramatic morality tale of enormous power. *Wormwood, A Drama of Paris,* concerns the horrors of absinthe addiction. Marie had a poor opinion of Paris and in a later book, *The Master Christian*, she dismisses Paris society thus: 'Paris has long been playing a losing game. Her men are dissolute, her women shameless – her youth of both sexes depraved, – her laws are corrupt – her arts decadent – her religion dead. What next can be expected of her?'[20] *Wormwood* is a terrifying exploration into the mind of a young man, an addict; his loss of moral judgement; the effect on him of alcoholic poisoning; and then a journey with him through his drugged hallucinations. The book is an eloquent diatribe against the evils of alcohol and drugs. Although today it seems overdramatic, it is a powerful book and the descriptions of sub-life in the Paris slums are shocking. Some of the background knowledge of the depravity of absinthe drinkers could have come from Dr Mackay's article on 'the unfortunate and crazy love of the French people, male and female', for absinthe, which he sent to *Blackwood's Magazine* in October 1889, just before he died. Marie abhorred any form of intemperance and wished her readers to be aware of its seductive dangers.

She wrote 'The action of absinthe can no more be opposed than the action of morphia. Once absorbed into the blood, a clamorous and constant irritation is kept up throughout the system, – an irritation which can only be assuaged and pacified by fresh draughts of the ambrosial poison.' Gaston is the name of the miserable hero, whose downfall commences when he discovers that his betrothed, Pauline, has betrayed him with his best friend, Silvio. Still obsessed by her beauty, he hides in the slums, and drinking to forget his pain, he becomes an absintheur. 'Whosoever has absinthe for his friend and boon companion has made an end of conscience, and for this blessing, at least, should thank the dreadful unseen gods!' As he loses all social conscience, he murders Silvio, and by confessing this deed to Pauline drives her to suicide. Marie then writes a fearful confession, by Gaston, of his downward path into a living hell:

I am a thing more abject than the lowest beggar that crawls through Paris whining for a sou! – I am a slinking, shuffling beast, half monkey, half man, whose aspect is so vile, whose body is so shaken with delirium, whose eyes are so murderous, that if you met me by chance in the day-time, you would probably shriek for sheer alarm! But you will not see me thus – daylight and I are not friends. . . . For twenty francs you can purchase me body and soul, – for twenty francs I will murder or steal, – all true *absintheurs* are purchasable! For they are the degradation of Paris, – the canker of the city – the slaves of a mean insatiable madness which nothing but death can cure.

Gaston's doctor implores him to give up drinking. 'It is a detestable habit, – a horrible craze of the Parisians, who are positively deteriorating in blood and brain by reason of their passion for this poison. What the next generation will be, I dread to think! I know it is a difficult business to break off anything to which the system has grown accustomed, – but you are still a young man, and you cannot be too strongly warned against the danger of continuing in your present course of life. Moral force is necessary, – and you must exert it.'

But Gaston is beyond salvation and continues on his downward path to a degraded end. Bentley was appalled by some of the passages but the agreement to publish *Wormwood* was signed on 1 September 1890. This time the terms were more favourable: £100 on signature and £300 on the day of publication. The public read *Wormwood* with a horrified fascination and the November first edition was sold out in ten days. The critics, predictably, slated it, *The Times* called it 'a succession of tedious and exaggerated soliloquies, relieved by tolerably dramatic, but repulsive incidents', but Marie was becoming resigned to their notices. She said, 'The Public itself is the Supreme Critic now, – its "review" does not appear in print, but nevertheless its unwritten verdict declares itself with such an amazing weight of influence, that the ephemeral opinion of a few ill-paid journalists are the merest straws beating against the strong force of a whirlwind!'[22]

After the publication of *Wormwood* Marie and Bertha resolved to take a holiday and Marie decided they would spend the winter at Clarens, near Montreux in Switzerland. She wanted it to be a complete holiday; she would do no work, but would only 'think and *dream*, and inhale the sweet mountain air, and listen to the tinkle-tinkle of goat bells'. She longed to show Bertha 'that lovely land of the lakes and eternal snow'. The plan was not a success; the snow was truly eternal; the damp cold chilled them to the bone; the heating was quite inadequate, and the house, which they had rented unseen, was impossible in the winter. Marie developed chills and blamed Bertha and they returned to England in March 1891, cold and cross.

Marie next set to work on another of her mystical novels, *The Soul of Lilith*, which she described in the preface as 'simply the account of a strange and daring experiment once actually attempted, and is offered to those who are interested in the unseen "possibilities" of the Hereafter, merely for what it is, – a single episode in the life of a man who voluntarily sacrificed his whole worldly career in a supreme effort to prove the apparently Unprovable.' Once again she writes of a mysterious Egyptian-looking hero, by name El-Râmi, who is a man of mystical powers. In a locked room upstairs, guarded by an old Arab woman, lies the body of a beautiful young girl who he has brought back from the dead by means of a secret liquid. At first it is a scientific experiment, to try and prove the existence of life after death, but now he wants more.

> Of what avail is it to propound questions that no one can answer? Of what use is it to attempt to solve the mystery of life which must for ever remain mysterious? . . . Every living creature who is not too stunned by misery for thought craves to know positively whether the Soul, – the Immortal, Individual Ego, be Fable or Fact. Never more than in this, our own period, did people search with such unabated

feverish yearning into the things that seem supernatural; . . . It would seem that this world has grown too narrow for the aspirations of its inhabitants; – and some of us instinctively feel that we are on the brink of strange discoveries respecting the powers unearthly, whether for good or evil we dare not presume to guess.[23]

This was much in tune with the Victorian fascination with mediums and table rapping, and there were many charlatans only too willing to take money from the gullible. In *A Romance of Two Worlds*, Marie wrote 'that disembodied spirits never become so undignified as to upset furniture and rap on tables. . . . Spiritual beings are purely spiritual; they cannot touch anything human, much less deal in such vulgar display as throwing about of chairs and the opening of locked sideboards.'[24]

El-Râmi, however, is a true scientist and only he knows how to communicate with Lilith, who lies motionless on a silken couch in a canopied room, and appears to be in a trance. He has the power to summon her spirit to him, then send it to seek information from other worlds. Heliobas, now the Supreme Head of the Brethren of the Cross, arrives to inform El-Râmi he has heard of his experiments, and that the girl must be allowed to die. Her soul is hovering and pleading to be free. El-Râmi refuses to comply with his demand, but decides that he will summon Lilith back from her trance-like state to be his soulmate. When he calls her, she warns him that if he persists she will disappear for ever. Believing in the strength of his love for her he insists on her return, but as he kisses her, sees her withering before his eyes. The skin blisters and the flesh blackens, 'the Body itself was crumbling into ashes before his very sight, helped into swifter dissolution by the electric potency of his own vaunted "life-elixir"'. Her soul is free at last. El-Râmi falls insensible on to the couch where all that is left of Lilith is a faint greyish-white powder. When El-Râmi recovers consciousness he is mad, and is taken to the Monastery of the Cross in Cyprus, where he is placed under the care of the Brethren.

The Soul of Lilith, published in 1892, was enormously popular. It combined romance and mysticism and a field of semi-scientific writing in which Marie was the leading, if not the only, female exponent. She was aware of her readers' demands for this. 'It so happens that when wielders of the pen essay to tell us of wars, of shipwrecks, of hairsbreadth escapes from danger, of love and politics and society, we read their pages with merely transitory pleasure and frequent indifference, but when they touch upon subjects beyond earthly experience – when they attempt, however feebly, to lift our inspirations to the possibilities of the Unseen, then we give them our eager attention and almost passionate interest. Critics look upon this tendency as morbid, unwholesome and pernicious; but nevertheless the tendency is there.'[25]

For *The Soul of Lilith*, Marie received £250 on signature, a further £250 on publication and 6s per copy after the sale of the first 1,500 copies. Three months after publication the book was into its fourth edition. This time Marie had hoped that George Bentley would have some influence with the critics, but when asked to intervene on her behalf, he replied, 'Good wine needs no bush and I am averse to associating your name or mine with a system of vulgar exploitation.' The critics were predictably unkind about *The Soul of Lilith*. The *Pall Mall Gazette* wrote, 'It would be impossible in columns of extracts to convey any idea of the platitude-in-extravagance which pervades this book from end to end. If it were amusing one could forgive it; but there is something so frigid and mechanical in the whole thing that it does not even raise a smile.' Marie in her rage threatened action, but Bentley wrote to calm her. 'Laugh at the review, and don't notice it to any of your friends. You have a good spirit of your own, and you don't mean to be crushed, and neither will you be. You will be the first to laugh this day six months for having been temporarily disquieted. As to law! Oh lor! Wouldn't your enemies, if you have any, rejoice to see you at loggerheads with the Press. No, no, that wouldn't do.'[26]

Marie's anger abated and in May 1892 she received a kind letter from Mr Bentley who now addressed her as Thelma. 'I am sure you will now see that the late attacks on "Lilith" will derive their importance only when you notice them. Even from those who do not like highly imaginative literature, I have heard the remark that the reviews in question were entirely one-sided, and left one to suppose that the English public was cracked in running after a writer without a solitary merit.' In July 1892 Marie, still smarting, began work on a secret plan to get even with the critics. Aided and abetted by Eric she kept her plans to herself.

Marie attracted around her a wide circle of young men, especially artists and writers, who enjoyed her company. Among them was the journalist Coulson Kernahan, and the popular poet, reciter and musician Clifford Harrison, who gave his recitals at Steinway Hall and had an almost cult following. Marie worried about Clifford Harrison, who had been unwell, and wanted to help him. She was concerned that if he became too ill to earn a living from reciting he would be in financial trouble and she had tried to encourage him to write a novel. Now she drafted a plot for him to use and wrote the outline in eight foolscap pages, as Coulson Kernahan described it:

> Every word is penned in her own beautiful handwriting, the plot itself is in black, the headings and side notes are in red ink, and the pages are fastened together with care that is almost sentimental by little bows of silk ribbon, of the colour she so often affected – a delicate pink. The manuscript opens with a romantically 'Lo! here behold!' There are two climaxes, each cunningly hidden away as in a casket. We come in our reading of the context to the words: 'He turns to raise and clasp her in his arms. She is ——' The rest is curtained from the reader's eye under a slip of paper inscribed 'Climax I', and secured by a bow of the same pink ribbon. Untying the bow, and drawing aside the curtain, we see the word – 'DEAD!' Or, in case a happy ending be chosen, under the slip, similarly tied, and inscribed 'Climax II', we read the words:– 'Perfectly happy with perfect lover and perfect love.'[27]

In the *Strand Magazine* there is a facsimile of the manuscript, which in itself is a work of art, with a transcription of the whole document. Clifford Harrison never did write his great novel, but he preserved the prototype until his death.

Coulson Kernahan remained a close friend of the two women, and when later in her life he asked Marie if he could write about her, she replied: 'Please, dear Coulson Kernahan, *never* allude to me in any book of "reminiscences"! it is *such* a bore! all *personal* recollections are to me a distinct mistake – the particular theories I hold are against them. Time for me is "*Now*" – Past and Future are in the *Present Hour*. Re your book – of course poor Conan Doyle's brain is diseased – with that of Sir Oliver Lodge – the mischief is slow and gradual, but it is working in both men – so we must have patience and pity.'[28] His article in the *Strand Magazine* was published after Marie's death, and he did not include her in his book *Celebrities*.

CHAPTER 4

Royal Patronage

In 1891 Marie was cheered to find a message from the Dowager Duchess of Roxburghe who had lent Queen Victoria her copy of *A Romance of Two Worlds* which Her Majesty had much enjoyed. Her Majesty would be happy to accept a presentation copy, and Marie, greatly flattered, organised this with Bentley. The Queen was delighted with the gift and commanded that in future all Marie Corelli's books be sent to her. Marie, overjoyed at this recognition, wanted to advertise the royal patronage but Bentley advised modesty as he feared it would be misconstrued as self-advertising. Naturally when the public did discover that the Queen was a fan of Miss Corelli's works, sales increased. Marie continued to find favour with royalty for in March 1893 she was summoned to meet the Queen's daughter, Empress Frederick, at Buckingham Palace. The Empress wanted to thank Marie for the pleasure her books had given to the Emperor, who had recently died.

The year before in 1892, Bertha, worried that Marie was heading for another bout of nervous exhaustion, had urged her to go away for a holiday and suggested that she go to Homburg where many of her friends were already enjoying the season. A week after Marie's arrival she wrote a happy letter to Bertha: 'The rooms are very pretty and comfortable. I have a balcony and a garden to myself, and I can sit and watch everyone go past, which is amusing, and the weather is quite glorious. You must come next time and see this fashionable and social rendezvous. I am sending you today a photograph of the lovely promenade, where your little friend is living *en luxe* like a small princess.'

She wrote again to tell Bertha that the next evening she had been the guest of honour at a dinner given by a Mr and Mrs Gabriel at the Kursaal and found that their table was next to that of the Prince of Wales. 'My seat faced him. He leaned back in his chair, smoking a cigarette, stroked his moustache, and fixed his eyes full upon me. He continued to look, much to the satisfaction of my host, who whispered, "I told you the Prince would not be long before spying you out." Well, H.R.H. then spoke in a low tone to Sir Christopher Sykes and Colonel Clarke, his Equerry-in-Waiting; when the Royal Party rose to go, the Prince passed, so did Sir Christopher, but Colonel Clarke, the Equerry, paused, and deliberately took off his hat to me with a profound bow. It was very curious.'[1]

The next day Colonel Clarke and Sir Charles Hall called on her and brought her an invitation to dine with His Royal Highness and explained to her how she was to behave. She was not to address him unless he first spoke to her, and in conversation she was to say 'Sir', and never speak or touch on the subject of religion or politics. All Marie's friends and acquaintances were abuzz. 'Congratulations have been pouring in upon me, and I have such a collection of magnificent sprays of flowers to wear tonight. I can't possibly wear them all! People are commenting and chattering and staring pretty considerably. It is too funny.' She went on:

The dinner was delightful. I sat on the Prince's left hand and Lady Sophia Macnamara on his right. He talked to me most of the time and was most attentive. He knew all my books and conversed about the different scenes in them; then he remarked on the smallness of my hand! He took it in his own to look at it, and called the attention of everyone to it and said, 'Out of small things what wonders rise!' After dinner we went out into the garden to hear the music. Really the Prince is charming, extremely courtly manners, a winning smile, and a peculiar way of doing things which is very 'taking'.

At saying 'good-night' I curtsied, but he gave me his hand and said, 'I am very pleased to know you; you must not stand on ceremony with me!' Altogether the whole thing was a success.[2]

Marie's letters to Bertha reflect her delight. Now she really was 'somebody'. His Royal Highness stopped to speak to her on the terrace and told her not to catch cold, 'We cannot be too careful of *you!*' He sent her his tickets for the Concert Room, and 'the Empress Frederick and her daughter, Princess Christian, and heaps of others were there. *You* will be amused to hear that when I went to that concert I was in my little white cotton wrap with the red Empire belt, the one you made. H.R.H. looked at your emerald ring the other day and said, "Who is the happy man?" I laughed and replied, "Your Royal Highness is looking at borrowed jewels. The ring is not mine, it belongs to a woman – my dearest friend."' Marie bubbled on to Bertha about the interesting people she was meeting and what everyone was doing and saying, she told

her how much the white wrap had been much admired, also the hat with
the edelweiss and that Sir Victor Holton raved about both hat and gown –
and then she rushed on:

> Oh! oh! oh! Just as I write this line I have got the most magnificent
> basket of roses from the Princess of Schleswig-Holstein. It occupies
> the whole of the centre table! I feel disposed to dance! . . . Oh! it is
> so lovely here! And such divine weather! You did well to pack me off,
> with all my 'dumps and dismals', as you call them. If I had known
> how delightful Homburg was I should have been here years ago.
> Mrs Skirrow has been here for thirty years. I have quite shaken off
> my old dormouse, stay-at-home sensations, and feel disposed to run
> all over the world!
>
> Remember, you have one true heart that loves you fondly and that
> would be quite miserable without you, in spite of all her naughty
> tiresome ways. We are far happier in our home than we quite realise
> – don't you think so?[3]

Marie had taken to Homburg her little Yorkshire terrier, Czar, given to
her by Eric and Bertha. Czar's party trick was to tear up newspaper
reviews. He was much admired and went with her to the Kursaal, and to a
concert where Marie reported he behaved remarkably well and only
howled once. Marie told Bertha, 'Czar is mentioned in the *New York
Herald* as the most beautiful small dog in Homburg!' When the Prince of
Wales invited Marie to lunch with him at the Ritter's Park Hotel, he
introduced her to his son, Prince George, who also enjoyed reading her
books. 'I sat next to the Prince of Wales. He was most attentive, kind and
delightful as usual.' She was asked by Colonel Clarke if the bad weather
would drive her away. 'His Royal Highness hopes you will be persuaded to
stay on until he himself leaves.' Of course she stayed. In a later letter she
wrote, 'The Grand Duke Michael is here. I am to be introduced to him.
Homburg life is very frivolous and rather fatiguing, especially for me, as I
am always in evidence and being pointed out to people; in fact I know
you will say I am my own advertisement; nevertheless, I shall be very glad
to be home again in dear old England. . . . The old Duke of Cambridge is
here and so are Mrs Stuart Wortley, Miss Fleetwood Wilson, Oscar Wilde
and Sir Archibald Allison.'[4] She invited Mark Twain to tea. Eventually the
season had to come to an end and when the Prince left, the party was
over. Marie returned to London and Bertha.

A book which she penned ten years later owed much to this visit to Homburg. She wrote *Temporal Power* after the death of Queen Victoria and the book was 'Dedicated with such devotion and true service as he alone may command to A KING'. In it she takes the roles of government and monarchy as her central theme. She challenges the people's demands on royalty:

> Kingship is a profession which cannot be abandoned for a change of humour, or cast aside in light indifference and independence because a man is bored by it and would have something new. A king is merely the people's Prisoner of State, – they chain him to a throne, – they make him clothe himself in sundry fantastic forms of attire and exhibit his person thus decked out for their pleasure, – they calculate, often with greed and grudging, how much it will cost to feed him and keep him in proper state on the national premises, that they may use him at their will, – but they seldom or never seem to remember the fact that there is a Man behind the King![5]

The king in *Temporal Power*, while still a prince, suffers from an arranged and loveless marriage to a beautiful princess. 'Every scribbler on the Press took special pains to inform the easily deluded public that the Royal union thus consummated was "a romantic love match".'[6] Twenty-one years pass, during which the prince becomes king, and his queen bears him three sons. His eldest son, twenty-year-old Crown Prince Humphry, is a caring and gentle man who tells his father: 'For God's sake do not make me a puppet on show before my time, – or marry me to a woman I hate, merely for the sake of heirs to a wretched throne.'[7]

The King begins to realise that he, too, is just a puppet of the state, locked into the sterility of Court protocol and out of touch with his people. 'He had lately come to wonder what would be the result, if with caution and prudence, he were to act more on his own initiative, and speak as he often thought it would be wise and well to speak.' He resolves to find out for himself what is happening among his people and one evening, using the assumed name of Pasquin Leroy, leaves the palace in disguise, with only two trusted courtiers as his companions. He learns for himself the appalling conditions under which the majority of his people live, and discovers the corruption in both government and Church. He realises that those in power are working for their own gain rather than for the good of the people, and slowly, with the cooperation of the chief of police, begins to plan some radical changes. He meets Lotys, a beautiful and commanding woman who is one of the leaders of the revolutionary Brethren. When he is attacked by a fanatic with a knife at a public ceremony, Lotys throws herself in front of him and is stabbed in his place. The King, who is deeply moved, comes to thank her and she tells him, 'Your flatterers tell you nothing. They are careful to keep you shut out of your own Kingdom – to hide from you things that are true, – things that you ought to know; they fool you with false assurances of national tranquillity and content, – they persuade you to play, like an over-grown child with the toys of luxury, – they lead you a mere puppet, round and round in the clockwork routine of a foolish and licentious society, – when you might be a Man! – up and doing a man's work that should help you to regenerate and revivify the whole country!'[8]

Popular opinion is divided between the King and the people and revolution is threatened in the city. At a meeting of the Brethren, Leroy reveals that he and the King are one and the same person, and how he had to be disguised in order to discover the truth. All he has done has been for the good of the people and he declares the Brethren will become the new Parliament. Underlying the political upheaval is a growing love between Lotys and the King, who has now achieved all he wished for his people but not for himself. He has a queen whom he does not love, and his passion for Lotys is not allowed. She tells him, 'You would not have our love defiled. Though I shall live apart from you all my days, my spirit is one with yours! God will know that truth when we meet – on the other side of Death!' *Temporal Power* rolls to its tragic end; Lotys is killed by a jealous rival and is mourned by the whole city:

> They all loved her! – and only now when she was gone did they realise how great that love had been, or how much that thought and tenderness for them all, had been interwoven with their lives! They had never stopped to think of the weariness and emptiness of her own life, or of the longing she herself might have had for the love and care she so freely gave to others. By and by as the terrible news was borne in upon them more convincingly, some began to weep and wail, others to kneel and pray, others to recall little kindnesses, thoughtful deeds, unselfish tendernesses, and patient endurances of the dead woman who, friendless herself, had been their truest friend.[9]

Her body is laid in its coffin on a boat covered with flowers and the people mass on the shore to watch and weep as it is swept out to sea by a fierce wind. Unbeknown to all who watch, the King has concealed himself on the boat to die with the woman he has come to love. As Marie declares to her readers:

> There is no greater slave in all the length and breadth of the world than a king! Bound by the chains of convention and custom, he is coerced more violently than any prisoner, – his lightest word is misunderstood – his smallest action is misconstrued, – his very looks are made the subject of comment – and whether he walks or stands – sits to give wearisome audience, or lies down to forget his sorrows in sleep, he should assuredly be an object of the deepest pity and consideration, instead of being as he often is, a target for slander, – a pivot round which to move the wheel of social evil and misrule. . . . Kings are prisoners from the moment they ascend thrones! And you never set them free.[10]

She received an advance of £5,000 for the book, which was released on 28 August 1902 by Methuen, who printed a first edition of 120,000 copies. Again the reviewers were not impressed. Much to Marie's displeasure W.T. Stead in the *Review of Reviews*, called it 'a tract for the guidance of the King'. Marie denied that this was her intention, but certainly two of the characters bore an uncanny resemblance to Joseph Chamberlain and the Marquis of Salisbury.

When Marie had returned from Homburg in October 1892 she had found herself embroiled in a controversy largely caused by her own hasty and misjudged actions. Marie, Eric and, it seems, Mr Labouchere, the proprietor of *Truth*, had between them written a satire lampooning fellow writers, public figures, and the press; called it *The Silver Domino*, and had it published anonymously. There was a lot of speculation in the newspapers about the identity of the author. Initially Marie had wanted George Bentley to publish the book, but she refused to let him read more than a few pages, and as he was worried about Eric's part in the venture, he refused to publish it unless he could read the whole. The book was then offered to Messrs Lamley & Co., who accepted the terms and agreed to publish. *The Silver Domino* is an outspoken attack on many of Marie's contemporaries. 'The literary puzzle of the hour,' said *The Literary World*,

'Who wrote *The Silver Domino?* The question of authorship apart, nothing at once so bitter has appeared since the days of Lord Byron. . . . The book is the most valuable contribution to our satirical literature that has appeared for many many years.'[11] *The Times* reported that '*The Silver Domino* consists of truly lengthy, candid sallies at the expense of men eminent in politics, literature and journalism.' Some of the book is clever, but much of it is trite. In one chapter, fellow writers are attacked and Rhoda Broughton's writing is dismissively rejected. 'The liberties she takes with the English language are frequently vulgar and unpardonable. Familiarity with "slang" is no doubt delightful, but some people would prefer a familiarity with grammar.' Mrs Henry Wood is 'always writing as one of my brother critics has aptly remarked, "in the style of an educated upper housemaid". And yet her books sell largely – partly because Bentley and Son advertise them perpetually, and partly because they "will not bring a blush to the cheek of a young person".' Marie Corelli herself is mentioned:

> Excellent BENTLEY! Stay thy lavish hand,
> Continuous trash were more than we could stand;
> Give prominence to Genius – publish less,
> Or rivals new thy 'house' will dispossess,
> In spite of folks who think the works of Shelley
> Inferior to romances by Corelli.

Other contemporary writers are praised or reviled: Thomas Hardy, Ouida, George Meredith and Oscar Wilde:

> Great Oscar! Glorious Oscar! Oscar Wilde!
> Fat and smooth-faced as any sucking child!
> Bland in self-worship, crowned with self-plucked bays,
> Sole object of thine own unceasing praise, . . .
> Thou hast swept other novelists away,
> With the lascivious life of Dorian Gray.
> Thine enemies must fly before thy face
> Thou bulky glory of the Irish race.[12]

Three years later Oscar Wilde went on trial for sodomy and was imprisoned in Reading Gaol. One day his warder asked him if Marie Corelli was a great writer and Wilde is reported as replying: 'Now don't think I have anything against her *moral* character, but from the way she writes *she ought to be here.*'[13]

Marie declared at the beginning of *The Silver Domino*, 'I want to take a passing glance at things in general. I shall whisper, mutter, or talk loudly about anything I see, just as the humour takes me. Only I will not promise any polite lying. Not because I object to it, but simply because it has become commonplace. Everybody does it, and thus it has ceased to be original, or even diplomatic.'[14]

She decried the pretence of morality: 'No nation can outrival the English in Sunday-show morality. It is the severest, grandest dullest Sham ever evolved from social history. And I, strutting idler as I am, stop an instant to stare and smile, and involuntarily I think of the Ten Commandments. I believe that on one occasion Moses was so angry that he broke the tablets on which they were graven. This was mere temper on the part of Moses; he should have spared the tablets, and broken the Commandments, every one of them; as we do.'[15]

In one description Marie outlined the way in which a publisher treated his lady authors, especially if they are young and inexperienced.

He has a soft voice and a conciliatory smile, and he gets on best with women authors. He tells them first how well they are looking – his next step is to call them 'my dear'. They are frequently much touched by this, and in the yielding softness of their hearts, forget to nail him down to 'terms'. . . . While at luncheon he advises you patronisingly, sagely, as to how you should write your next book. You have your own ideas, but it is also advisable for you to bring those ideas into keeping with the ordinary public taste. Ordinary, mark you! Not extraordinary. . . . But nothing shall be drawn too strong; you understand? no luscious colouring of any sort – keep the imagination well in check – tint the canvas grey – and make the book one that will be bought by stout, moral-minded parents, for slim, no-minded young women, and it is sure of sale – sure![16]

It is possible that when Marie was despatched to Homburg she had not seen the finished manuscript, which was left in the care of Mr Labouchere to tidy up before being delivered to the publisher. Problems arose when the rumour became widespread that *The Silver Domino* was Marie's doing, and many of her acquaintances who had been pilloried were outraged and ceased to call. Bentley was angered at the attack on his reputation and felt Marie had played him a poor trick. He wrote to his son, Richard, 'I have seen her disloyalty, and so I leave it and her.' For six months there was a chilly silence, and then Marie asked friends to intervene with Mr Bentley on her behalf. In May 1893 she confessed to him that she was part author of the book, but told him that she sold only 150 pages of manuscript to the anonymous author, who then wrote the rest. She assured him that in her part there was no reference to Bentley & Son. Bentley's answer, received in June 1893, was unforgiving: 'The literary world attributes to you the authorship of *The Silver Domino*. How much or how little is written by you is a question of minor importance, since the volume appears with your sanction. It is, I think, nearly a year since it has appeared, and during that time you have taken no step to disassociate yourself in the public mind from a volume wherein some of your friends are attacked. You cannot be surprised that this disloyalty is resented. I have not troubled you with any remarks upon it, and should not now trouble you, but that you appeal to my courtesy and to our past friendship.'

On reading the book today it seems that Marie's claims could be true. The book falls into a variety of styles. Some of the early part is lightly amusing and portrays a quizzical view of society as seen by the wearer of the Silver Domino, the watcher in disguise, but the latter part of the book deteriorates into bad doggerel and petty and spiteful prose. Not only was Eric suspected of being one of the authors, and it is the sort of escapade which would have appealed to him, but there is a strong possibility that another contributor was Henry Labouchere, the controversial editor of *Truth*.

Labouchere's association with Marie and Eric went back to Fern Dell days. His parents lived at Broome Hall, near Dorking, and Labby, as his friends called him, was four years older than Eric. As a child, Labby was a born rebel and hated discipline, declaring that he 'would rather be deformed than unnoticed'. Very much the black sheep he went to America and then to Mexico, where he fell in love with a circus girl, joined her troupe, dressed in pink tights, and was billed as the 'Bounding Buck of Babylon'. He was extricated from this situation by his family, joined the Diplomatic Service and for the next ten years travelled the world creating a certain amount of confusion in diplomatic circles. In 1865 when Marie was ten, he returned to England and was elected to Parliament. He became the manager of the Queen's Theatre in 1867 and lived with one of the actresses, Henrietta Pigeon, whom he married two years later, but because of this irregular liaison he was socially ostracised. In 1869 he inherited £¼ million from his uncle, Lord Taunton, and bought a quarter share in the *Daily News*. In 1877 he founded *Truth*, a magazine which specialised in the exposure of humbug and fraud.

It was Labouchere's amendment to the Criminal Law Amendment Bill of 1885 which was the unwitting cause of Oscar Wilde's downfall. Labouchere, who was a fierce radical, was irritated more by the wording of the bill than its content, the primary object of which was to 'make further provision for the protection of women and girls'. He proposed an amendment prohibiting all forms of sexual activity between men, possibly hoping it would force the withdrawal of the bill. He misjudged the mood of the House. It was late, the few MPs present were not interested, and there was little debate. The bill was passed, almost by default, and was not repealed until the Sexual Offences Act of 1967. Labouchere, because of a whim, had carelessly imposed 'the blackmailer's charter' on generations of homosexuals.

Labby and his wife were close friends of Marie and Bertha, who frequently attended the receptions held at his home at 5 Palace Yard. These parties were famous for their lack of formalities. Guests were not introduced, and Labby was notorious for his sharp sense of humour. He wore old clothes, didn't drink, ate sparingly, and was always mocking society. No reputations were safe and many considered Labby's receptions as a modern School for Scandal. There is a revealing quote towards the end of *The Silver Domino*. 'I am the member of a House, the adherent of a Party, and the promoter of a Cause, and your biggest men, both in politics and literature, know me well enough.'[17] *The Silver Domino* is just the sort of joke which would have appealed to him.

Marie's relationship with George Bentley, who was old and unwell, never recovered from *The Silver Domino* affair. His son, Richard Bentley, who had now taken over the publishing business, had little consideration for her foibles and she disliked him. She began to question some of Richard's decisions on her behalf, possibly at the instigation of Eric, who had appointed himself her business manager. Marie still handled all her own contracts, which were becoming ever more complicated. There were not only many different English editions of each book, but many of them had been translated and sold in Europe and the East. *Vendetta*, for example, was translated into Japanese. There were also the colonial and the American editions. Richard Bentley seemed to have little interest in the overseas sales, and from the few records of the American returns available it appears that Marie was quite right in questioning the honesty of the American agent. As a result of this growing animosity Marie Corelli decided to part company with Bentley & Son and her next book, *Barabbas*, was placed with Methuen.

Marie, who saw herself as a moral crusader, wrote *Barabbas* as a dramatic and emotional re-telling of the crucifixion story from the point of view of the pardoned thief, who watches and records all the subsequent events. The writing is powerful, passionate and purple. Interestingly, Marie suggests that Judas, rather than being the betrayer of Jesus, was in fact himself betrayed. She gives Judas a sister, Judith, who is loved by Caiaphas, the chief priest. It is Judith and Caiaphas who plot Jesus's downfall, and Judas is merely the unwitting tool. Peter too is flawed because of his denial. 'Alas for thee, Peter, that thou too must serve as a symbol! A symbol of error, – for on thy one lie, self serving men will build a fabric of lies in which the Master whom thou hast denied will have no part. . . . T'were hard that Judas should be evermore accursed and thou adjudged the apostle! Yet such things happen – for the world loves contrarys and falsifications of history, – and while perchance it takes a month to spread a lie, it takes a hundred centuries to prove a truth.'[18]

Jesus is portrayed as a figure of immense strength and virility. 'Still as a statue of sunlit marble He stood, erect and calm, His white garments flowing backward from His shoulders in even picturesque folds, this displaying his bare rounded arms, crossed now on his breast in a restful attitude of resignation, yet in their very inertness suggesting such mighty muscular force as would have befitted a Hercules. Power, grandeur, authority and invincible supremacy were all silently expressed in His marvellous and incomparable Presence.'[19]

To read this book now is like watching a huge Technicolor epic unroll. It is full of wide panoramas, strong passions, love and betrayal. There is a message for the reader that Christianity is corrupt and obsessed with power; if Jesus returned now he would be crucified again, and the reader is exhorted to listen to His message. 'Upon that hill of Calvary . . . hath been mystically enacted the world's one Tragedy – the tragedy of Love and Genius slain to satisfy the malice of mankind. But Love and Genius are immortal; and immortality must evermore arise, wherefore in the dark days that are coming let us not lose our courage or our hope. There will be many forms of faith, – and many human creeds in which there is no touch of the Divine, – keep we to the faithful following of Christ, and in the midst of many bewilderments we shall not wander far astray.'

Barabbas was published in October 1893 and received mixed reviews, some calling it a masterpiece and some an attack on Christianity and a 'gory nightmare', but it was just the sort of pseudo-romantic religion the public loved. By the end of 1894 it was into its fourteenth edition. *Barabbas* was translated into over forty languages, and it continued to be one of Marie's most popular books. It was quoted from pulpits and the scene of the resurrection was often read in church as a 'lesson' on Easter Day.

One can understand Marie's rage and frustration at her treatment by the critics. On the one hand her books were selling more copies than any others on the market, and on the other the critics either ignored her or belittled her work. As Marie saw it, an attack on her work was an attack on herself, and she was deeply hurt. Her friends told her to ignore the reviews; surely the booming sales were proof enough of her popularity, but for her it was not enough to be popular, she wanted to be critically acclaimed. What began as an almost childlike need for approval changed, with this constant rejection, into a declaration of war.

In March 1894 Marie and Bertha went to the south of France for a much needed holiday. They went first to Marseilles, then on to Cannes where they stayed at the Metropole Hotel. There they discovered that the well-known critic, Edmund Yates, and his wife were fellow guests. He had much influence in journalistic circles and wrote under the pseudonym 'Atlas' in the weekly society newspaper, The *World*, which he had founded. He had also been editor of *Temple Bar*, and contributed to *All the Year Round* and the *Observer*. He was one of Marie's main detractors and had written slashing reviews of her books. After dinner on that first night Edmund Yates was introduced to Marie, and sat down by her side and talked in such a cheery way that after twenty minutes Marie fell under the spell of his charm and told Bertha later that she felt as though she had known him all her life. The ice was broken. Yates told her, 'You are not the least like what I fancied you might be. You don't look a bit literary – how is that? You've taken us all in! We expected a massive, strong-minded female, with her hair divided flat on each side, and a cameo in the middle of her forehead!'[20]

He had a droll way of talking and they used to walk together slowly up and down the terrace of the Metropole while he told her stories and Bertha sat and chatted with Mrs Yates. They became such firm friends that they wished to prolong their time together, and arranged to travel in each other's company to San Remo on 12 March and then on to Genoa and Pisa. From there the Yateses went to Rome and Marie and Bertha went, as planned, to Florence. They were reluctant to part and Mr Yates wrote to Marie from Rome on 22 March 1894: 'My Dear Little Chap, – What a mournful little plaint! Has it got blue little puds and frost bitten little toes! I think that possibly by this time warmer weather will have softened your views of Florence and that you will be willing to stay there a bit. My Marion does not like Rome and will be glad when our time here is at an end. It seems to suit me and I enjoy it. . . . Last night we dined with the Baroness B.C. and found her reading *Thelma*. I have lent her *Barabbas* now, and was warm in the praises of our "little chap". Let us know your movements and your address, and with love to yourself and Bertha – I am always, affectionately, Edmund Yates.'[21] They all met again in London in May and at one of their meetings Yates took one of his slashing criticisms of Marie out of his pocket and waving it to her said, 'Never again, little chappy'.

The Yateses were looking for a country house where they hoped that Marie and Bertha would visit them at the weekends. Edmund Yates called at Longridge Road on 19 May, but Marie was away. At the Garrick Theatre that night he had a sudden heart attack, and died the next morning. Bertha wrote to Marie at once, to Oatlands Park, Weybridge, where she was staying. Marie replied: 'I am perfectly sick with horror and grief at the terrible news. I can think of nothing else. Poor, dear, kind old fellow! What a pity he came back to take any part in the silly distractions of London! I have indeed lost a friend for whom I cared very much – it seems so incredible, so cruelly sudden. . . . Go at once and, even tonight, enquire how Mrs Yates is, and try and see the maid, Jeannot. – Your most sorrowful little Marie.'

She wrote again to Bertha and said she did not know when she had felt more utterly grieved. On the night Yates died she had been unable to sleep, and had read the *Letters to Dickens*. When she was reading one written to Edmund Yates she had thought she heard someone calling her name very softly, but then had assumed it was someone else of the same name who was being called. 'I feel dreadfully miserable, cold and stupid and can do nothing at all. The skies are as leaden as they can be, and I keep on picturing Mrs Yates. The horrible details of the funeral arrangements – oh dear! I know it all, and how one's heart is nearly breaking with all the ghastly formalities and chill.'[22]

As so often happened, Yates, one of the foremost critics, changed his attitude to Marie upon meeting her, but to critics who had never met her,

her outspoken writing gave the impression of her being a 'strong-minded massive female', asking to be attacked. As Marie wrote in *The Sorrows of Satan* about her author, Mavis Clare: 'One longs to make her miserable! But how to do it? . . . I see how perfectly she has won her public – it is by the absolute conviction she has herself of the theories of life she tries to instil. What can be done against her? Nothing! But I understand why the critics would like to "quash" her – if I were a critic fond of whisky-and-soda and music-hall women, I should like to quash her myself for being so different to the rest of her sex!'

After the success of *Barabbas*, and the increasing financial rewards, Marie began to contrast this income with returns from Bentley & Son. She asked for a complete list of all her accounts from Bentley. There is a memo in the Bentley papers recording that on 11 June 1894, 'a packet of nearly one hundred accounts was sent to Miss Corelli made up by Mr Cousens to show the total sales and the Foreign and Colonial sales of each of her works during the last four years'. There is a note at the end of the copied letter 'For which pains taken, the following characteristic acknowledgement was sent (to Slough).' To George Bentley on 14 June: 'I'm afraid I did not think when I wrote to you whether my letter was "pretty" or not; I was only conscious of an immense surprise that my *one* book *Barabbas* should sell me more in eight months with Methuen than all my *six* books together in a whole year! And the surprise still remains. No "special" or 3/6*d* edition has been issued by Methuen for Australia or the Colonies. We put a clause in our agreement that "special" terms *might* if demanded "be arranged on consultation with the Author", – but we have found all the Colonial houses ready to take a work of mine on any terms owing to the popularity of my name. . . . Please exonerate me from any thought of wishing to vex you and believe me. Always sincerely yours, Thelma.'

Marie was still writing to George Bentley at his home in Slough, as she had always done. She had no wish to correspond with Richard Bentley, but she was still not satisfied, and so George Bentley wrote to her again on 9 July 1894. 'Dear Miss Corelli, Will you kindly address your purely business letters, such as the one which is now before me dated Sunday July 8th to 8 New Burlington Street [the publishing house]. I have carefully read your letter and can come to no other conclusion in spite of your recent letters than that you doubt our accounts. If therefore you will authorize the expenditure, we will call in a chartered accountant who shall render you a certificated account. Yours truly, George Bentley.'

On 25 July the following note appears: 'Explanation of accounts to Marie Corelli – cheque has been paid in. Amount of royalty is correct. Richard Bentley.'[24] It was difficult for Marie to oversee what was happening to her royalties, for they were complicated by foreign editions and colonial printings. George Bentley had always, until now, been an avuncular and kindly figure and she had been too indebted for his various kindnesses to question her financial affairs. With the advent of Methuen she realised just how much money she could earn, although with the loss of most of Methuen's records in the bombing of the Second World War it is now hard to make an exact assessment of the situation.

There was one further fight with Richard Bentley over the colonial copyrights. On 2 October 1894 a letter was printed in the South African *Cape Times* concerning the many pirated copies of popular English works published in South Africa, which had been imported from America with no payment of copyright. Marie Corelli's *A Romance of Two Worlds* was particularly mentioned. The Collector of Customs argued that he had not received notification of these works being copyright. This situation had arisen because of the omission on the part of the English publishers, 'if such notification be immediately sent to the Commissioner of Customs in accordance with the Imperial Act, and such list be sent to the Collector of Customs here [Cape Town], we shall be fully acting within the provisions of the Colonial Act of Parliament and shall be able to prevent any further sale of works . . . so that you will see that promptness is required on your part, and we trust that you will act immediately'. By 1 January 1895, fifteen publishers had replied, and forwarded lists of copyright works which they had published, to the Commissioner of Customs. It seems that Bentley & Son had not included Marie Corelli's works in their list, and she was not pleased.

28 January 1895
Dear Sirs,
I think that if it was technically unnecessary to enter my books on registration at the Customs-house you *might have told me so long ago.*

I was not supposed to know these 'technicalities' – on the contrary, *you* were, it being quite in your business to protect *all* the rights of the author whose works you publish. This is plain justice. If you had registered other people's books you should have registered mine – or if you did not choose to take that trouble, you should have informed *me* that it was necessary to do so.

Marie Corelli.

Richard Bentley retaliated.

28th January 1895
Dear Madam,
This is strictly speaking a technicality which should have been carried out by you, and though we have registered a large number of books during the present reign at the Custom House (of which the conditions of publication were different) we did not in the first instance enter your novels, thinking it probable that you had done so.

Richard Bentley.

There is one last letter from Richard Bentley on 29 January: 'Being aware of the attention you usually devote to all matters of business, until we were actually informed of the circumstances it did not occur to us that you had omitted to make the entry of copyright at the Customs required by the Order in Council. We might perhaps have risked appearing officious. . . . We should have hesitated to ask you lest it might have been taken as an imputation of negligence though, in technical matters such as these, a very probable one where a lady is concerned. . . .'[25]

The correspondence ceases and the relationship with Bentley & Son was finished. George Bentley was ill and had now retired; it was time to sever the connection. Marie withdrew all her previous books from the firm, as she controlled the copyright, and placed them with Methuen. 'It is quite impossible for me to permit my books to remain where they do not produce what should be their value at a time when my work commands almost the highest terms on the market', she wrote in 1895. George Bentley died a month later.

CHAPTER 5

Queen of the Bestsellers

In August 1895, Marie Corelli finished what was to be her most successful book so far, *The Sorrows of Satan*. It was published by Methuen in one 6-shilling volume, instead of the usual three-volume format, and it became the first example of what later came to be called the bestseller. Until now, the publishers, before issuing a new book, had first negotiated deals with the major circulating libraries that controlled the distribution of new works. The circulating libraries such as Mudie's, therefore, had considerable power over the titles of books to be published and the price they were prepared to pay the publisher. This meant that initially the authors' payments were largely dictated by deals between the libraries and the publishers. Books were not issued in the cheaper one-volume form until several months later, when they became available to the general public.

This changed in the middle of 1894, when the circulating libraries announced that from the beginning of 1895 all new books were to be issued from the start in the cheaper one-volume format and would be available immediately to the general public through both the libraries and the ordinary bookseller. As they no longer had exclusive rights for the distribution of new books, they would reduce their payments to the publishers, and they would expect that no cheap editions would be issued for at least one year after publication,

This announcement had far-reaching consequences. Now that books were issued into an open market and the payments depended on the number of copies sold, publishers were keen to attract authors with wide popular appeal. To encourage them they were prepared to offer large advance royalty payments. The consequences for the more traditional and less popular authors were unfortunate, but for writers such as Marie Corelli, who had an immense following, it meant a considerable rise in income.

This freeing of the market was one of the major reasons for the upsurge in popular novels at the end of the nineteenth century and the decline in sales of more intellectual works. The class of reader was changing too, for when machines took over some of the routine jobs, the workers acquired more leisure, and as the general public became more literate they had time to read, not only newspapers, but uplifting and romantic literature with which they could identify.

The Sorrows of Satan was Marie's first book launched under the new distribution system, and it became the most discussed and the bestselling book of the year. There was another factor which ensured maximum publicity. Marie, tired of the unremitting sneers of the literary critics, decided that she would no longer allow her publisher to follow the accepted custom of issuing free review copies. She refused to pay to be insulted and she inserted a special notice at the top of the first page: 'NO COPIES OF THIS BOOK ARE SENT OUT FOR REVIEW. Members of the press will therefore obtain it (should they wish to do so) in the usual way with the rest of the public, i.e., through the Booksellers and the Libraries.'

The initial sales of *The Sorrows of Satan* in 1895 were greater than any previous novel written in English. In it Marie combines many of her favourite themes: authors, newspaper critics, the corruption of society, publishers' wiles, the position of women, the power of money, and above all, the power of Satan in the guise of handsome Lucio Rimanez. The story is told by Geoffrey Tempest, a poor and unsuccessful author, who asks the reader:

> Do you know what it is to be poor? Not poor with the arrogant poverty complained of by certain people who have five or six thousand a year to live upon, and who yet swear they can hardly manage to make both ends meet, but really poor – downright, cruelly, hideously poor, with a poverty that is graceless, sordid and miserable? Poverty that compels you to dress in your one suit of clothes till it is worn threadbare -- that denies you clean linen on account of the ruinous charges of washerwomen – that robs you of your own self-respect, and causes you to slink along the streets vaguely abashed, instead of walking erect among your fellow men in independent ease. This is the sort of poverty I mean.[1]

Geoffrey Tempest has just finished his first book and, unable to find a publisher, he is contemplating suicide. Into his world comes Lucio Rimanez, a sinister but charming millionaire, who befriends Geoffrey and when Geoffrey mysteriously inherits £5 million, takes him under his wing. Lucio introduces Geoffrey to the beautiful Sibyl Elton, who agrees to marry him for his money and explains; 'Marriage for me *is* a sale, as far as my father is concerned – for you know well enough that however much you loved me or I loved you, he would never allow me to marry you if you were not rich, and richer than most men.' Lucio also explains to Geoffrey how, with money, he can now have his book published and well reviewed. Marie divulged how popularity could be purchased for mediocre books.

Lucio: 'In the first place I should suggest your getting yourself properly paragraphed. . . . There is an Agency for the circulation of paragraphs – I daresay they'll do it sufficiently well for about ten or twenty guineas.
Geoffrey: 'Oh is that the way these things are done?
Lucio: 'Do you think anything in the world is done without money? Are the poor hard-working journalists your brothers or your bosom friends that they should lift you into public notice without getting something for their trouble? If you do not manage them properly in this way, they'll abuse you quite heartily and free of cost – that I can promise you! I know a 'literary agent', a very worthy man too, who for a hundred guineas down, will so ply the paragraph wheel that in a few weeks it shall seem to the outside public that Geoffrey Tempest, millionaire, is the only person worth talking about.[2]

The book is duly 'boomed' and becomes a success. Lucio explains to Geoffrey how the publishing business creates its own publicity. The publisher launches a first edition of 250 books and gives them all away. He then inserts a 'leaderette' into 800 to 1,000 newspapers in England and America, to announce that a second edition is to be brought out. He has, in fact, already printed several thousand. The second 250 are all released to provincial booksellers on 'sale or return' and so the book is once again out of print. A third edition of 250 copies is then issued on demand, and this playing of the market will continue until the sixth or seventh edition is reached, each edition being only 250 books. At this stage the one-volume or cheap edition is issued, and the book appears to have been hugely successful.

The Sorrows of Satan is about corruption: in publishing; in society; in marriage. Everyone has their price, everyone and everything can be bought. Everyone, that is, except the famous novelist Mavis Clare. Mavis is another of Marie's heroines who is small and fair-haired. She has two dogs at her cottage in the country and one, a Yorkshire terrier called Tricksy, tears up critical reviews. Mavis is immensely popular with the public, and Geoffrey is jealous of her skill as a writer. 'If this Mavis Clare was indeed so "popular", then her work must naturally be of the "penny dreadful" order, for I, like many another literary man, laboured under the ludicrous inconsistency of considering the public an "ass" . . . and therefore I could not imagine it capable of voluntarily selecting for itself any good work of literature without guidance from the critics. Of course I was wrong; the great masses of the public in all nations are always led by some instinctive sense of right, that moves them to reject the false and unworthy, and select the true.'[3] Geoffrey visits her with Lucio and is amazed to find her young and beautiful. 'The writer of such a work, I imagined, must needs be of a more or less strong physique, with pronounced features and an impressive personality. This butterfly-thing playing with her dog, was no type of "blue stocking".' Mavis jokes to the two men about the condemnation of her work by the critics and, to illustrate how little she cares, takes them into her garden to see her pet doves. The doves are called after the names of journals such as the *Saturday Review*, *Pall Mall*, the *Spectator*, the *Morning Post*, the *Standard* and the *Daily Telegraph*.

After his wedding to Sibyl, Geoffrey discovers he has married 'a beautiful feminine animal with the soul of a shameless libertine', and the drama of his loveless marriage unrolls. Geoffrey, waking one night, discovers that Sibyl is not by his side. Going in search of her he finds her in the moonlit great hall, kneeling at the feet of the handsome Lucio and imploring him to make love to her. Lucio savagely mocks and spurns her and she runs to her room and locks the door. Geoffrey leaves the next morning with Lucio, but is recalled by a telegram from Mavis Clare: 'something is wrong – come at once'. He returns to find the door of Sibyl's room locked and commands the servants to break it down. Inside he makes a gruesome discovery. They find Sibyl's dead body, propped upright in a chair, staring into the mirror. Geoffrey sees her written confession spread out on the table in front of her – the pen thrown on top of the papers, in which she recounts how she married Geoffrey but loved Lucio. Her life is empty and she must end it. She drinks poison and as she dies slowly and agonisingly, writes of the horror she has just discovered. She knows '"at last WHOM I have loved! – whom I have chosen, whom I have worshipped! . . . Oh God have mercy! . . . I know WHO claims my worship now, and drags me into yonder rolling world of flame! . . . his name is ——" Here the manuscript ended – incomplete and broken off abruptly – and there was a blot on the last sentence as though the pen had been violently wrenched from the dying fingers and hastily flung down.' Geoffrey, horrified, rushes from the room.

After the funeral Geoffrey sets out on a cruise to Egypt with Lucio on his boat, *The Flame*, but Geoffrey begins to have hallucinations and at night dreams of Sibyl. Wanting to escape his nightmares, he tries to shoot himself, but as he raises the pistol to his head, Lucio enters and tells him, 'I am your Enemy'. In the wild storm which follows Lucio reveals himself as Lucifer, Prince of Darkness, who lives in torment:

> What would be the sorrows of a thousand million worlds, compared to the sorrows of Satan. . . . To be shut out of Heaven! – to hear all through the unending aeons, the far-off voices of angels whom once he knew and loved! – to be a wanderer among deserts of darkness, and to pine for the light celestial that was formerly as air and food for his being – and to know that Man's folly, Man's utter selfishness, Man's cruelty, keep him thus exiled, and outcast from pardon and peace! . . . Christ redeemed Man – and by his teaching, showed how it was possible for Man to redeem the Devil![4]

Lucio tempts Geoffrey to choose his way instead of God's, but Geoffrey chooses God. 'From the brightening heaven there rang a silver voice, clear as a clarion call – *"Arise, Lucifer, Son of the Morning! One soul rejects thee – one hour of joy is granted thee! Hence and arise!"*' The heavens change from gold to crimson and then to shining blue, and Lucifer, the beautiful angel, rises to spend his hour of freedom in heaven, earned because his temptation of Geoffrey has failed. The yacht sinks, Geoffrey is shipwrecked then rescued, only to find when he returns to England that his lawyers have swindled him of all his money. He is strangely relieved, as he can now start his life anew, and will begin another book. One evening he walks by the Houses of Parliament and sees Lucio but does not acknowledge him; he turns and watches as Lucio greets a well-known Cabinet minister and, 'arm in arm they disappear within the House of England's Imperial Government – Devil and Man – together!'

The book was enormously popular. It is absorbingly written and some of the descriptions of heaven and hell are wondrous. The reader is carried with the author, Geoffrey Tempest, along his own path of temptation and eventual redemption. When the manuscript was sent to the printer, Marie was exhausted and miserable; she thought her writing unworthy of the theme. However, the public did not agree. Sermons were based on *The Sorrows of Satan*. Father Ignatius, a monk at Llanthony Abbey, near Abergavenny, wrote to Marie, 'I have been reading your book, *The Sorrows of Satan,* in my quiet monastic cell, among these solemn, silent hills. I want to thank you for writing it; for your faithful delineation of the fallen English Upper Ten, for the exposure of the trickeries and frauds of the Press to the Literary World of these "Last Days".' He gave two very popular sermons on *The Sorrows of Satan* at the Portman Rooms in Baker Street. Marie and Bertha went to the one on 19 April 1896, where they had the foresight to reserve themselves two seats, for the hall was full to overflowing and many were turned away. A continuous stream of carriages arrived and the doorkeepers were hoarse with shouting out that every seat was taken. People who could not find seats stood shoulder to shoulder, and crowds blocked the streets. Father Ignatius first read evening prayers with hymns and the lesson, which concluded with the words 'The Lord shall sell Sisera into the hand of a woman'. This text he used for his sermon.

Of late years the Divinity of Christ has been constantly called in question, to be arrogantly doubted and rejected, and the servants of the Lord have cried unto Him, and have been unheard. Then, all at once, like a clap of thunder, Marie Corelli's book, *The Sorrows of Satan,* bursts on us. . . . Yes, Marie Corelli is doing more for the faith than Archbishops and Bishops and convocations put together. . . . It is said that our author dislikes the clergy. I am sure she would not dislike an honest clergy; it is the clergy who decline to go against Sisera she would dislike. . . . I say there are thousands upon thousands throughout English speaking Christendom who will bless the pages that Marie Corelli has penned. Is the power of this book merely to be accounted for on some hypothesis?

Where did the courage come from that made this woman so bold that the Personality of God, the Divinity of Christ, the sanctity of marriage, and the necessity of a religious education should spring from her pen?

Let all our clergy have a copy of *The Sorrows of Satan* on their literary tables. . . . Why do the Press, as a rule, stand aloof from our author and do all they can to hinder instead of help? . . . But our author stands out quite independent of the Press, quite independent of opinions. She forces people to read her books; she makes you listen, you cannot help yourself. In this sense she is a queen. . . . *The Sorrows of Satan* is flung down into the midst of English Society, as it is constituted at present, as an heroic challenge to that society and to the Church.[5]

This was clerical endorsement indeed, but the press gave grudging approval to the book's narrative skills and the greatness of the theme. W.T. Stead in the *Review of Reviews* wrote, 'If after she has achieved her success, sold her scores of thousands, and avenged herself to her heart's content upon her critics, she would then be so good as to take the book, tone it down, omit her superlatives, and cut out of it every solitary word that relates to reviews, reviewers, and other woman novelists, she will have produced a book which will live long after much of the ephemeral literature of the day is forgotten. Otherwise *The Sorrows of Satan* will be sunk by the sorrows of Marie Corelli, which, however interesting they may be to our little contemporary world, cannot be expected to be entertaining or edifying to posterity.'

Strangely, it is just this in-fighting, illuminating the relationship between the press and the artist, which makes the book so entertaining for readers today. Until 1895 most newspapers had been concerned with the serious reporting of parliamentary affairs and court cases. However, the *Daily Mail* was launched on 4 May 1896, under the ownership of Alfred Harmsworth, and this heralded the beginning of a different approach to news. This 'new journalism' paper promised it would not consist of 'four leading articles, a page of parliament, and columns of speeches', as the conventional papers did. The new *Daily Mail* was aimed at the masses, and because of this Lord Salisbury dismissed it as 'a journal produced by office-boys for office-boys'. Costing only ½d the paper specialised in sensational gossip and class-based politics, and the sales were huge.

It was not only newspapers that were changing, so was transport. The first car to be seen in England was an imported Benz in 1894 which caused such a sensation that the driver was stopped by the police when he drove across London. In 1895 Herbert Austin designed a car to be built by the Wolseley Sheep Shearing Machine Company in Birmingham. There was much excitement about the manufacturing of the first English four-wheeled motor car. When Parliament did away with the 1878 Highways and Locomotives Act, no longer did a mechanical vehicle have to be preceded by a man on foot carrying a flag, and the speed of the vehicle was not restricted to four miles an hour. The increase in the speed of travel and the accessibility of hitherto remote places, which came with the advent of the motor car, blurred the sharp divide between town and country. Londoners would motor down to the country for the day or for the weekend, and bring their new-fangled ideas to rural areas. The face of Victorian England was changed for ever.

In the summer of 1896 Marie was asked to turn *The Sorrows of Satan* into a play. She was busy and Eric suggested that a friend of his, Captain Herbert Woodgate, take charge of the adaptation. Captain Woodgate, in turn, suggested that a Mr Paul Berton should help him with the writing. Marie agreed, but stipulated, 'under agreement with myself and Messrs Woodgate and Berton, that nothing was to be done respecting this play without my distinctly declared approval'. The 'final version' was read in Marie's and Bertha's presence, to Mr Beerbohm Tree, who, after listening patiently for a couple of hours, told the dramatisers, Messrs Woodgate and Berton 'that the play as it stood was *unactable*'. Marie fully agreed with him and offered to rewrite portions of it, but her offer was rejected. The plot was melodramatic, badly written and poorly adapted. On 2 September 1896 an agreement was made between Woodgate, Berton and Eric with the Grosvenor Theatrical Syndicate, who planned to produce the play at the Shaftesbury Theatre. Marie was unhappy with the arrangement but could do nothing, as her agreement with Eric only gave her the right to read but not to veto. Later in September, Bertha took her away to Scotland for three months in the hope that the matter would resolve itself, and found a house for rent at Killicrankie. Marie wanted 'quiet – no boating' but she wanted to fish. They returned to London in November feeling much refreshed.

While they were away Woodgate and Berton gave a revised version of the play to the Grosvenor Theatrical Syndicate without telling Marie, and £500 was paid into her account for the theatrical rights. Marie had written to the Syndicate saying that she 'left the matter to Messrs Woodgate and Berton, trusting to the knowledge and experience they professed to have of the stage that they would alter and revise the play not only to make it worthy of the admitted success of my book, but also of the prestige of my name'. She was not pleased with the result and in a letter to the backers, Marie dismissed the badly written Woodgate and Berton version which they planned to produce.

In December 1896 they were invited by Mr Berton to meet leading actors Lewis Waller, Evelyn Millard and Rose Dupré, who had been engaged to play the parts of Lucio Rimanez, Sibyl Elton, and Mavis Clare. Marie was present at the first reading at the theatre and was distressed to find that the new version was even worse than the first. As Marie reported: 'At the close of the reading of the second act Miss Evelyn Millard and Mr Lewis Waller rose abruptly and left the reading, calling me outside to tell me with great vehemence that they could not on any account risk their reputations by acting in such a play. I was entirely of their opinion, and the whole incident gave me the greatest pain. The play has again been altered and the first act submitted to me through my lawyer, merely by way of form, – and I have only to say that each alteration makes it worse.'[6]

Marie did her best to stop the production. She refused the £500 cheque from the Grosvenor Theatrical Syndicate but the agreement with Eric tied her hands. Her lawyers told her there was nothing more she could do. She refused to attend any of the rehearsals or to be present at the final production. 'I am leaving town next week [24 December] and do not intend to return until early in February. . . . I cannot see anything ahead of the proposed production but disastrous failure.'[7]

Against all Marie's wishes, the play was produced on 9 January 1897 at the Shaftesbury Theatre and received reviews which condemned it as melodramatic and farcical. The public assumed that Marie was the author and Clement Scott, who had published her first poems and always been her staunch champion, wrote in the *Whitehall Review*, 'Do let us be fair to Marie Corelli. . . . It has been said that the play has been written without the sanction of the authoress. That can scarcely be the case when she has superintended every detail of it.' No doubt he wished to help. Copyright laws were only just beginning to be enforceable, and seldom covered overseas productions, but following the fiasco of *The Sorrows of Satan*, Marie was determined to take all possible steps to protect her future work. Henceforth she organised a dramatic reading of each of her books soon after publication, to register her performance copyright over the text.

It had not been a good year. Marie was not well and complained of headaches and severe stomach pains; she refused to consult a doctor, and Bertha could find nothing to give her relief. Marie had been working long hours and was exhausted. Bentley had earlier been sent an anonymous letter which warned, 'She has parties living on her, I know, who would like such pressure to be put on your firm, who have alone been more than kind to her, and to them I attribute this cramming. I wonder she allows herself to be so badly abused.' This had referred to Marie's ceaseless production of books in order to obtain advances, which she then paid to Eric, 'the party living on her'. In 1896 and 1897 she produced five books: *The Mighty Atom, The Murder of Delicia, Cameos, Ziska*, and *The Strange Visitation*.

Marie had put up with considerable bullying from Eric. He demanded money, he mocked her appearance, he belittled her writing, and he tried to make trouble between her and Bertha. He took advantage of her generosity while she continued to do all she could to further his career, which included writing to influential friends to propose him for the next Poet Laureate. However, since the dramatisation of *The Sorrows of Satan*, she had begun to have reservations.

The Murder of Delicia is more than just another of Marie's romantic novels. Delicia's relationship with her husband, Lord Carlyon, mirrors Marie's relationship with Eric: 'She was the hiving bee – he the luxurious drone that ate the honey. And it never occurred to him to consider the position as at all unnatural.' Delicia is a successful and popular writer but much prefers to stay at home while her husband swans around in society, attends the races and entertains actresses. She is quite happy to provide for all his monetary needs and, trusting him implicitly, gives him anything he asks for. As Marie writes in the introduction to *Delicia*:

> To put it bluntly and plainly, a great majority of the men of the present day want women to keep them. It is not a manly or a noble desire; but as the kind of men I mean have neither the courage nor the intelligence to fight the world for themselves, it is, I suppose, natural to such inefficient weaklings that they should, – seeing the fierce heat and contest of competition in every branch of modern labour, – gladly sneak behind a woman's petticoats to escape the general fray. But the point to which I particularly wish to call the attention of the more thoughtful of my readers is that these very sort of men, . . . are the first to run down women's work, women's privileges, women's attainments and women's honour.[8]

This was a good description of her relationship with Eric, who mocked her behind her back. Coulson Kernahan was present on one occasion when Eric was spreading vicious rumours about the relationship between Marie and Bertha, and accused him of being a liar and a scoundrel, saying that if he spoke one more word against 'those brave and dear women', he would knock him down. Victorian women were expected to play a supportive and passive role in life and, if they stepped outside this role, then they were dismissed as having passed beyond the boundaries of normal womanhood. As Marie stated in *Delicia*: 'The woman who paints a great picture is "unsexed"; the woman who writes a great book is "unsexed"; in fact, whatever woman does that is higher and more ambitious than the mere act of flinging herself down at the feet of man and allowing him to walk over her, makes her in man's opinion unworthy of his consideration as a woman; and he fits the appellation of "unsexed" to her with an easy callousness, which is unmanly as it is despicable.'[9]

Eric spread other malicious rumours, the most persistent of which claimed that he was the real author of Marie's books. Men of all classes in Victorian society were united an attempt to curb and control women. The demands made by husbands, fathers and brothers on their female relatives were confining and unrealistic. Marie refused to be silenced. She gave her definition of literature as: 'Power! The power to make men and women think, hope and achieve; the power to draw tears from the eyes, smiles from the lips of thousands; the power to make tyrants tremble, and unseat false judges in authority; the power to strip hypocrisy of its seeming fair disguise, and to brand liars with their name writ large for all the world to see!' *Delicia* was Marie's answer to Eric. 'The greatest loss that can befall a woman had befallen her – the loss of love. Her love had been deep and passionate, but the object of that love had proved himself unworthy – hence love was dead and would never revive again. . . . It is so hard . . . for a woman to be quite alone in the world! To work on, solitary, wearing a bitter laurel crown that makes one's brow ache; to be deprived, for no fault of one's own, of all the kisses and endearments so frequently bestowed on foolish, selfish, ungrateful, and frequently unchaste women – to be set apart in the cold Courts of Fame, – a white statue, with frozen lips and eyes staring down the illimitable ways of Death – Oh God! is not an hour of love worth all this chill renown!'[10]

Marie's own pain and disillusionment show clearly throughout the book. In it Delicia shuts herself in her room and, refusing to see anyone, she writes until, eventually, worn out by work and despair, she dies. As Marie says 'There are thousands of such "murders" daily happening among us – murders which are not considered "cruelty" in the eyes of the law. There are any number of women who work day and night with brain and hand to support useless and brainless husbands; women whose love never falters, whose patience never tires, and whose tenderness is often rewarded only by the most callous neglect and ingratitude.' Marie did not die, but she did become seriously ill.

By March 1897 Marie was suffering, not only from headaches, eyestrain and betrayal, but also from an internal complaint. In the hope that Scotland might restore her to health, she and Bertha went again to Killiecrankie for three months. It was obvious that she was still seriously ill, but she refused to see a doctor. She insisted on sitting for two portraits as a gift for Bertha, one painted by Helen Donald Smith and one by Ellis Roberts. In some of the sittings she was in such agony she nearly fainted and nothing Bertha could do relieved the abdominal pain. Marie was told that she must have an operation – or she would die. Surgery was still very primitive, operations were performed in the patient's home, and, as almost all doctors were men, many women preferred to suffer rather than to expose their bodies to the eyes of a stranger. Marie was eventually persuaded to see one of the most famous surgeons of the day, Sir John Williams, but insisted on knowing exactly what he proposed to do and questioned him closely. He resented her attitude but as Marie said, 'It is my life at stake, and I must know.' This eminent gentleman said to Eric, when talking about the pros and cons of the operation, 'Once I get her into my surgical home I will be a match for twenty Marie Corellis.' This was reported to Marie and when the eminent gentleman's nurse arrived the next day to set up one of the bedrooms at Longridge Road as an operating theatre, Marie sent her away. She was frightened that she would die during the operation, and took a house at Hove hoping that by some miracle the sea air would cure her.

The miracle came, not in the form of sea air, but in the person of Dr Mary Scharlieb. Marie and Bertha had known Dr Scharlieb for nearly ten years as a friend. Her cousin, Charlotte, was married to Henry Bird, the well-known organist, who had played before the Queen and Prince Consort, and the Birds lived in Longridge Road. Dr Scharlieb, too, was musical and spent every Saturday afternoon and Sunday with her cousins in Longridge Road, where she had met Marie. Dr Scharlieb was a woman of great courage. She had married and done her early medical training in India before she returned to London. After the early death of her husband she completed her training as a doctor at the Royal Free Hospital, the first hospital in England to open its wards to women. In 1882 she became a Bachelor of Medicine and Surgery and in 1887 bravely opened her own rooms at 149 Harley Street. Women doctors were rare and viewed with great suspicion, and patients were reluctant to attend her surgery. She worked with Elizabeth Garrett Anderson at the New Hospital for Women in Marylebone and in her memoirs she reported that the staff were excellent, but because they were women, under-trained. When Dr Garrett Anderson retired, Dr Scharlieb was put in charge of the New Hospital for Women and specialised in abdominal and gynaecological surgery. Marie trusted her enough to ask her to perform the necessary operation, almost certainly a hysterectomy, and before the operation said that if anything went wrong she would bear the blame. She and Bertha went to Hove in October, and the operation was performed on 29 December 1897. Dr Scharlieb, helped by her assistant Dr Frampton, probably saved Marie's life. When Marie was well enough to be moved she and Bertha went to the King's Private Hotel in Brighton for three months to convalesce under the care of Dr Scharlieb. By March 1898, Marie was slowly recovering.

Two years earlier, before Marie had become aware of Eric's duplicity, she had asked Hutchinson's to publish a book of Eric's poems, *Arrows of Song*, which they agreed to do only on the condition that she wrote a novel for them. Eric's poems were not a success, but Marie's book was enormously popular. *The Mighty Atom* was released in March 1896, and the first edition of 20,000 copies sold out almost immediately and was quickly reprinted. The book is an attack on the modern education system, which would not allow religion to be taught to Board School children. Marie wrote in her dedication 'TO THOSE SELF-STYLED "PROGRESSIVISTS" WHO BY PRECEPT AND EXAMPLE ASSIST THE INFAMOUS CAUSE OF EDUCATION WITHOUT RELIGION, and who, by promoting the idea, borrowed from French atheism, of denying to the children in Board Schools and elsewhere, the knowledge and love of God as the true foundation of noble living, are guilty of a worse crime than murder'.

The book is melodramatic and full of Victorian sentiment, but it was immensely popular, and many wept over the death of the two innocent children, Lionel and Jessamine. The character of Reuben Dale, the father of Jessamine and the sexton of the little church at Combe Martin, was based on that of James Norman, a charming man whom Marie had met when she and Bertha stayed at Ilfracombe in 1895 and went to visit the church. Marie sent him a copy of the book and he wrote: 'I am sure I am highly favoured, I get scores of people daily to see me and the old church through you. . . . I hope if you ever come down to this part you will call upon me. . . . I conclude with kind love from your old friend. Reuben.' James Norman had a postcard picture of himself taken as Reuben Dale, which he sold to visitors. In March 1898, while Marie was still convalescing at Brighton, she learned that James Norman had died. Marie wrote to H.W. Toms, the Rector of Combe Martin, to send her condolences. The Revd Toms replied:

4 March 1898

Dear Madam,

I received your letter this morning and am very glad that you are recovering from your serious illness. Our late sexton had a bad attack of pleurisy in the end of 1896; he became much better last summer and autumn, but was never the same again. . . . Consumption was his illness. He was quite aware that he could not live long and was conscious to the end, for which, we trust, he was prepared. He spoke of your great kindness to him, and much valued the book you sent him and your letter that accompanied it. . . . I enclose a copy of our Parish Magazine, in which you will see that we intend to place a memorial on his grave. I also enclose a photo taken by a lady in the village which I hope you will accept. He made a good deal by the sale of these photographs last summer.[11]

The following article in the *Daily Mail* of 18 March 1898 shows how they chose to report the incident.

The trouble has arisen out of the recent death of Norman, the old sexton of Coombe Martin [*sic*], who was the prototype of the character of 'Reuben Dale' in 'The Mighty Atom'. . . . No special mention of Norman's death and burial was conveyed to Miss Corelli. Suddenly the rector of Coombe Martin was surprised by the receipt of an indignant letter from the author of 'The Mighty Atom' complaining that she had not been personally informed of Norman's death . . . but for her, as she represented, the worthy sexton would never have emerged from the mists of his native obscurity. The rector of Coombe Martin was a sensible man, and a humorous, so he replied to Miss Corelli to the effect that it was intended to erect a monument to the departed sexton, and that her subscription, if she sent one, would be duly acknowledged. To this Miss Corelli replied with instructions concerning the monument. It must be a plain cross, she declared, and in lieu of the name of Norman, it must bear the name of Reuben Dale, with a note explaining that Reuben was the hero immortalised in 'The Mighty Atom'.

But, alas for her complacent intentions! The rector, evidently a cleric of much logic and little imagination – observed to her in final response, that in consigning the sexton to the earth he had buried a man and not a myth, and that, moreover, his churchyard was not available for gratuitous advertisements.[12]

It seems Marie's distrust of the press was well founded. Not only is she is misreported, but there is an unpleasantness in the manner of writing. Marie had no one who was in a position to champion her except Eric, and from evidence it seems that he was doing nothing but harm to her reputation.

After Marie's operation Dr Frampton had remarked that 'she could not even own to illness without being accused of self-advertisement'. Marie wrote again to the Revd H.W. Toms, to ask if he knew anything about the *Daily Mail* article. He replied from Combe Martin by return of post.

I beg to acknowledge your letter of 22nd; and to inform you that the article in the Daily Mail, to which you refer was not written or published by my authority: nor do I know by whom it was written.

The only letter I have written to you was on March 4th, in which I replied *fully* to your letter received that day, but nothing was said in it as to 'the Churchyard not being available for gratuitous advertisements'. I did not read your letter of 5th as to intimating that you intended subscribing to a memorial to James Norman, but that you should write to the leading Devon paper and put the facts before the public in such a manner that they might be able to decide for themselves as to whether any mention of *how* he became famous should be put upon his tombstone.[13]

The press hounded her relentlessly. In response to a letter of commiseration from Frederick Henry Fisher, the editor of the *Literary World*, Marie wrote from the King's Private Hotel, Brighton.

23 March 1898.
I have been so dangerously ill, – having had to undergo a critical operation, – and the portals of the next world stood so close and open to me, that newspaper lies and other mundane matters have rather ceased to move me. . . . The 'silly story' – respecting the rector of Combmartin [*sic*] is a pure *fabrication of the 'Daily Mail'* – which is never so happy as when inventing lies about me. I have *never* had any such letter as the DM describes from the Vicar of Combmartin – nor have I given any 'instructions' or had any 'wishes' respecting poor old 'Reuben Dale's' grave. I did not write an 'indignant letter to the Vicar', – my secretary wrote to him merely asking for particulars of the old man's illness and death. Herewith I send you an exact copy of his reply, the only letter I

have as yet received from him. . . . I may add the old sexton wrote to me for Christmas a letter of 'grateful thanks for all I had done for him –' . . . he also said that he had been compelled to put his autographed copy of 'The Mighty Atom', into a case screwed against the wall, to prevent tourists from taking it. He added that I had been the means of bringing 'hundreds and hundreds of visitors to the Parish Church', and that he had 'made many friends' through my book, saying that he was able to make 'quite a tidy bit' through the sale of his photographs as 'Reuben Dale.' . . . I must thank you for your consideration and sweetness. The 'beautiful panther' is alas! not strong enough to 'spring' – but she lies *couchant*, and her eyes are very watchful. I am leaving London for good and giving up my house there, – I shall probably settle in the country when I am quite in health again. London air is poisonous, – and the venom and spite and meanness does not purify it! –

    Very kind regards to you from

        Yours gratefully and sincerely,   Marie Corelli.[14]

She wrote to him again a few days later. 'Thanks for all your kindness and advice. But I have had to suffer "libel" and other misrepresentation at the hands of the press for a continuous ten years, – and I really have become – well! – contemptuous of so much "littleness" and petty spite, and feel that it is rather "going down in the mud" to argue with well-known *banded* calumniators. Your health rules are very imaginative! But I may not "cycle" yet for some months, as I had to go through a very risky *internal* operation, and you know that means great rest and care for a *long time* afterwards.'[15]

Marie decided not to return to Longridge Road after her three months' convalescence at Brighton, but to move to the Royal Hotel, Woodhall Spa, where she engaged a suite and planned a long stay. She and Bertha arrived in April 1898, and settled in. Their rooms faced the woods, and on the far side of the woods were miles of heather-covered moorland. It was a welcome retreat from London and all the petty worries of her life there. The hotel was large and very comfortable, designed by the owner, Mr Came, an architect. There was an impressive Winter Garden, 1,000 yards square, where tall palms, camellias and grapes grew. Marie became fond of Mr Came's small daughter, Ida, and often walked with her around the grounds.

She consented to be interviewed by a Mr Arthur H. Lawrence for the *Strand Magazine*. He arrived at the end of April and Marie liked him. He was suitably impressed by 'her magnetic charm, rare strength of character, her refreshing sweetness of manner, and, not least, the intense womanliness which indeed one might have anticipated – but for our friends on the press.' The article claimed to be the only 'interview' granted by the novelist, and in it Mr Lawrence expressed the hope that 'it will be possible for me to do something to negative the extraordinary caricatures of the charming novelist which so many of my "friends" on the Press have so industriously circulated'. He reveals that when she was convalescing in Brighton she was the victim of 'some particularly virulent attacks'. Marie told Mr Lawrence that 'for some time past she had considered the suite of rooms in the Royal Hotel, as home', and that she was giving up her town house in Longridge Road. Lawrence asked her about her legendary fight with the critics and Marie told him that the critics started it, but by not sending *The Sorrows of Satan* out for review she had simplified matters. The critics seldom read her books and so for the future she had saved them any further trouble, and her publishers a great deal of expense. In the article Lawrence said, 'I am glad to be able to assist in giving currency to her authoritative denial of the suggestion which has been made in the Press that the title of her next book will bear the blasphemous and revolting title of "The Sins Of Christ". At the time of writing, this statement has been given a publicity which utterly untrue statements so often achieve.'

This was in answer to a damaging paragraph in a magazine called *Literature*, stating that Marie's next book was to be called *The Sins of Christ*. This caused unbelievable consternation, and for a while the implications of blasphemy halted all sales to the colonies, and caused a huge falling off in sales at home. Where the rumour came from was not known. The editor of *Literature*, H.D. Traill, published a grudging apology, but the damage was done. Arthur Lawrence ended his article by saying that he felt 'bound to point out that Miss Marie Corelli's imperturbable sweetness of manner and unfailing good humour are the natural outcome of strength of character. It is no effort to her to be kindly, charming and gracious – she is naturally so.'[16] It is clear from this interview that Marie now considered Woodhall Spa her new home.

All these plans were suddenly overthrown when Marie received a telegram from Longridge Road. Eric had developed septic pneumonia in the last week of May and had died from heart failure on 2 June. Bertha's half-brother, Frank Vyver, was present at his death, as was Dr Scharleib, who signed the death certificate.

Marie and Bertha returned at once to London, but Marie was so distressed and weakened by her recent operation and the shock of the news that she collapsed. At the suggestion of Frank Vyver, she and Bertha went at once by train to Inverness and from there to their favourite cottage at Killiecrankie where they stayed for three months. When they returned to London in September Marie found evidence among Eric's papers that he had been systematically cheating her and blackening her name to friends, to the press, and to all their acquaintances. Marie's hurt and shame was such that she wrote a savage denunciation of Eric refuting all his allegations, which she had printed, intending to circulate it to their friends and acquaintances, but Bertha and Coulson Kernahan both urged her to reconsider and she agreed to destroy all the leaflets. She wrote to Kernahan:

I am grateful to you my friend, for the few but sincere words of sympathy you have given me. I cannot express to you quite how much I value them. Yes – I have passed through the 'Vale of Tears' and my written theories of life have had to be put into daily hard practise. I thank God that when I came face to face with death I felt no fear. But Eric! His loss I mourn – but not so much as the *way* he was lost! If you knew all you would indeed be sorrier still in your good heart, and you would realise that after being scorched in such a furnace of affliction, all personal ills from henceforth can only seem poor trifles. The agony heaped upon me *after* Eric's death was far worse than the death itself. From that day when I met him *first* – (I a child of twelve, he a man of forty five when he returned to his father's house from Italy penniless), I had worked *for* him and tried to persuade him to retrieve his wasted days; I thought he had done so – and was content *still* to work on for him, – but then – to find all was wasted! – to discover that the home I had tried to keep up was blackened by treachery – and to have to turn away from it forever –, – ah! – heap what the world will on me, *no* trouble can hurt me as *that* hurts, and *will* hurt always. Forgive me – I have no right to trouble *you* with this – let it go.[17]

Marie no longer wanted to remain in London. They went back to the King's Hotel at Brighton, but because of Marie's distress she found it impossible to write. In early 1899 Dr Scharlieb was consulted and she strongly recommended that Marie must spend at least two years in the country.

CHAPTER 6

'A Fairy Stirring up the World'

Marie and Bertha chose Stratford-upon-Avon, where they had been so happy eight years earlier. They heard that a Mrs Croker would be willing to rent her house, Hall's Croft, to them for six months. Marie wrote to her from Brighton, 'I am a very quiet little person, devoted to flowers and home-things, and am only seeking peace and comfortable surroundings in dear Shakespeare-land in order to finish my new book.'[1] Several letters were exchanged concerning the state of the drainage and the number of pots and pans and jelly-moulds, but eventually all was deemed satisfactory. By mid-May they were settled into Hall's Croft.

Stratford-upon-Avon in 1899 was a sleepy little country town. The cultural centre was the Shakespeare Memorial Theatre, built in 1877 on a riverside property given to the Town Council by Charles Edward Flower, a local brewer and landowner. It was, initially, a controversial addition to the town. When the theatre first opened the *Daily Telegraph* reported indignantly: 'They have no mandate to speak in the name of the public or to invest with the attribute of a national undertaking a little mutual admiration club whose object is to endow Stratford-on-Avon with a spic and span new Elizabethan building . . . to be half theatre and half mechanics institute. . . . [The] Governors and Council are respectable nobodies.'[2]

In the first few years the theatre had a variety of presentations, but with the advent of Frank Benson and Company in 1886, the Memorial Theatre acquired its own visiting theatre troupe. Edgar Flower succeeded Charles Edward Flower in 1892, and in 1897 the one-week Spring Festival was extended to two weeks, with a major celebration on 23 April, Shakespeare's birthday, when the streets were lovingly decorated with flowers and Mr and Mrs Frank Benson and Company were welcomed like long-lost friends.

Nearby Warwick Castle, the home of Lord and Lady Warwick, was the most stately of stately homes, and there were other country estates at Alscot and Ettington and Admington, where the favoured were invited to garden parties with croquet, tennis, and strawberries and cream. Footmen handed round iced lemonade and tea. Marie, regarded as a visiting celebrity, was invited everywhere. In the rustic peace of Stratford, she had begun to write again.

Stratford society was narrow and prone to scandalous gossip. There was the shocking tale of Dr Latimer Green who, when on house visits, had an irresistible urge to grab at the ankles of young parlourmaids when they were unfortunate enough to precede him upstairs. For this he was excommunicated for a period of six months by the Revd George Arbuthnot, the vicar of Holy Trinity Church. There was more local gossip about Revd Arbuthnot, who lived with his wife in a large house, The Firs, on Grove Road. There was some speculation among his congregation concerning the particular nature of his interest in a nineteen-year-old orphan girl whom he took under his wing, and for whom he later found a position in Mr Parkhouse's drapery shop. However, the Revd Arbuthnot, an imposing figure who ruled his choir with a rod of iron, quelled the gossip in one memorable sermon during which he challenged any member of his congregation who wished to discuss the matter to come and speak to him in his vestry after the service. Nobody appeared. Labouchere wrote in *Truth* that 'he received a hundred complaints against the Vicar of Stratford to one against any other cleric. The churchwardens should organize a "Society for the Suppression of the Vicar".'

There were a number of schools in Stratford-upon-Avon. Trinity College was a private boarding school for the sons of gentlemen, many of whose parents were serving in India. The headmaster was a Mr Beckwith. There was also the boys' Grammar School where Shakespeare had been a pupil. Girls from good homes went to private day schools, one of which, opposite Hall's Croft, was run by a Mrs Cameron Stuart, who was not pleased to receive a note from Marie one day, requesting silence from the schoolgirls as she was working on her book, *Boy*. The children of ordinary working people went either to the National School, founded by the Anglican National Society, or to the public Board Schools, of which Marie disapproved because the teaching of religion was forbidden.

The *Stratford-upon-Avon Herald* enjoyed having a visiting celebrity but printed some strange pieces of trivia about her doings. On 16 June they reported: 'Mary Anderson has a close friend Marie Corelli who has thought out several of her novels in M.A.'s rose garden. They are very fond of walking and take long tramps over the sweet smelling English moors. For walking Mary Anderson wears a short bicycle skirt; but she does not cycle. She started to learn, but mishaps were so many that she gave up in despair.'

Sarah Bernhardt visited Stratford to play Hamlet at the Memorial Theatre, and Marie was one of the party who met her at the station. Bernhardt stayed with Marie at Hall's Croft and together they visited Shakespeare's grave. This was of course reported in the *Stratford-upon-Avon Herald* which provoked the following 'Note by an Outsider' on 7 July 1899. 'Why on earth Miss Marie Corelli cannot be left to a peaceful existence at Stratford is another of those things that no man can understand. Why every newspaper hack should chronicle every little incident that affects her, why again that because she met a brilliant sister in Madame Bernhardt, and entertained her as a good comrade should another, and why two of our most distinguished women (I prefer that word to ladies) cannot hobnob without interference, is to me an uncracked nut.'

Annie Davis, a part-time reporter on the *Stratford-upon-Avon Herald* had been asked by the paper to cover the event and she contacted Miss Douglas, Marie's secretary, to find out the correct name for the lace on Marie's gown. Marie, impressed by her thoroughness, sent for Annie to ask if she could help her in any way. When Annie told her of an outstanding debt of £2 10s on the Technical School Cricket Club, for which she was collecting funds, an envelope was sent to Annie the next day containing £5 and a letter. At the bottom of the note Marie had written 'Go on with a brave heart, you are sure to succeed.'

Marie was swept into local activities and was frequently asked to be the guest of honour at public functions. She opened a bazaar in aid of parish church funds at Henley-in-Arden. She wrote to the headmaster of the Grammar School offering to pay for the entire school to go to the circus, which offer was accepted with much gratitude. She called on Mr Flower to introduce him to her dear friend Wilson Barrett, who was appearing at the Memorial Theatre. She planned to have a copy made of Shakespeare's gold signet ring, which was to be awarded to the first Hamlet to play the part to artistic perfection. Who was to be the judge of this is uncertain! In September Marie presented a window to the parish church, Holy Trinity, in memory of Eric Mackay. She opened a bazaar at Birmingham organised by commercial travellers in aid of their National Benevolent Institution, and in October gave a speech at a prize-giving in Leamington for Trinity College students. In December Marie was asked to distribute prizes at a PSA (pleasant Sunday afternoon) gathering, again at Leamington, in front of 1,000 people. She was a good speaker and always drew large crowds. Marie much enjoyed her new life as a visiting celebrity, and she and Bertha decided that they would like to make Stratford-upon-Avon their home. They told Richard Savage of the Birthplace Trust that they would like to buy Hall's Croft, and restore it to its old state. Unfortunately, Mrs Croker, about to return to her home, did not wish to sell and so they moved down the road to the Dower House (now called Avon Croft), while they looked for somewhere permanent to live.

On 1 January 1900, 1,000 children of the Stratford-upon-Avon National Schools were invited by Marie to a party at the Memorial Theatre. The theatre trustees were loath to allow their theatre to be invaded by village children but Marie was very persuasive, and the party was organised with military precision. The children were to meet at the schools and were under the sole supervision of their respective teachers. There were seven different coloured standards for the girls and seven for the boys, and each child had pinned to his or her coat a piece of ribbon to match the colour of their standard; they then marched, in order, to the theatre. The girls were seated in the body of the theatre and the boys in the gallery. When assembled, the curtains went up and a huge Christmas tree, donated by Domerick Gregg, was displayed on the stage, which was illuminated by electricity supplied from Birmingham, as there was none in Stratford. The children were entranced. They sang 'Rule Britannia' which in turn was followed by selections played to them by the town band. At the end of the performance all sang 'God Save the Queen' and the children filed out of the theatre strictly in order. As they left each child was given a cracker, containing cakes, sweets and an orange, as they were allowed no food in the theatre. Marie's friends the Laboucheres helped her with the organisation and it was a great success. At the end Mr Arbuthnot moved a public vote of thanks to Miss Corelli, but added privately to her afterwards that she should not expect any thanks from the people of Stratford.

On 6 January, Marie provided a party for 500 needy Birmingham youngsters at the Cinderella Club and paid for all the food and entertainment, and on 12 January she provided another party for the 270 children of the Stratford Infants' School, which was not held in the theatre as they were considered too young. Again there was a large Christmas tree laden with gifts which were given out by Marie, Bertha, Mr Fernan Vyver, Bertha's half-brother, Miss Wilson and Miss Douglas, Marie's secretary.

Marie often had visiting actors from the Memorial Theatre to stay, and Herbert Halliwell Hobbes became a great friend. He was originally from Stratford, so Marie could gossip with him about the vagaries of Stratford society. On 19 March she wrote, 'I told you I often had strange letters from odd people – I had one today from a "family grocer" who says that he and "his own true wife" fear I am "not in a state of grace" and they pray for me that the "proper spirit of godliness" may be "imparted" to me – etc etc. I should say he is a grocer who gives short weights and puts sand in the sugar!'[3] Marie's religious beliefs had been the subject of some local speculation. She had become friendly with the Revd George Arbuthnot, and in reply to a letter from him she explained her position.

Avon Croft, 28th April 1900
Dear Mr Arbuthnot, – It is very sweet and kind of you to write me such a nice letter, and though I do not belong to your form of the Christian Faith, nor to the Roman Catholic form either now, I have the greatest respect and reverence for both. I am one of a very numerous 'fraternity' (we are perhaps between 50,000 and 100,000 altogether) – who are bound to try our best to follow the teachings of Christ as enunciated by Himself – and we are not, by the rules of our Order, allowed to attend public worship, 'That we may be seen of men.' Our rules are somewhat difficult and arbitrary, and render us liable to a good deal of misconception – hence we have chosen as our motto, 'In the world ye shall have tribulation, but be of good cheer – I have overcome the world.' If you would like to form an idea of what we *try* to do, I will copy the 'Daily Paradise' from my little private Manual (each member of our Order has one), as I think it will rather interest you. We are all at one in our Faith in the Divinity of Jesus Christ and His Message, as being the only way to truth and life: of final salvation, so far as this earth and its inhabitants are concerned, and any doubter of this first grand principle would be requested to resign his or her membership. But we do not accept any of the Church forms. We simply, as far as it is humanly possible to do, obey the *words of Christ* as spoken by himself – even at all risk of inconvenience to ourselves and misjudgement by our friends. . . . Please forgive me for taking up your time in this way, but your letter was so kind that I felt impelled to tell you a little of myself, that you might not altogether mistake me, and judge me perhaps wrongly.[4]

Because of her illness Marie had produced no books for three years, but had worked hard since her arrival in Stratford. At the beginning of 1900

Jane was published, followed by *Boy*, in June, which in turn was followed by *The Master Christian* in August. She had worked on the latter book since before her illness. *Jane* is a short morality tale of a spinster who inherits money and leaves her quiet country cottage for the fashionable life in London. She finds society corrupt and rude and returns thankfully to the country.

Boy was well received. An insert in the front of the book explained: 'This NEW LONG STORY is the *most important* volume by MARIE CORELLI published for some years, and the first issued since the Author's serious illness.' Once again her dedication was to Bertha. 'To my dearest friend in the world, Bertha Vyver, who has known all my life from childhood and has been the witness of all my literary work from its very beginning, this simple story is gratefully and lovingly dedicated.' In *Boy* Marie explores the effect of drunken and slovenly parents on an innocent child. 'From the earliest beginnings of childhood, all the seeds of his present misery had been sown, – by neglect, by carelessness, by bad example, by uncomfortable home surroundings, by domestic quarrellings, – by the want of all the grace, repose, freedom, courtesy, kindness and sympathy, which should have given every man's house the hall-mark of "Home". His childhood had been sad and solitary – his boyhood embittered by disappointment, followed by the excessive strain of "competitive cram", which had tired and tortured every little cell in his brain to utter exhaustion, – he was old before he had time to be young.'[5]

Boy suffers many disappointments, falls into bad company and runs up heavy debts. He steals from the one person who has been kind to him, a middle-aged spinster who refuses to press charges. He is so ashamed that he enlists in the army, fights in the Boer War, and is killed in battle having distinguished himself by saving the life of his boyhood friend. Marie did not believe that war solved problems. She explores this in *Boy* in an interesting exchange between one of the surgeons at the front and his nurse.

Surgeon: It is a relic of barbarism . . . indeed, it is almost the only vestige left to us of the dark ages. The proper way for civilized nations to behave in a difficulty is to submit to peaceable arbitration. War – especially nowadays – is a mere slaughterhouse – and the soldiers are the poor sheep led to the shambles. The real nature of the thing is covered up under flying flags and the shout of patriotism, but, as a matter of stern fact, it is a horrible piece of cowardice for one nation to try murdering another just to see which one gets its way first.

Nurse: I'm glad you think as I do. It is surely better to serve Queen and Country by the peaceful arts and sciences, than by killing men wholesale!

Surgeon: Yes, nurse, but you must remember that the arts and sciences are very seldom rewarded – whereas if you kill a few of your human brethren you get notice and promotion![6]

England was in the midst of the Boer War and nationalistic passions ran high, but Marie believed that little benefit could come from the war being fought in South Africa. Her story of the gallant death in battle of the young man given no chance in life touched the heart of her readers. A fellow writer, Robert Hichens, who had written a satire on Oscar Wilde, *The Green Carnation,* but who was best known for his macabre stories and his desert romances, was generous in his praise:

Marie Corelli occupies a peculiar position among the notorious ones of the world. For years she has been famous. For years she has made more money than almost any literary man or woman. For years she has been worshipped by – shall I say millions of readers! For years she has been discussed, condemned, praised, pilloried. In the midst of all this hubbub she continues to write as she feels, to express her temperament on paper, and to put forth, with amazing vivacity, her opinions. . . . People say she is small and fair. So she ought to be – a fairy stirring up the world with a wand dipped in ink. Does she wish to be adored or revel in being hated? Who knows? Perhaps she laughs to herself in some shady hermitage, and marvels at the good people who grow dishevelled around her footstool. . . . But she always puts into her work the same peculiar and abnormal vitality. . . . Yes, tears will be shed over *Boy.* . . . He wanted to be a real English boy. He wanted to act on the square . . . but again and again in this story Miss Corelli surprises me by the effects she obtains without any apparent effort, without any attempt at eloquence, elaboration, or rhetorical power. In simplicity she has won a new success and found the way to a fountain of tears.[7]

He also wrote directly to Marie and advised her not to read criticisms. 'I have over and over again longed to say this. I believe the less you read of attacks, the better and better you will write, the mellower and mellower the fruit of your brain will become.'

The Master Christian, released in August 1900, is a thinly disguised series of sermons on the deplorable state of the Church generally, but particularly the Church of Rome. Cardinal Felix Bonpré is the elderly saint-like hero. 'What he saw, and what sincerely and unselfishly grieved him, was that the people of this present age were unhappy – discontented – restless, – that something of the simple joy of existence had gone out of the world. . . . Universal weariness of life seemed a disease of the time, – there was nothing that seemed to satisfy.'[8]

Angela Sorrani is famous throughout Europe as a painter and, using her as a mouthpiece, Marie once again states her feminist credo. 'Oh, a woman! Only a woman! *She* must not give a grand lesson to the world! She must not, by means of brush or pen, point out to a corrupt generation the way it is going! Why? Because God has created her to be the helpmate of man! Excellent reason! Man is taking a direct straight road to destruction, and she must not stop him by so much as lifting a warning finger! Again, why? Only because she is a woman! But I – were I twenty times a woman, twenty times weaker than I am, and hampered by every sort of convention and usage, – I would express my thoughts somehow, or die in the attempt!'[9] Marie fiercely denounces the corruption in the Church of Rome: 'He had perceived the trickery, the dissimulation and hypocrisy of Roman priestcraft, . . . he had watched with sickening soul all the tawdry ceremonial, so far removed from the simplicity of Christ's commands . . . he could only remain a dumb spectator of the Show in which not the faintest shadow of Christianity according to Christ, appeared.'[10] There are many sermons in this book, but it much in it which is passionate and moving. 'So little is needed! – Simplicity instead of ostentation – voluntary poverty instead of countless riches, spiritual power instead of the perpetual cry for temporal power, – the doctrine of Christ instead of the doctrine of Church Councils – and the glad welcoming and incorporation of every true, beautiful, wise and wonderful discovery of the age into the symbolic teaching of our Creed.'[11]

The book is an impassioned plea for a return to a decent and simple way of life, and it was very popular; within the next two years the book sold 160,000 copies. The critics dismissed it as tawdry, badly written rubbish and the *Saturday Review* on 16 September 1900 declaimed: 'There is practically no plot, only a number of impossible incidents strung together to afford standing room for a crowd of ranters. . . . As for her typical ecclesiastics . . . she abuses them as "pagan" and we feel that she would have been equally convincing had she denounced them as isosceles triangles. . . . Whenever a Roman comes into the room he is made to say "buon giorno" though the rest of his remarks are obligingly translated into a kind of English. . . . The French of Marie is only surpassed in inaccuracy by the Italian of Corelli.' However, the public disagreed and Marie, joyfully spending her royalties on the children of Stratford-upon-Avon, chose to ignore the critics.

Marie was hostess to the Whitefriars Club on 29 June, for a magnificent luncheon in the Dower House gardens, where Winston Churchill was one of her guests. He later wrote to her: 'I often look back to the time when I had the pleasure of sitting beside you at the Whitefriar's dinner, and of listening to a speech the rhetorical excellence of which almost disarmed my opposition to Female Suffrage.' This speech was well reported by Annie Davis, the young reporter on the *Stratford-upon-Avon Herald*: 'A more charming hostess than Miss Marie Corelli it would have been difficult to find, and many people who had not previously met her, and who, perhaps, by reason of her fame as a novelist, had expected to see a learned-looking lady of severe and elderly aspect, must have been considerably surprised to be welcomed by so dainty and youthful a figure.' Marie liked Annie and was soon sending her pieces of information for the paper. In 1901, after the death of Queen Victoria, Marie's permanent secretary, Miss Douglas, left to get married and Marie employed Annie in her place for four days a week. Annie stayed with her for thirteen years.

In July Marie paid for an excursion and treat for over 600 of the National School children to visit Rugby Park; she also gave a talk on temperance in the courtyard of Dudley Castle to raise money for the Temperance Institute. In her first year at Stratford the list of Marie's public engagements, and the number of charities which benefited from her generosity, is astonishing. She needed to become part of the community, and now that she had money, she wanted to use it for the benefit of others. Mr Boyden, the editor of the *Stratford-upon-Avon Herald*, gave her advice on which charities and causes she should support. The paper revealed on 5 October, 'So many reports having obtained circulation respecting the movements of Miss Marie Corelli, perhaps outsiders would like to know that the popular novelist is still in Stratford, and that she is likely to remain here. This is an announcement that we make with a good deal of pleasure, inasmuch as Stratford cannot afford to lose one who has filled the role of Lady Bountiful so admirably.'

As Marie and Bertha were determined to make Stratford their permanent home, it was necessary to find a house they both liked before the owners of the Dower House returned. They looked at several possible houses, but found it difficult to find just what they wanted. One of them, Alveston Leys, was quite decided on and a deposit was paid, but then Marie realised that it was too close to the Avon and would be very damp. Eventually they settled on an eighteen-month lease (with the option of purchase), on a house in Church Street called Mason Croft. The house had many drawbacks, not least that it was bordered on two sides by Trinity School and its playing fields. It had once been an old farmhouse of Elizabethan origins, and in the grounds was a little watchtower and an old double sundial on top of a stone archway. The house was owned by Mr J.C. Tregarthen, who also owned Trinity School. Marie signed the lease, but it would be several months before they were able to move in, for the house had been badly neglected and it needed considerable repair work. Now that Marie was to become a permanent resident of Stratford she wanted to take an active interest in town affairs.

She learned there was a large outstanding debt on Shakespeare's church, Holy Trinity, and wrote to Ellen Terry with a view to raising a fund to pay this off. Ellen Terry replied, 'I'll do what I can to help, but at the moment I am ill and confined to my bed, but what a disgrace – this debt! I enclose my contribution (£15) and £1 each from Edith Craig and Gordon Craig. I don't quite know how to beg, but I'll try. People should rush forward longing to do each a little in such a case. Shakespeare!

Well – well! . . .

A performance would be good – as you suggest – but how many performances am I not "down" for between now and April! I've already promised more than can be – probably – performances. I have never played in Stratford!'[12]

While still trying to raise the money, in October 1900, Marie discovered that Sir Theodore Martin proposed to erect a memorial in Holy Trinity Church to his late wife, the actress, Helen Faucit. This was to take the form of a large bas-relief on the chancel wall which would dwarf the bust of Shakespeare on the opposite wall. Sir Theodore, who had already donated a large pulpit in green marble to his wife's memory, also offered to pay off the outstanding church debt. On discovering this Marie immediately wrote a letter of protest to Mr Arbuthnot. 'I am in a position this morning to offer you the instant payment of the £900 needed to close the debt on the church, if you will use your authority to prevent the inclusion of a modern bust into Shakespeare's Chancel, and relegate it to some other place in the church. You are asked to do this as a matter of *national sentiment* and hallowed history. The cheque is at your service on these conditions. All Shakespeare lovers feel very strongly the intended act of vandalism.'

Mr Arbuthnot called to say he was regretfully unable to accept Marie's offer as it would mean offending a wealthy patron. His decision was supported by the Bishop of Worcester who had already approved the placement of the bust. Marie was determined not to allow this desecration to take place, and made the issue a national talking point by writing letters to more than fifteen major newspapers, thus stirring up a storm of protest. She discovered that to erect the Faucit memorial in the chancel would entail the removal of a memorial tablet to a previous vicar, whose wife's permission had not been obtained. On the strength of this she took the matter to the Court of Arches and won the case. Helen Faucit's memorial bas-relief was not placed in Holy Trinity but in a far more suitable place, the Memorial Theatre.

The matter aroused a great deal of antagonism in Stratford, and a great deal of support outside the town. Marie was criticised for interfering by Mr Cuming Walters of the *Birmingham Gazette* and she replied on 27 October. 'I personally gain no advantage by calling the public attention to what I and many others consider to be an unnecessary intrusion into the greatest historic corner in England; but I am content to lose friends and gain foes, if such be the result of my disinterested effort to save Shakespeare's shrine from molestation.' Mr Cuming Walters wrote a courteous response, and Marie replied: 'I am glad to have crossed swords with a "foeman worthy of my steel". I should like to see you. . . . Yes I am a "hard hitter" – but one must hit hard to make the dense world start – especially when such obtuse old gentlemen as Sir Arthur Hodgson & Sir Theodore Martin parcel out Shakespeare's church according to their liking!'[13] Marie invited him to visit her at Stratford, and after a cautious beginning they became friends. Cuming Walters, who had judged Marie by press reports and hearsay, was disarmed when he met her in person.

She was also condemned by her old enemy, the *Daily Mail*. 'The future historian will probably find it necessary to record that Stratford is noted not only for Shakespeare but for Miss Corelli; for the gifted lady seems determined to give it new claims to fame. She has declaimed her loudest against the intended violation of Shakespeare's shrine, shrieked against an act of sacrilege, and from her ample armoury of invective drawn forth the deadliest weapons of speech with which to assail the desecration of Shakespeare's chancel.' Marie defended herself: 'Had there been a male representative of the literary craft in Stratford I should have left the matter to him. But there was not. So, I raised what my critics kindly called a "shriek". However, I myself have always regarded a shriek as being more satisfactory than a snuffle.'[14] She received support from Sir Sidney Lee, a noted Shakespearean scholar and editor of the *Dictionary of National Biography*. He wrote: 'No one can be in any doubt that it was your own energetic intervention which caused the satisfactory solution of the difficulty. Your active pursuit of the matter undoubtedly led me to consider it more closely and greatly reinforced my sense of the incongruity of the situation. Most of the London papers, as far as I have seen them, with perfect rightness, consider that you have saved a national monument from a serious peril. The victory is certainly yours.'

The following appeared on 30 October, in 'Mr Clement Scott's new paper' to 'the fair (and unbiased) authoress of "Manners Gentlemen!"'

> This lady wins the laurel
> For capacity to quarrel,
> And batter 'Fourth Estate' men to a jelly –
> So here is a suggestion,
> Which should pass without a question,
> That, marry, she should sign herself Quarrelli![15]

The *Birmingham Post* supported her stand. 'Miss Marie Corelli deserves hearty thanks for courageously and promptly protesting against this proposed "second" Faucit Memorial being erected in the chancel of Holy Trinity Church Stratford-on-Avon. The charges of "shrieking", self-advertising, notoriety hunting, and such like ill-mannered and ungallant impertinences have fallen flat, and died a natural death. We are all willing to give credit for good intentions, honour and truthfulness to the actors of this drama.' Not everyone in Stratford was quite so willing to give credit. Marie had involved the town in unwanted notoriety in the national press, and made the council appear negligent in their care of Shakespeare's legacy. Some of the councillors were not happy. Lady Bountiful was expressing her thoughts rather too strongly.

The new home at Mason Croft needed considerable work. First the inside of the house had to be made comfortable and clean. Marie and Bertha planned to glass over a large area at the rear of the house leading out of the drawing-room, and turn it into a winter garden similar to the one at the Royal Hotel, Woodhall Spa, though on a much smaller scale. The house was dark with a multitude of small rooms; the winter garden would give them the warmth and light they needed. It was a major effort to get the furniture and possessions transported from London, but they moved into Mason Croft at the beginning of 1901.

Marie had become one of the 'sights' to be visited in Stratford-upon-Avon and whenever she left her house was cheered by a waiting crowd of sightseers. She drove out in her carriage at a set time each afternoon and, like a modern pop star, was greeted by adoring fans. She began to suffer from intrusive journalists and photographers, constantly seeking a 'story'. Arthur Bridges, the butler, became very skilled at deflecting unwanted and importunate visitors. There were problems with their neighbours: Marie was angry when she found the neighbours to the right, Dr Earnshaw Hewer and his young wife, spying on them over the fence; the Trinity College boys on the left of Mason Croft were even more difficult. The sons of well-to-do army officers serving in India, the boys tended to be unruly. They deliberately kicked rugger balls into the garden and damaged windows and the glass roof of the winter garden. In November 1901 Marie complained to the acting headmaster of Trinity College, the Revd Harvey Bloom (Mr Beckwith was on sick leave). Mr Bloom called on Marie to apologise and was most persuasive. On finding that he, too, was an author, Marie invited him to dinner – one week with Mr Methuen, and the next with Mr Fisher Unwin – as a result of which Mr Bloom was offered contracts for two books. He introduced his young daughter, Ursula, to Marie, who was charmed by her and invited her to stay at Mason Croft.

The ladies entertained a great deal, for Marie liked to gather around her eminent friends in art, literature and politics who were good talkers and active-minded thinkers. Because she was musical she was invited in 1901 to become President of the Stratford-upon-Avon Choral Union and organised a concert at the Memorial Theatre featuring Dame Clara Butt and Kennerley Rumford, Mlle Albertini, and Monsieur Johannes Wolff, supported by the Choral Union. The guest artists stayed at Mason Croft, and the concert was sold out.

Herbert Halliwell Hobbes stayed with them in April while appearing with the Benson troupe at the Memorial Theatre. Marie wrote in July to tell him of some of her other doings: 'I got up such a pretty concert on the river with illuminated boats – it was such a pretty sight. Stratford is about as usual – jealousies running high, and people scratching each other like cats! It is a matter of real injury that I should have made myself such a pretty home, and have got the liking of the "townspeople" as well! What a funny world it is! Sir Arthur is well and still obdurate! I am halfway through a new novel. And I am looking forward to seeing you again at Christmas!'[16]

Marie hadn't finished with the Town Council and attacked them for filling up the Bancroft Basin in front of the Memorial Theatre. The council had decided that the shallow lake was a danger for children and so had drained the water leaving a stagnant pool which Marie considered to be a health hazard. On 6 September 1901 she wrote to the *Stratford-upon-Avon Herald*: 'The foolish intermeddling of persons who must be busybodies or nothing, has completely spoilt the before charming expanse of river-mead and water so generously given to the town by the late Charles Flower, and whatever small risk there used to be for children playing round the pretty and safely shallow lake was nil as compared to the present danger of an epidemic of disease. Typhoid, scarlet fever, diphtheria and measles are all in the process of comfortably undisturbed germination in the stagnant mud, which is all the "improvers" have left us.' The council tried to ignore her, but it was the beginning of troubled times. They resented the way in which she threw her money around, though it was for good causes. Many considered that she was unnatural because she was unmarried and successfully earned her own living. Marie was fearless, outspoken, contentious and becoming a problem.

The next year was to change many things. Marie, at the height of her fame, embarked on an immensely popular series of talks and lectures. She was invited to address the Philosophical Society of Edinburgh which was a singular honour, as the last speaker had been Charles Dickens. She gave a rousing address on 'The Vanishing Gift', the loss of the imagination caused by the rush and bustle of life. 'There is something humorous in all this modern hurry-skurry – something almost grotesque in this desire for swift movement – this wish to save time and to start work; but there is something infinitely pathetic about it as well. . . . It is very certain that where there is no time to think, there is less time to imagine – and where there is neither thought nor imagination, creative work of a high and lasting quality is not possible. . . . The art of conversation is almost a lost one. People talk as they ride bicycles – at a rush – without pausing to consider their surroundings.'[17] She refused a fee but was given a large silver rose bowl: 'Presented to Miss Marie Corelli by the Edinburgh Philosophical Institution, in grateful recognition of the brilliant address delivered by her on the 19th November 1901.'

Shortly afterwards she received a letter from W.H. Wilkins, who asked her if she would honour the Royal Society of Literature by reading a paper: 'if you accept, you are the first lady who has ever lectured to them'. She accepted with pleasure. She was invited to Glasgow to speak to the Scottish Society of Literature and Art at St Andrew's Hall on 20 February 1902. More than 3,000 people attended and she lectured them on 'The Signs of the Times'. Again she refused a fee and was presented with a pair of antique silver candlesticks. She wrote to J. Cuming Walters who had become a close friend: 'Quite a sensation here! *Crowds* of people disappointed! There never was such a "crush" even for "Patti" in her palmy days!!' Three days later she wrote again: 'I so wish you had been in Glasgow! My audience was simply *wonderful*. A packed sea of human heads. I never thought I should be able to face such a multitude. I had a truly *magnificent* reception – no statesman could have had a finer one.'[18]

There is a child-like joy in these letters. At last she was speaking directly to her public; not through her books as the mysterious author who declaimed from the pages of her novels, but as Marie Corelli: short, middle-aged and beautifully dressed. She spoke to an audience of over 4,000 people for the Royal National Lifeboat Institution in the City Hall at Leeds, and the hall was so full that the doors could not be closed. She gave 'A Little Talk on Literature' to the Literary and Philosophical Society in Manchester. She was deservedly acclaimed as a public speaker, and the public thronged around her to look, to listen, and even to kiss the hem of her gown. One who was there, M.E. Sadler, described her manner of delivery. 'She made every *letter* tell, but without undue mouthing or emphasis. There was a delicate modulation of tone. She read, but the effect was of slow intimate speech. The technique of the business was admirable . . . everyone listened very respectfully and solemnly. It was like a well-given mediocre sermon without a text or "And now" at the end of it. But the general effect was to make one feel better and stronger.'[19] He felt that the content was banal but that the tone was good.

When she first arrived in Stratford-upon-Avon after her operation and long convalescence, Marie had been petite and slim, and she was still a handsome woman, as we can see from a series of photographs taken by Bertha in March 1902. She was an indefatigable hostess and continued to entertain a wide circle of friends at Mason Croft. Ellen Terry was the star of that year's Shakespeare Festival; she played Katherine at the Memorial Theatre to much acclaim, and lunched with Marie on 25 April.

In July, Marie's carefully created world was threatened from a very unexpected source. Marie and Bertha had planned to attend a flower show in Town Meadow and asked Harvey Bloom if his seven-year-old daughter, Ursula, could come with them. Marie had made a pet of Ursula and was encouraging her to write; she was a frequent guest at Mason Croft. Ursula was invited to lunch that day and during a pause, thinking she was making conversation, asked Marie if she was divorced. She had overheard some servants' gossip at home, but had no idea what the word meant – or the effect that it was to have on Marie. The implications of divorce in 1902 were dire. It meant that you could not be received in society, were ostracised by the Church and, most vital of all for Marie, could not attend any royal function or enter a royal enclosure. The coronation of Edward VII was to be held in early August and she had received the singular honour of an invitation. Any shadow of scandal would jeopardise both her invitation and her career.

She and Bertha were both deeply shocked to realise that for Ursula to utter those defamatory words, someone must have discussed the possibility in her presence. Marie reacted impulsively. The carriage and pair were ordered and Ursula was taken home to her father's rectory at Whitchurch where Marie intended to have the matter out with Harvey Bloom. Finding both Bloom and his wife out, she summoned his servants into the parlour and demanded to know the origin of the story. Leaving Ursula in tears at the rectory and the place in an uproar, Marie returned to Mason Croft. This was the start of a bitter and damaging war between Marie and her erstwhile friend Harvey Bloom. The next morning Bridges, Marie's butler, cycled over to Whitchurch Rectory with a letter:

Dear Mr Bloom,   Private and Confidential.
I think it advisable that you and Mrs Bloom should know the following facts. When your little girl Ursula came here yesterday, she had scarcely been seated two minutes at luncheon, before she stated that I was a divorced woman and said that all Stratford knew it! She was told this by your servant, Annie, whom I confronted yesterday, *myself*, with Ursula, and find that your late cook had started this *wicked, scandalous lie*.

I will not dwell on the *infinite pain* it is to me, to find that my name has been so falsely and *cruelly* mishandled in your house; that is a matter for my solicitors; but the most *pitiful* experience that I have ever known is to think that such a very young child like Ursula, should be stuffed with such *calumnies and falsehoods*, against one, who honestly sought to be her friend and yours. You must be perfectly well aware that I am, and always have been *un*married; I have never even been engaged! and most *devoutly* do I thank God that I have nothing to do in life, with such common and base ideas as appear to have poisoned the mind of your poor little child! I have hundreds of friends who know *me*, and my *life's history*, (many of whom will be the first to resent the injury, *most cruel and undeserved*, done to me in your house which I entered as a friend), *in all ways*. You must understand that it is not my fault that our acquaintance must cease.
Faithfully yours,
Marie Corelli. Mason Croft. July 27th. 1902

The Revd Harvey Bloom, a clever but flirtatious man, always ready to steal a kiss from a pretty woman, thought Marie Corelli was making an unnecessary fuss. He wrote to apologise for Ursula's unwitting behaviour and for the gossip of the servants. 'We knew nothing about it, of course, neither I nor my wife know what the servants talk of. Had we known, we should at once have told the young woman that she had no right to take away character.' Marie's answer came back on 31 July: 'I am afraid you have not quite grasped the position. "A child's babble" of the kind reported may have a very serious result in the case of one, whose position is so public as mine. Ursula distinctly said that *both you and her mother knew all about it*. She also said that both you and Mrs Bloom often talked of the way I was "hated". *She is perfectly aware of what divorce is. Perfectly conscious* that it is a disgrace, and that this disgrace is attached to me. . . . I felt as one in a wild dream, branded as a criminal by those I had honestly and lovingly sought to benefit and serve, and Miss Vyver could scarcely restrain her tears at the *venomous cruelty* of this little child whom I had loved, and been kind to.'[20] Marie handed the matter over to her solicitor, and in her efforts to clear her name, wrote letters to the newspapers. She made a permanent and unpleasant enemy of Harvey Bloom.

In order to understand her reaction it is only necessary to look at her past. She had spent an unhappy childhood tainted by the knowledge that she did not know her parents, and was probably illegitimate. That this was a barrier to any possibility of marriage was borne out by an uncorroborated story that when young, she had been engaged to a naval officer whom she met in Scotland, who had thrown her over for another woman with better prospects. She had managed, by sheer hard work, to build a name and a successful career for herself, only to see it nearly destroyed by Eric, and on that occasion had reacted quickly and impulsively to salvage her reputation. Her ignorance of her true identity meant that she had been forced to create herself, to stand alone, and to defend herself against probing questions – for to be illegitimate was to be an outcast. She moved to Stratford to create her own home; had been lavish with her money and time and had become a well-known feature of Stratford life. She was receiving deserved adulation for her lectures. Now, once again, out of the blue, she found herself threatened by someone she had tried to help. The Revd Harvey Bloom was a philanderer of enormous charm and easy morals, as his daughter later acknowledged. He had charmed Marie and she had introduced him to her publishers, but further than that she would not go. She wrote in 1904, in a book which carried a bitter caricature of Harvey Bloom, that her heroine had been the subject of a rumour that she was 'peculiar' because she wouldn't marry. She goes on 'it does make me so angry! For when people get hold of the word "peculiar", it is made to mean several things. It's a way some modern men have of covering their own rejection and defeat. The woman in question is branded through the "smart set" as "peculiar", "difficult", "impossible to deal with" – oh yes! – I know it all!'[21] Marie's crime, it seems, was not only to be without a husband, but to be successful, something which her detractors could not tolerate. To explain her unusual status they needed to find another, preferably scandalous, reason for it.

Queen Victoria had died on 22 January 1901 and the Empire mourned. Marie wrote *The Passing of the Great Queen*, which she dictated to Annie Davies, who was now to work permanently as Marie's secretary. 'Strange indeed it is to think of England without the Mother-Queen of the great British people; – to realize that she, the gentle and beneficent Lady of the Land, has left us for ever! We had grown to think of her as almost immortal.'[22] The Prince of Wales, who had waited for so long, had been criticised and hounded by the press and Marie called for more understanding. 'During the brief time that has elapsed since our late glorious Sovereign's death, there has been far too much dragging-in of the King's name, to matters "theatrical and sporting", in the Press, – and it is of far more interest to the nation to remember how ardently he, as

Prince of Wales, has worked for good and charitable aims, how much he has worked to promote the cause of the poor, the weak and the aged, and how generously and promptly he has always given his personal aid and influence to relieve any immediate suffering. I do not think it is possible to appeal to the King for a good cause in vain; I have never heard that he has turned a deaf or callous ear to the cry of sorrow.'[23]

Marie did attend the coronation in Westminster Abbey at the particular request of Edward VII who still viewed her with affection, and it was a magnificent occasion. It was reported that she was dressed 'in the very simplest attire of white chiffon and lace, she was one of the most unobtrusively dressed ladies present, as she wore no jewels, and had nothing indeed about her costume that could attract the slightest attention, though she was the "observed of all observers" at the luncheon held in the House of Peers after the Abbey ceremonial, not for her dress, but for her fame'.

In October 1902, Marie and Bertha went to Scotland for their annual visit to Braemar and stayed at the Invercauld Arms Hotel from where she went with a party of friends to the Braemar Highland Gathering. In the social report in *The Gentlewoman*, Marie was mortified to see that her name had not been included in the list of those who had been invited to the royal enclosure. She wrote at once to the editor, marking her letter *Private and Confidential*:

Miss Marie Corelli presents her compliments to the *Scottish Gentlewoman*, and notes with some surprise that her name has been omitted from the list of friends invited by Mr Farquharson of Invercauld to the Royal Enclosure at the Braemar Highland Gathering. She notes the name of her friend, Lady Byron, is included and wishes to point out that as she (Miss Corelli) was the means of taking Lady Byron to the Gathering, and as Mr Farquharson's invitation was for 'Miss Corelli and party', without any allusion to Lady Byron at all, Miss Corelli can only conclude that her name was purposely omitted. Miss Corelli begs to say that the omission has caused the greatest surprise and offence to many persons, including Lady Byron, who is at present staying at Braemar as Miss Corelli's guest. This letter is confidential, but an explanation is requested, as Miss Corelli was with Lady Somers and Lady Kennard.

Marie, suffering from many slights, both real and imagined, had played right into her detractors' hands. The editor may have purposely omitted her name, but now he heaped insult on injury. He wrote to her:

142, Strand, London.   October the 6th. 1902
The Editor of *The Gentlewoman* presents his compliments to Miss Marie
Corelli, and begs to acknowledge her letter from Braemar without date.
He assures Miss Corelli he at once realises that an apology for
misunderstanding her is clearly due. But he thinks that Miss Corelli had
forgotten a letter, also without date and also from Scotland, which she
addressed to this office in the year 1898. And indeed, in all those of her
books which the Editor has been able to read, Miss Corelli has glorified
in the opportunity of expressing her contempt for the Press, and in
particular those 'snobs' (Miss Corelli's favourite word) who seek
newspaper notice in any of the social, literary, or other relations of life.

Miss Corelli's conjecture that her name was 'purposely omitted' from
the account sent by *The Gentlewoman*'s Scottish correspondent, describing
the party at the Royal Enclosure at Invercauld, is perfectly correct. In
deference to Miss Corelli's expressed opinions on 'newspaper puffs', the
Editor long since gave instructions that her name should not be
mentioned in *The Gentlewoman*. Now he realises that Miss Corelli has been
misunderstood, and that it would really have gratified her to be named as
being present in the 'Royal Enclosure'. The Editor begs forgiveness for
pointing out, however, that he does not comprehend why 'an explanation
is requested' because 'Miss Corelli was with Lady Somers and Lady
Kennard'. No such titled companionship was necessary to induce the
Editor to give this frank explanation. He can only plead, however, some
little excuse for his mistake because of the apparent sincerity of Miss
Corelli's letters and writings on the subject of 'snobs' and newspapers.

Logical consistency obliges the Editor to understand that the word
'Private' at the head of the letter should be read 'Public', unless, indeed,
he has again misunderstood, and that Miss Corelli's letter is not, as it
appears to be, a request for publicity. The Editor proposes, by way of
making reparation and emphasising his apology, to print Miss Corelli's
letter and this reply in *The Gentlewoman*.

Marie had walked right into the trap and there was nothing that she
could do but wait for the inevitable. In the next issue of *The Gentlewoman*,
both the letters were printed in full with a further covering letter by the
Editor.

It is due to the readers of *The Gentlewoman*, as well as to Miss Marie
Corelli, to explain, by publishing the two following letters, why the name

of that distinguished lady has been omitted from this paper. Miss Corelli's letter is marked 'Private'. Under all ordinary circumstances it would be a breach of good taste to print a letter marked 'Private'. But these circumstances are extraordinary. The very purpose of Miss Corelli's letter is personal publicity.

I am quite willing that Miss Corelli's letter should be the medium of announcing to the world her presence, 'by invitation', at Mr Farquharson's place. Personally I cannot quite understand the pleasure of being within elbow distance of Royalty, even in an 'enclosure', to an individual who habitually writes with such sneering disrespect of royal personages. However, I have frankly made amends to Miss Marie Corelli for misunderstanding her in the past.[24]

This, printed in one of the leading women's journals, was revenge indeed. One of her supporters, J. Cuming Walters, wrote in her defence: 'Miss Corelli has been the victim of much misunderstanding in the past, of some injustice, and – alas that it should have to be said – of deliberate malevolence. . . . Her influence is vast and far reaching – She writes with a purpose. . . . May this valiant woman, standing alone, battling for the right, yet add to her conquests!' Marie thanked him for his kind article: 'I am *deeply touched* by your very great kindness, and I do assure you that I shall never forget it. . . . *Temporal Power* has sold out its first edition. Another 30,000 is being rapidly prepared. The absurd injustice with which certain quarters of the press still continue to treat me, is becoming very sickening to the public.'[25]

While in Scotland she fulfilled one of the early dreams which she had shared with Bertha. They had wanted a small carriage pulled by two Shetland ponies with a black fox fur rug to keep them warm. She bought two ponies while in Aberdeen and they were delivered to her in Stratford on 21 November 1902. The ponies were christened Puck and Ariel and every day, at a certain time, the chaise would be drawn up outside Mason Croft and Marie and Bertha would set out for their daily drive. This event became popular with tourists who waited for the two ladies to drive out in the little carriage pulled by the small ponies with bells on their harness. A spiteful piece of gossip was circulated in Stratford, that the Warwickshire inspector of the Royal Society for the Prevention of Cruelty to Animals was called upon by concerned residents to stop the chaise and check the weight of the two ladies. The story went on that it was only because of the intervention of Marie's enemy, the Revd Harvey Bloom, that the inspector was dissuaded from carrying out his duty. It seems more likely, in view of Bloom's relationship with Marie, that the story was invented by him to embarrass his enemy.

The young actor Halliwell Hobbes spent Christmas 1902 at Mason Croft. Marie liked him and was keen to help him with his career. She wrote to him on 4 January: 'I will write to Ellen Terry today and tell her about you – perhaps she will be able to find room for another!! It is so kind of you to say that you like coming to Mason Croft. I can assure you that you are always a welcome guest, and we are unfeignedly sorry when you take your departure. I am hoping you will be with Benson in the Shakespeare week, as we might really have some fun! They are preparing "a Civic Welcome" for me in Manchester! it is an appalling prospect. "Me and the Lord Mayor! – !!!"' Marie arranged an interview for Hobbes with Ellen Terry, and he was offered a part which he accepted. She was genuinely interested in his progress and later offered him some wise advice. 'Concerning what you say of *ambition*, it is certainly *not* "a sin"! It is the only thing that gives salt and savour to life – it also intensifies all emotions and affections. Aim at the highest *always*! If one flies for the moon, and only reaches a tall tree, the tree is better than the barren desert of commonplace. Yes – *aim high*!'[26]

On 19 January she was the guest of honour of the Lord Mayor of Birmingham. Her editor friend, J. Cuming Walters, was to be present and she wrote to him. 'You ask me if you could do anything for me – well, I am very nervous of *crowds*, and all I want, is to do my sight-seeing *quietly* and *unobserved*. I want to "slip in" to the hall where I am to speak by a door that *no* one outside knows! and "slip out" in that same way. It always makes me quite wretched to have to pass through any group of sight-seers!'

The talk was reported in the *Stratford-upon-Avon Herald* on 23 January and gives a good picture of the author. 'No-one who was present at Heaton Chapel on Monday night is likely to forget the occasion. For a woman to entertain an audience for over an hour with a lecture on Literature is itself a remarkable feat, when it is added that the address was delivered in clear liquid tones, with emphasis and expression, with true oratorical grace, and with scarcely a reference to notes, then it becomes more than remarkable – it is perhaps unique.' There is a description of Marie from 'One Who Was Present', who describes her as 'a daintily-dressed, sweet-faced woman [who] stepped onto the platform and amid a breathless silence began to talk to us about Literature. It is seldom that the author of "The Master Christian" lays aside the pen in favour of "silvern speech". "Silvern speech" is no mere exaggeration in the case of Miss Corelli, whose clear, musical voice and charm of diction would ensure her an attentive audience on the part of most prejudiced listeners. . . . She speaks with perfect distinctness and with the most delightful simplicity; she uses no involved phraseology, and one is never in doubt as to her precise meaning. The language of her address on Monday night resembled – if she will forgive the parallel – her plain white evening gown in its freedom from ornament, and she gave one the impression from beginning to end of absolute sincerity.'[27]

The lecture was a great success and Marie returned to Stratford with her confidence restored. However, an event was brewing at the end of 1902 which was going to eclipse all the previous arguments and disasters, and which is still known as 'The Henley Street Controversy'. It split Stratford into warring factions and created precedents in town planning which are still acknowledged today. The controversy became a personal and bitter fight between commercialism in the form of the Stratford Town Council and conservationism led by the intrepid Miss Corelli.

'An authentic likeness of myself, as I truly am today.' The first 'official' portrait of Miss Marie Corelli taken by Gabell in 1906 for the frontispiece for Treasure of Heaven *and used by Marie for the rest of her life*

Mary Mills/Minnie Mackay aged three-and-a-half in 1859

Marie Corelli aged thirty-three on the staircase at Longridge Road in 1888. Bertha, using the pseudonym 'Adrian', was the photographer

Sketch of Marie Corelli by Dudley Hardy in 1903, the year of the Henley Street Controversy

Bertha Vyver in about 1906

Annie Davis, Marie's secretary for thirteen years from 1901 to 1914 (courtesy of John Wells)

Marie's portrait before correction

Marie's 'official' portrait after correction

...arie Corelli in her gondola on the River Avon

...e library in Henley Street (author)

Mason Croft in 1905

The music room at Mason Croft

The winter garden at Mason Croft

orelli on the front page of the Sketch, 1905: 'a photograph
a lady who would not be photographed' (by permission of
e Syndics of Cambridge University Library)

Marie Corelli and Mrs Docker in 1910

Marie Corelli and Bertha Vyver at a fete in 1916

Marie Corelli's funeral bier in the rain outside Mason Croft in 1924

The angel on the grave (author)

The shield which still remains over the fireplace in the music room at Mason Croft (author)

CHAPTER 7

The Battle for Henley Street

Before Marie had left for Scotland in late 1902, there had been some discussion in Stratford-upon-Avon about setting up a local library. Edgar Flower was Chairman of the Executive of the Birthplace Trust, and his son, Archibald Dennis Flower, a recent Mayor of Stratford, was Chairman of the Library Committee. While Archie Flower was still mayor, he had approached the American millionaire philanthropist, Andrew Carnegie, to ask if he would donate a free library to Stratford-upon-Avon. Carnegie consented and two sites were suggested, one at Market Hall and the other in Henley Street near Shakespeare's Birthplace. Marie's opinion was asked for, among others, and she declared her preference for Market Hall, as she thought Henley Street should be preserved. For Shakespeare lovers this was a sacred site.

On her return from Scotland in October, she learned that Henley Street had been chosen and that five old cottages next to the Birthplace were to be demolished to make way for the library building. Marie, still smarting from her humiliation at the hands of *The Gentlewoman*, decided not to intervene. On 7 December 1902 she received a letter from Lady Colin Campbell, imploring her to help to save the old cottages. Marie refused, but explained her reasons. 'I could save Shakespeare's Chancel from mutilation, because I was able to prove the interference illegal, but I can do nothing here. The only way would be to get up a "literary agitation" about it, and *I* must not do this, as my kind friends (and Mr Flower probably) would say I wanted to "advertise myself".'[1]

For a while she kept out of the argument and went on with her own life. She continued to be asked to intervene in the matter of the free library and against her better judgement was eventually persuaded to help. She wrote to the *Morning Post* on 11 February 1903 and declared that she was only writing in response to 'several literary people and lovers of Shakespeare [who] have asked me to say a word of protest against the further pulling down and modernising of this unique old town'. She deplored the proposed demolition 'in one of the most traditional quarters of the town'.

On 14 February Ellen Terry wrote to the *Morning Post* to endorse Marie's views: 'It seems to me that even the advantages of a free library would be dearly bought by the ruin of something which can never be replaced. . . . Free libraries can be built anywhere at any time – and a great benefit I believe them to be – but when the street at Stratford, now such a fitting setting for the humble and glorious birthplace of Shakespeare, is once changed, a thing of peculiar value will be lost for ever.' Ellen Terry suggested putting the free library near the Memorial Theatre and the museum, 'the three together forming a striking tribute to the aims of modern art and architecture, and this without pulling the dear old place to pieces'.[2] This all seemed eminently sensible and *Vanity Fair* commented: 'Miss Ellen Terry's and Miss Marie Corelli's action in drawing attention to the vandalisms which are about to be committed at Stratford-on-Avon should be met with the active support of everyone who is interested in Shakespeare's town.' Letters of support from around the world were received and printed in various newspapers.

However, there were opposing forces at work, not least of which was that Stratford Town Council were getting very tired of Miss Corelli telling them what to do. Mr Archie Flower replied through the columns of the *Daily Post* on 28 February. 'As this question has been taken up by some who are evidently not acquainted with the locality, it is apparently necessary to make a further statement of the actual facts. In January 1902 the Mayor wrote to Mr Carnegie asking if he would contribute a free library in Stratford-upon-Avon. On 18 February he received a reply from Mr Carnegie, from America, saying that he would feel it an honour to give the sum necessary to erect the structure of a free library, if the Act were adopted and a site provided.' Mr Flower explained that the Act was adopted on 11 February 1902, and the site was selected by the Town Council. 'The Market Hall was suggested, but found too small for the purpose, and it was therefore decided to build on the land adjoining the Technical School [erected in 1898] in Henley Street. Part of this was bare space (owing to a fire some years ago); part was occupied by a china shop and owned by the Corporation. There are three cottages standing between this site and the garden of Shakespeare's house.' In the autumn of that year Mr Carnegie bought the cottages and presented the land to the Trustees 'to be added to and preserved as part of the birthplace property'. Archie Flower avowed that the cottages were not Shakespearean but modern, and that 'The china shop, undoubtedly, contains some old timbers', but that it 'has an ugly modern front, and is in a perfectly hopeless state of decay. . . . It is thus abundantly clear that this building must either fall down or be pulled down, and it was therefore decided to utilise the space for the erection of the free library.'[3]

This was the nucleus of the problem. It seemed that the Council and the Library Committee had accepted the gift of a free library and the cottages, and the site was therefore a *fait accompli.* Now here were Marie Corelli and her literary friends demanding that the library be situated elsewhere, for they believed that to build a library in Henley Street and to demolish the Shakespearean cottages was an act of vandalism. The Council had not considered the historical implications of the site before accepting the gift, but they did not feel they could now go back to Andrew Carnegie and ask him for land elsewhere, for they had been given Henley Street.

The actor Wilson Barrett, writing to the *Daily Post* on 28 February, supported Marie: 'Has Mr. Andrew Carnegie insisted on the proposed site, or has it been suggested or chosen by another? If so who is that other? No man has a right to arrogate to himself the power to meddle or muddle in any way with Shakespeare's house, his tomb, or any of the few relics of his life and times. They should be held sacred, and guarded zealously and jealously. . . . A public library for Stratford is a very desirable thing. To dedicate such an institution in the place of his birth to the greatest poet of all time is wise and fitting, but let it be on some other site. There are scores equally available and eligible.' There may have been 'scores' of other sites. But the council had committed themselves to Henley Street. All they could do was to try and bluff it out, and hope that they could discredit Marie Corelli and her supporters.

The *Birmingham Daily Mail* supported Wilson Barrett on 1 March. 'Mr Barrett takes a large view of the subject which, we hope, may in the course of time penetrate into the rather parochial minds which seem to flourish in what, after all, should be one of the most cosmopolitan towns on earth. . . . Possibly, on broad grounds, the authorities at Stratford who are so desirous of placing a modern free library – presumably filled with modern literature, only the most flimsy part of which will be read – would be ready to protest with most monstrous zeal that they would be the very last people in this world to dream of any departure from the great all-ruling principle. Would they be vandals? Would they desecrate the memory of their well-beloved Shakespeare? Perish the thought!'[4]

Marie was the subject of a poem by H. Chance Newton entitled 'Avonic Agitation – The Reign of William and Marie':

> On my mem'ry 'tis engraven
> How at Stratford-upon-Avon
> (You must always say 'upon' when at the Birthplace),
> As the 'Birthday' was approaching
> I there found, alas! encroaching
> Dire discussions like to move that modest mirth-place,
> Yea, alarums and excursions
> Came to damp the proud diversions
> In which we bardic pilgrims go engaging.
> For, behold! a casus belli
> Found by Novelist Corelli
> Has set an awful rumpus there a-raging!
>
> I hold with Marie (very),
> And also with Ellen Terry
> That the library (if built) should be erected,
> Not near the Old Bard's cottage
> (Which helps pay Stratford's pottage)
> But where its Newness can't be so detected.
> And when ye go a-Barding
> With deep reverence regarding
> That Poet who has helped the World's expansion,
> Also (leftward from the station)
> Go and pay your adoration
> At that other Stratford Shrine – Sweet Marie's Mansion.[5]

A woodcut of the proposed library had been prepared and published the previous August in the *Stratford-upon-Avon Herald*. It shows a Victorian Tudor building in the style of the Technical School built in 1898, to which it was to be attached. The proposed frontage, of 61 feet, would involve the demolishing of Birch's china shop (built in 1563) and all the old cottages. For conservationists there were good reasons to be alarmed. It became quickly obvious to the Shakespeare-lovers that the Board of Trustees and the Town Council were not going to be swayed by any emotional considerations, and that if this outrage was to be prevented it would have to be by legal means. On 9 May 1903 a letter was printed in the *Birmingham Daily Post*.

In the controversy that is raging respecting the demolition or preservation of the cottages nearest Shakespeare's Birthplace – two of the four tenements given by Mr Carnegie for the purpose of extending Shakespeare's garden and more completely isolating the poet's house – the writers have been rather handicapped in being unable to view the interior of the premises. True, access has been afforded the public through the first cottage, adjoining Birch's china shop, to the back of the four cottages in question, and, seen from this point of view, and also seen from the street, the ordinary observer would no doubt come to the conclusion that the cottages were not worth saving; but yesterday, finding the front doors open of the two cottages nearest to Shakespeare's garden, our Stratford correspondent entered, made a careful inspection of the interior of the premises, and was astonished at what he saw.

The writer discovered old beams and fireplaces and massive timber framing on the walls. In the attic was discovered 'a finely-timbered roof of massive black oak beams, certainly centuries old, some of the rafters being from a foot to fourteen inches in thickness. . . . There can be no doubt, therefore, that these two cottages are contemporary with Shakespeare, and some portions much older, and that they ought to be preserved.' The writer went on to state that they were previously one house 'of some importance', and that the front of 'substantial but plain brick' had been added in the last hundred years.

This, now, was the information needed to halt the demolition. But it was barely in time. The Council had planned to pull down all the old buildings during the Festival Fortnight in April but the mayor, Mr Bird, decided that the houses would not be touched during the festival, 'because it was thought to be inadvisable to fill Henley Street with dust and debris when there were so many visitors about. Besides – and he admitted that there was dissatisfaction in some quarters – the destruction of the cottages might wound the feelings of some of the visitors.'[6] It seems that the Birthplace Trustees had not investigated the situation sufficiently before accepting Mr Carnegie's gift. The ancient deeds which proved the real age of the cottages were already in the possession of the Trustees and they could have been read. 'But instead of doing so, they deliberately resolved . . . to entirely destroy property *of which they held valuable deeds testifying to its antiquity and connection with Shakespeare.*'[7]

Marie was now in the forefront of the campaign to save Henley Street. She believed that the truth of the controversy was being deliberately kept out of the pages of the *Stratford-upon-Avon Herald,* and so she issued a magazine called the *Avon Star. A Literary Manual for the Stratford-upon-Avon Season of 1903.* This was a collection of articles by various writers on Shakespeare and his work. There was quite a substantial section, however, by Marie herself, on rambles round Stratford; hotels, shops, historic houses in Stratford, the charms of the river, and the paintings of Mr Quatremaine. She also used it as a vehicle for her opinions about the placing of the Helen Faucit memorial, and included an article on 'The Present Mayor and his Public Spirit'. This was a report on a recent meeting of the Shakespeare Club during which the mayor, Mr Bird, proposed that a public banquet be held at the Town Hall on the occasion of the Bard's birthday and that the club ask some well-known literary men to make the principal speeches. Marie was asked to invite Sir Beerbohm Tree. Mr Harvey Bloom was the only one to object to the scheme. 'It will be seen from the above that the only "dissentient" to the proposed Celebration was a country parson, who objects to "foreign influence" in the Shakespeare Club [wrote Marie]. It is, however, precisely what the Stratford-upon-Avon Shakespeare Club needs badly – "foreign influence" with plenty of "foreign funds".' The main article in the magazine was called 'The Spoliation of Henley Street', which was a cogent 26-page exposition of the facts up to publication date, and which reproduced the main letters and press opinions.

Harvey Bloom saw that here was a chance to have his revenge on Miss Corelli. Working around the clock, he produced a counter-magazine, the *Errors of the Avon Star,* which was released on 22 April, the eve of the Shakespeare birthday celebration. In this he made fun of many of the articles in the *Avon Star.* He sneered at Mason Croft: 'Her own dwelling, with its porch, and glass appendage in the style of an Earl's Court tea kiosk, which she calls a Winter Garden'; he upbraided her for narrow-mindedness and hinted at her questionable parentage, because she had denigrated Ben Jonson for not being Shakespeare, 'and even rates at his lowly birth, which, in that he was born in lawful wedlock, is at least as respectable as many a birth in higher walks of life'. He also mocked her for her lack of education: 'What has her education been? There are rumours of a convent school, and of private governesses. How they fitted her for her task her writings show.'

It was an unpleasant and very personal attack. Marie commented in a later publication, *The Plain Truth,* 'The lampoon was written by a clergyman whose family I had benefited in various friendly ways, and to whom I had been the means of financial and social assistance. On the same day ribald rhymes against me were sold in the street, but as I was fully informed of the sources from which these senseless attacks emanated, I paid no attention whatever to them, beyond regretting so publicly displayed evidence of the lack of education and good manners.'

To read this today makes it seem trivial and rather petty, but to realise the full implications of the Revd Bloom's attacks one has to remember that the Victorian reaction to illegitimacy was to exclude the victim from genteel society. Marie was at the peak of her literary and public-speaking fame – her reputation as the upholder of moral values meant that she was in a particularly vulnerable position – and it is hardly surprising that she reacted strongly. On the day of this attack from Harvey Bloom, Marie was a 'distinguished guest' at the Shakespeare Club luncheon, to which she had, as promised, invited Beerbohm Tree, who was appearing with Constance Collier in *Antony and Cleopatra*. She responded to the toast of 'Literature and Art' with a talk about literature. It must have been an ordeal, as among the other guests were many, including Harvey Bloom, who were now her opponents. In his speech of reply, Beerbohm Tree referred to his exchange of letters with the committee that had invited him to bring his company to Stratford for the Shakespeare Fortnight in 1904. The committee denied that they had issued such an invitation and took exception to his speech, after which Beerbohm Tree declined to have anything more to do with them. Such was the mood of the committee that Marie was blamed for the misunderstanding, although she strongly denied this. She 'declared openly that there would be no worthy Memorial Theatre until it was divorced from purely local management, and put into the hands of a competent national committee'.[8]

What had seemed initially to be a straightforward attempt to relocate Mr Carnegie's free library now became a bitter and personal fight between the Town Council and 'the outsiders'. The Town Council had no wish to change the location, and without the controversy would have demolished the old cottages during the Festival period; now they changed their story. On 11 May Edgar Flower wrote to the editor of the *Morning Post*: 'I beg to say that if in proceeding with the alterations of the cottages, after removing the decidedly new buildings, any portion proves of sufficient interest and value, the retention of such portion will, of course, be considered, but the details of removal and preservation have not yet been decided, nor can they be until certain portions are exposed.'[9]

Marie's attempt to save the cottages was backed by historians, by Sidney Colvin of the British Museum, by Dr William Martin of the London Shakespeare Commemoration League, by the Selbourne Society and by Lord Warwick. It was established without doubt that the pair of cottages had belonged to Shakespeare's granddaughter, Mrs Nash. Marie joined the National Trust, as it was a 'Society for the Preservation of Historic Sites and Places of Beauty or Interest' but found them ineffectual. She offered, through them, to buy Birch's china shop anonymously for £1,000 but the offer was refused by the Town Council at their meeting on 12 May.

Marie had written personally to Andrew Carnegie, hoping that she could persuade him to intervene, but he replied that he had nothing to say. Marie wrote again to suggest it was only fair that he should see her, as he saw Archie Flower constantly, and she managed to organise a meeting with Carnegie on 12 May at the Langham Hotel in London. It must have been an unusual meeting, between two strong-minded, self-made people, both committed to getting their own way, and both very short. Marie reported that Carnegie did all the talking. He was unaware of the location of the site and did not care about it. 'He furthermore stated that if Henley Street were "*as old as Christ*" he would pull it all down, if any part of it were in dangerous proximity to the Birthplace, in any way of menace from fire.'

While Marie was safely in London with Andrew Carnegie, a resolution was passed by the Town Council to erect a library on the site chosen and to preserve Birch's china shop as far as it was possible. At five o'clock in the morning of the following day, 13 May, before the conservationists were aware of the plan, two of the houses in Henley Street were stripped of their roofs and the demolition began. In response to a surge of public indignation, a special meeting of the Executive Committee of the Shakespeare Birthplace Trustees was held; Edgar Flower presided. The *Birmingham Daily Gazette* of 16 May reported: 'During the last few days, by the removal of adjoining buildings and the stripping of the internal plaster inside the tenements contiguous to the Birthplace, indisputable proof was forthcoming that most of the original ancient timber-work remained. . . . The gift of Mr Carnegie, therefore, is of even greater value than was at first contemplated, and Miss Corelli will derive some satisfaction from the knowledge that in a measure her strenuous efforts have met with success.'[10]

There was considerable concern that the trustees would try and pull down the two remaining cottages. Legal proceedings were set in motion by the British Archaeological Association 'to show Breach of Trust on the part of the Birthplace Trustees, in attempting to deal arbitrarily with property, the Shakespearean value of which, despite their possession of the deeds pertaining to it, they were professedly ignorant'. This stayed the demolitions in Henley Street for a short period. When legal proceedings commenced, the Executive Committee of the Birthplace Trustees quickly announced that the cottages in Henley Street had not yet been officially handed over to them by Mr Carnegie. The doors of the cottages were locked and would-be visitors were told that the cottages 'did not yet belong to the Trustees'. Proceedings against the trustees were now not possible, and the intended action was withdrawn. As soon as the action was withdrawn, the work in Henley Street recommenced.

In the *Stratford-upon-Avon Herald* of 10 July the following appeared: 'We know not what led to the abandonment of the proceedings, but the discovery has doubtless been made that the Trustees have quite as much reverence for the buildings entrusted to their care as meddling outsiders. With regard to the property Mr. Carnegie has presented, or intends presenting to the Trust, he could impose what conditions he pleased, and the cottages which have been demolished were given for the express purpose of affording greater protection to the Birthplace.'[11]

Archie Flower made a quick trip to Scotland to visit Andrew Carnegie to clarify the legal position. On 16 July he wrote to Sidney Lee, 'My visit to Skibo was quite successful – he signed the deeds without even glancing through them – the conveyance to the Trustees is absolute and unconditional with an extra promise (for what it is worth) that they in their absolute discretion may alter or pull down or treat the cottages in any way they think fit.'[12] The trustees were determined to have their own way and the *Stratford-upon-Avon Herald* was supporting them. However, Marie had partly won her campaign for without her intervention all the cottages, including Birch's china shop, would have been demolished and a mock-Tudor library erected on the site. It now seemed that because of the public outrage the two oldest cottages and Birch's shop would be restored. She was unable to have the library relocated, but a resounding blow had been struck for conservation. No Stratford Town Council for some time to come would lightly undertake the pulling down of any old building. At the end of her clearly set out history of events of the controversy she writes: 'I have steadily maintained, and still maintain, that to destroy or alter genuine old houses of Shakespeare's time for the sake of erecting any modern thing whatever, is nothing less than a National

Scandal, and a grave discredit to all those wilfully concerned in it. That such destruction was fully intended, and that such alteration is now in progress, can be proved by the plain truth of all the circumstances.'[13]

There was, by this time, a strong anti-Corelli faction among the worthies of Stratford-upon-Avon, including Flower, Bloom, and Boyden, the editor of the *Stratford-upon-Avon Herald,* which accused Marie of self-advertising and suggested, in an editorial in May, that Marie's opposition to the scheme was only because it was to be a Carnegie Library and not a Corelli Library. 'There is another fly in the ointment. Mr Carnegie committed the work to the hands of gentlemen who have lived in the town for very many years, and whose names are identified with nearly every scheme for the preservation of the ancient places of Stratford. To speak plainly, Miss Corelli does not like these people. In her own eloquent diction she designates them the "Pro-Beer Party", and suggests that they are utterly unworthy of the great responsibilities which are cast upon them. This, of course, is Miss Corelli's opinion, formed after a residence in Stratford of about three years!' The bureaucrats were closing ranks.

In early June a letter of support for Marie Corelli appeared in the *Stratford-upon-Avon Herald* from A.J. Stanley, to whom she had donated £200 to restore his house to its original Tudor condition. It was he who had printed the *Avon Star.* One of the governors of the Technical School, Fred Winter, who had a drapery shop in the High Street, saw that this letter from Stanley might be put to good use. He wrote a letter to the *Herald* dated 12 June 1903.

Sir, – The letter from Mr A.J. Stanley in your last issue recognising the generosity of Miss Marie Corelli in restoring Tudor House for him leads me to record the circumstance that occurred some time ago, and which shows how anxious Miss Corelli has always been to add to the beauty and attractiveness of the ancient town. Before any mention was made of the proposed gift of a Free Library to Stratford-on-Avon by Mr Carnegie, I was asked to obtain for Miss Corelli the price for the piece of land (then belonging to Mr John Wright) adjoining the Technical School in Henley Street for the purposes of a Free Library. I did so, and it was submitted to Miss Corelli, who replied that the price was too high. The negotiations therefore ceased, and Mr. Flower afterwards purchased this land at the price asked and presented it to the Corporation. I think this fact 'deserves public recognition', as it throws a little light upon the motives for the recent agitation, and proves, at least, that Miss Corelli was, at that time, in favour of a Free Library in Henley Street. It would have been a 'Corelli' instead of a 'Carnegie' Library.

The *Stratford-upon-Avon Herald* published this letter, with their unflattering editorial comment, and on the same day a copy of that letter, plus the editorial from the *Herald*, was sent to every major newspaper in the country. With them was a covering letter from Fred Winter asking that they should both be published. Marie decided that she now had no option but to bring a libel action against the *Stratford-upon-Avon Herald*, and Fred Winter.

The battle was turning into a schoolyard scrap. The facts were uncorroborated but the inferences were unmistakable. If Marie couldn't be silenced, she would be discredited. The trustees consulted and enlisted the help of Sir Sidney Lee who, in January 1903, had been elected a Life Trustee of Shakespeare's Birthplace Trust. Andrew Carnegie wrote from Skibo Castle to Lee, who had been asked to prepare a paper arguing the trustees' side of the question. 'Glad you are going to look into the Stratford Tempest. I had nothing to do with site – never do have – bought the cottages.' All through June letters flew to and fro between Archie Flower, Harvey Bloom, Arthur Hutchinson and Sidney Lee, suggesting amendments and additions to the pamphlet he was to write. Arthur Hutchinson wrote to thank Sidney Lee for the corrected copy of the typescript and said he had given one copy to Archie Flower. He told him to be careful on two points: Miss Corelli's injunction to the press about Winter's statement and the writ still current against the trustees. He warned that editors might be shy on technical grounds.

Archie Flower wrote on 26 June about the lawyer's advice that the 'trustee' element ought to be kept down for the moment, 'possibly also the legal proceeding against Winter will make it desirable to omit that point – but the paragraph touching it could come out at the last quite easily'. Archie Flower wanted a shortened version, 'so that the *whole* of your letter could be printed *in the local* paper on the earliest possible date'. Constable & Company were engaged to print the pamphlet and 'by dint of printing through tonight the copies of the pamphlet will be all off the machine on Monday. We shall have 250 bound copies here on Wednesday, 750 on Thursday and further supplies daily.' When the pamphlet came out on 19 July it received scant attention. On 27 July, Constable & Company wrote to Sidney Lee: 'Trouble with S.L's pamphlet no-one wants to take it. Messrs Smith & Sons decline to take it on the bookstalls, even on "sale or return". Neither will Army & Navy Stores, Messrs. Hatchards, Messrs. Denny, Messrs. Truelove and Hanson.'[14] It seems the public had lost interest in the affair.

In a letter to Cuming Walters on 29 September, from Braemar where she and Bertha had gone for their annual Scottish holiday and to escape from Stratford, Marie gave her opinion of the trustees. 'Colbourne is an innkeeper, Pearce a jeweller, Bird, a wine and spirit merchant whose interest is in bowing down to Mr A.D. Flower. Dr Mason is a silly old man who knows absolutely *nothing* about Shakespeare, or literature at all – Arbuthnot *you* know! And Mrs Flower does nothing but gabble! Oh my dear Mr Walters, *go on* and prosper – all the world is on your side! . . . And remember, if it had not been for *me*, Shakespearean houses, of which these Trustees hold the records (which they never read!) would all have been razed to the ground last April.'[15]

It worried her that the fate of buildings of national heritage importance was left in the hands of a group of people who she felt were totally unqualified to appreciate the situation. Stratford was still a small country town, governed, in the main, by the local shopkeepers and the Flower family. She had still not given up the fight to stop the building of the library, and was appealing to everyone she could. Again she wrote to Cuming Walters from Braemar:

I have just had a private talk at *Balmoral* on the subject of Henley St. The King is *deeply displeased* that there should be any modern 'library' introduced there, and takes a surprising interest in the fight I have been making. He has spoken to Balfour, but Balfour says it would require an Act of Parliament to buy the old house and cross the Stratford Town Council. . . . But – *Flower* learning this goes to Lady Elcho, a great friend of Balfour's – she lives near Stratford and begs *her* to *prevent* his taking it up! Good! – *he obeys* – and pays her no more attention – setting aside the King's desire even – by saying that he 'does not see his way' – to making a new Act. Now please *keep this* matter of the King's feelings, *strictly to yourself.* . . . Mention me as little as possible. I am like a red rag to the vandalistic bulls. . . . It is a cause that should have been warmly, even enthusiastically supported –, and I should not have been treated as if I did not know what I was talking about. . . . But if you work on it *now*, in every possible quarter, we may yet cry 'rescue' at the last moment.[16]

Did she go and see the King? It is quite possible, for they had been friends ever since she met him at Homburg, and it was by his special invitation that she had attended his coronation the previous year. Arthur Balfour and Lady Elcho were both members of the 'Souls', an exclusive clique of upper-class intellectuals who had reigned supreme over social and aristocratic London from the group's inception in 1893. Initially a salon of ladies of remarkable ability and high social position who later allowed men into their hallowed circle, the 'Souls' considered themselves the *crème de la crème*. Once they had closed ranks, Marie's political campaign was lost.

On 16 December Marie's defamation case came up for hearing at the Birmingham assizes. The main defendant was Fred Winter. What had started off as a simple attempt to relocate a library had gone sadly awry. The trial became a national news story. 'Widespread interest was taken in the case, and the accommodation of the court was taxed to its utmost capacity. The application for seats from people from all over the country was unprecedented.' There were between thirty and forty pressmen present. 'The majority of spectators who got in by special ticket were ladies.' Just before 10.30 Marie arrived, accompanied by Bertha, Annie Davis and Marie's solicitor, Mr Balden. The *Daily Mail* reporter described the scene.

> It was a unique experience to be allowed to gaze without let or hindrance upon a face and figure which to the general public has so long remained a tantalising mystery, and there was a gasp of expectation when Miss Corelli left her seat next to her solicitor to enter the witness box. It was certainly difficult to believe that this plump, rosy, fashionable little lady was in reality the popular novelist whose name had been called.
>
> She prepared herself for the fray by removing her jacket of thick grey fur. Then she stood up radiant in a pale blue silk blouse overlaid with lace. She wore a wondrous black hat with drooping ostrich plumes, and her black silk skirt had a train so immensely long that as she stood erect in the witness box her flounces trailed all the way down the steps.

The *Evening Dispatch* noted that when Marie was called to the box, 'a strange hush fell on the court. She is not at all the slight, pale figure that such gossip as has leaked out from her privacy has led the world to suppose. She is below the medium height, and decidedly buxom, with a round face that has a sad expression in repose. Her light brown hair is low on her face, and her eyes have a dreamy half awake expression. Blue eyes and a large mobile mouth are her most expressive features.'

Miss Corelli's counsel was Mr Marshall Hall KC, and the defendants were represented by Mr Hugo Young KC. Mr Marshall Hall outlined the events leading up to the present case and stated that the main battle had been to save the two old cottages and that had now been successful, the two cottages had been spared, 'and so far Miss Corelli's main object was achieved; so far as she was concerned the matter would have been at an end. She had fought her battle and she had won.' Marshall Hall now 'turned to Mr F. Winter's letter and said he wanted to show where the malice came in. Mr Winter, Mr Flower and Mr Boyden, were no doubt all keen partisans to the scheme of placing a Carnegie Library in Henley Street. What happened? They wanted to have a dig at Miss Corelli, who had beaten them.' He told how Mr Winter prepared a letter, 'and they would see how that libel, conceived in jealousy, born in envy, and nurtured in malice, grew into the form in which it was afterwards circulated for the purpose of damaging Miss Corelli's name and reputation'.

He then quoted Mr Winter's letter and asked 'if any fair-minded man who read the letter could have the smallest doubt that it was malicious to the last degree, and intended to attack the only thing that the writer could attack about that lady – her motives and reputation; a lady who was entirely dependent on the public favour for her literary success, and one who – he did not say it offensively for one moment – was not beloved too much by a section of the Press, but who even dared to beard the critics in their own dens.' She had a large public who liked her works and looked upon her as an honest woman, but in this case the honesty of her actions was impugned and she was held up as a person who was driven by hypocritical and unworthy motives, and whose opposition was merely actuated by petty pique and spite. 'The suggestion was an unworthy one, and was one of those things which were far better left not said, but Mr Winter did not leave it there. He could not get the best of her in that way. His own tongue, no doubt, was insignificant and powerless to use that little story by way of slander in Stratford, and so he had recourse to the Press.'

The trial went on all day with charge and countercharge. It was suggested that Mr Flower, Mr Winter and Mr Boyden had planned this assault on Marie's reputation in order to discredit her. In response, Mr Hugo Young alleged that Miss Corelli played with the same weapons, and 'that they were hardish knocks that he had read'. Miss Corelli replied that they were deserved. Hugo Young's examination of Marie Corelli was aggressive.

1. *The defendant Mr Boyden.* 2. *The Ladies' Gallery.* 3. *Miss Corelli and Mr Justice Channell.* 4. *The defendant Mr Winter.* 5. *Miss Davies.* 6. *Mr Marshall Hall KC* (*from the* Birmingham Weekly Post)

'You don't agree that you are the defenceless woman your counsel suggests you are?'

'I don't think that has anything to do with the case,' retorted Miss Corelli, with dignity.

'But you mustn't start with me like that,' said Mr Young. 'Although attacks have been made upon you, you have given them back, pretty well – just as a man would. You knew that he [Mr Carnegie] had to give £2,000 for these two cottages because the lady who held them was about to turn them into refreshment rooms, and said it was a very valuable position for such?'

'I know nothing about that, he told me he gave £2,300.'

'Never mind about the price – you knew what was in contemplation by that lady!'

'I was told afterwards.'

'I don't care what you were told. In your judgement would it have been more desirable to have a teashop there and an ordinary modern shop built on the vacant site than what was now going to be done?'

'That has nothing whatever to do with it. In my judgement nothing modern should be erected on that site.'

'Would you prefer a tea shop and an ordinary common boot-shop rather than a Free Library?'

'I have no preference either way.'

After Marie had been standing in the witness box being questioned for an hour and a half, a gentleman among the spectators interrupted to ask if the plaintiff could be offered a seat. He was told by the judge to leave the court if he could not behave himself. The cross-examination then finished.

Annie Davis, 'a pale young woman with auburn hair', was next in the witness box and shook so much from nerves that she had to sit down to be examined by Hugo Young.

Hugo Young: I'm sorry to hear you have been ill and I suppose your memory at the present moment on these things that happened some time ago is not of the best. Your memory is not very clear about some of these matters.

Annie Davis: Why should it not be?

Hugo Young: I thought you were in a state of bad health at the present time.

Annie Davis: I have bronchial catarrh, but that does not affect my memory.[17]

She corroborated all Marie's statements. She stated that she had been employed as a teacher of typewriting and shorthand at the Technical School since 1895 and had only worked for Marie since May 1901. She also revealed that Mr Flower had asked her if Miss Corelli had always been against a Free Library, and if Miss Corelli had once wanted that piece of land. Flower had said to her, 'If you search through Miss Corelli's private letters you will find one giving the price of the land for a Free Library.' Annie Davis had answered 'I have nothing whatever to do with Miss Corelli's letters.'[18] As both a long-term resident of Stratford and an employee of Miss Corelli Annie Davis was in an invidious position. She staunchly backed Marie.

When Fred Winter was examined he insisted that the letter had only been written by him and that there had been no collaboration with Mr Flower and Mr Boyden. He stuck by all his allegations. He did not know what had happened to the original letter which had disappeared from Mr Boyden's office. Marshall Hall asked him if he could explain how Mr Boyden had lost the letter, and Fred Winter replied, 'I should say he has burnt it.'

When the judge summed up at the end of the day he said he thought the letter clearly imputed dishonourable motives to the plaintiff, so the question for the jury to consider was whether there was justification. The plaintiff had taken a very prominent part in the controversy, and it was for the jury to decide whether the libellous letter had been provoked.

At 7 p.m. the jury retired and returned after only twenty minutes with their verdict. They had found for the plaintiff – but assessed the damages at one farthing. The *Daily Mail* reported that 'Miss Corelli laughed with the rest and disappeared apparently quite satisfied, for her counsel had pointed out that she did not seek damages, but merely a verdict to vindicate her reputation.' The judge remarked, 'I take it that the verdict informs us it is an action which ought never to have been brought.'[19]

It was an unhappy situation. Marie had won a hollow victory but had alienated herself from the mayor and corporation and quite a number of prominent people in Stratford. It seemed that her fervent wish to become part of the community had suffered a severe setback. Marie Corelli's enemies were mainly small-minded bureaucrats, and the press, who manipulated her image as they chose. To be a woman of passionate convictions in this male-dominated environment was an enormous handicap, as the suffragettes were about to discover. She had detractors, and she could be dogmatic and argumentative, but she was also a woman

Miss Corelli in court (from the Evening Despatch*)*

of great charm and intelligence with many loyal and loving friends. Marie went home to Mason Croft to the comfort of Bertha, while the farce played itself out.

On 18 December, Marie's solicitor wrote to Fred Winter.

Dear Sir, – We shall be obliged if you will let us have the coin of the realm which represents the amount of damages given herein.

Yours truly – Balden & Son
21 December 1903.

Fred Winter's solicitors replied:

Dear Sirs,
We are in receipt of your letter of the 18th inst., and on Saturday morning sent a clerk to see Mr Winter with same. As the latter was aware that our Mr Gibbs, who attends to the matter, was away from home, he went down to Miss Corelli's residence, and saw the butler, and told him he had come to pay the damages, and handed him a form of receipt for

your client's signature. Miss Corelli declined to see Mr Winter, and referred him to you. We now enclose the coin of the realm which represents the amount of damages given herein. On his handing us the coin, Mr Winter requested us to inform you that the particular coin was sent to him from a little girl in the town.

Yours truly – Slatter, Son and Gibb.

23 December 1903.

Dear Sirs,

We have received and now beg to return the coin of the realm representing the damages in this case. We are instructed by our client, the plaintiff in the case, to inform the defendant that she is happy to present him with the damages granted by the jury as a contribution to one of the many Stratford charities he no doubt supports.

Yours truly – Balden & Son.

Winter established a Farthing Fund for the benefit of a Stratford hospital, but when Marie sent him her contribution of 12,000 farthings, Winter returned it. What had started out as a well-intentioned crusade to save a valuable old building, thus degenerated, through petty bickering and malice, into an unpleasant personal squabble. Neither side emerged from the controversy with much credit.

CHAPTER 8

Bitter Consequences

Marie and Bertha, who had arrived in Stratford-upon-Avon with every hope of being accepted, now found themselves less welcome. When they first moved to Stratford they tried to fit into a world about which they knew very little, for Marie's previous experience of life had been either in the unhappy solitude of Box Hill, or as an emerging celebrity in London. She had no experience of living in a small community and found her position in the town had now changed; she was looked on as a meddling outsider. Marie's passionate defence of old buildings in Stratford and her plea for the preservation of the countryside was unusual for that time. Her motives were simple and straightforward – to preserve history for future generations – but her critics were unfamiliar with the concept. Many of the papers were biased in the way they reported her activities, and those whose interests she threatened attacked fiercely. In the face of what she saw as ignorant opposition, she became irritated and fought with every weapon at her disposal. Once backed into a corner she lashed out at her attackers, sometimes unwisely, and she never forgave what she saw as their betrayal.

She was in many ways out of step with the thinking of her day, which is perhaps why she found much solace in the creation of her own fictional worlds. In her first book she foretold how things would be. 'You need not be one of the rank and file unless you choose, – . . . but you must take the consequences, and they are bitter. A woman who does not go with her time is voted eccentric; a woman who prefers music to tea and scandal is an undesirable acquaintance; and a woman who prefers Byron to little Alfred Austin is – in fact, no measure can gauge her general impossibility!'[1]

Marie's gifts were fame and money, and she used the first in order to be generous with the second. This gave her much pleasure and her generosity was at first welcomed, though later found threatening by the Stratford municipal bodies. When the Henley Street controversy was over, she had split the town into warring factions, and the committees and trusts and councils wanted no more to do with her. It seemed this would never be the haven for which she so desperately longed, and she would always remain an outsider. She tried to ignore the critics, wrote articles, entertained her London friends, went for daily drives and started on her next book. In an anonymous article in Annie Davis's papers, an unknown admirer wrote: 'Like every other Genius who climbs the Hill of Fame, she has surrounding her a howling pack of critics, some who openly insult, others who condemn her works, through insufficient acquaintance, and the few who appreciate and esteem. Yet she stands today, like the Statue of Liberty in New York harbour, holding out the lamp of Truth and Right, fearlessly outspoken and ignoring the wild ocean waves of jealous literary critics raging at her feet.'

In March 1904 Marie and Bertha went for a holiday to Cornwall, which was a welcome change from the bitterness of Stratford. They took Puck and Ariel with them but the Cornish hills proved too steep for the little ponies and so they were sent back to Stratford. In April the two friends went on to Wales.

Marie's attacks on the Church became more outspoken. In *Pagan London*, written in June 1904, she wrote; 'What of the ordained ministers of Christianity who are un-christian in every word and act of their daily lives? What of the surpliced hypocrites who preach to others what they never even try to practise? . . . What of the spiteful, small-minded, quarrelsome little "local" parsons? . . . On their "ordained" heads be it! For "pagan" people are merely the natural outcome of a "pagan" priesthood.'[2]

She was now working on her next book, *God's Good Man*, her fictional revenge on barely disguised figures from Stratford-upon-Avon. The story is centred round a small country town, Riversford (Stratford-upon-Avon), where the villains are the *nouveau riche* inhabitants of the large country houses, portrayed as nobodies, and the heroine is a young woman, Maryllia, who is vilified and misunderstood. Like Marie, 'She looked much younger than her twenty-seven years, her child-like figure and face portrayed her as about eighteen, not more. She stood rather under than over the medium height of a woman, yet she gave the impression of being taller than she actually was, owing to the graceful curve of her arched neck.'[3]

The Revd Harvey Bloom is caricatured as the Revd Putwood Leveson, 'whose truly elephantine proportions were encased in a somewhat too closely fitting bicycle suit, and whose grand-pianoforte shaped legs and red perspiring face together presented a most unclerical spectacle of the "Church at large".' Putty Leveson is no friend of Maryllia's; he spreads a vindictive story about her morals, and when challenged declares: 'I've a perfect right to speak of the Abbot's Manor woman *if* I like and *as* I like!

All men have the right to do the same – she's been pretty well handed round as common property for a long time! Why, she's perfectly notorious! – everybody knows that!'[4] Marie comments:

> So the drops of petty gossip began to trickle, – very slowly at first, then faster and faster, as is their habit in the effort to wear away the sparkling adamant of a good name and unblemished reputation. The Revd Putwood Leveson . . . rode to and fro on his bicycle from morn to dewy eve, perspiring profusely, and shedding poisonous slanders almost as freely as he exuded melted tallow from his mountainous flesh. . . . Mordaunt Appleby, the Riverside brewer, and his insignificant spouse . . . were readily pressed into the same service and did their part of the scandal-mongering with right goodwill and malignant satisfaction.[5]

The initial disagreement in this book between Maryllia and other residents of Riverford is about the unwarranted cutting down of a stand of beautiful old oak trees. In *Free Opinions* Marie wrote 'Nothing can be more pitiful to see than the ruthless and stupid cutting down of noble trees all over the country, under the rule that their branches shall not hang over the road. . . . Our ancestors, more individually free, showed finer taste. . . . They left us a heritage of many lovely and lasting things; but it is greatly to be feared that we shall not do likewise to those that come after us. We are destroying far more than we are creating.'[6]

The happy ending of *God's Good Man*, is Edwardian soap opera. Maryllia is forced to leave her country home, driven away by malicious gossip of an affair she is alleged to be having with the local vicar John Walden. When she finally returns, she is injured in a hunting accident, caused by the deliberately careless riding of one of her enemies. John Walden has always been secretly in love with her, and fearing that she will die, finally declares his love. Maryllia recovers to live happily as the wife of the Revd Walden. The book is fluently written and easy to read. Into it Marie incorporates several of her favourite causes. She disapproves of motor cars rushing through the country roads; of cutting down old trees; of various forms of religion, and of absentee landlords. However, she approves of simple Christianity, of country customs, and of conservation and preservation. The critic W.T. Stead wrote of *God's Good Man*:

Her atmosphere is one of vehemently self-assertive Christianity. She is in her way a revivalist preacher and hot-gospeller. She has her own creed, and she preaches it with fiery, although it must be admitted somewhat feline fervour. The pussy-cat, the ill-natured, spiteful, malicious feline, comes out in her pictures of Smart Society. Of course Marie Corelli is quite unconscious of any spite in her delineations. . . . It is probable that the secret of Marie Corelli is to be found neither in her Gospel nor in her Inferno, in her dissertations on the nature of the Deity, nor in her caricatures in the life of the upper classes. There is in her books, despite all their overdone extravagance and unrestrained verbosity, a touch of human nature which appeals to the heart and meets with immediate response. She is human, intensely human, and her foibles contribute, equally with her virtues, to keep her hold on the public. And, above all, she believes in herself with a whole heart fervently, and that, perhaps, is the central secret why so many believe in Marie Corelli.[7]

The publication of this book in September did not improve her relationship with the town. In an article on 'The Happy Life', written by Marie in July 1904 for *Strand Magazine*, she quotes an article written by the elder Disraeli in 1840. 'Of all the sorrows in which the female character may participate, there are few more affecting than those of an Authoress – often insulated and unprotected in Society – with all the sensibility of the sex, encountering miseries which break the spirits of men.' She comments: 'But if the woman concerned has studied her art to any purpose she will accept calumny as a compliment, slander as a votive wreath, and envy, hatred, and all uncharitableness . . . as so many tokens of her admitted power. And none of these things need disturb the equanimity of the Life Literary.'[8]

By 1904 Marie was the author of nineteen books and two booklets as well as numerous articles. Many of her books had been translated into other languages. Most of them had been published in special colonial editions and were sold widely in Australia, Canada and South Africa, and her American market was huge. The reprints were numerous and she was the single bestselling author, male or female, in Britain at that time. It was an almost impossible task for Marie to control this empire and she realised that she could no longer manage the wide ramifications of her publications. In September 1904, she obtained the services of the well-known literary agents

A.P. Watt and Son; it was one of the wisest decisions she could have made. On 12 October she wrote to them: 'One month's experience of your prompt and admirable business methods has saved me a whole year of worry. "For this relief much thanks."' It was a move she never regretted.

One of the things which irritated Marie in Stratford was the way in which the Shakespearean scripts used at the Memorial Theatre had been sanitised. She commented about it in a review of a performance of *As You Like It*: 'Some people wondered last night whether Miss Terry as Rosalind was affected by excessive prudery, as she omitted many of the sparkling witticisms of her part, till it was suggested that the actress was probably playing from the "Memorial Theatre Edition" of the comedy, edited by the late Charles E. Flower, and completely "bowdlerized", with such changes as will adapt it to our times.'

It wasn't only the scripts which were censored. The Theatre Committee had invited Sir Henry Irving to perform with his own company in *The Merchant of Venice* at Stratford in 1905, but the engagement was cancelled, and this was blamed on ill health. Marie attributed his non-appearance to the attitude of the committee.

> Perhaps he is not to be blamed for putting a wide distance between himself and the histrionic building on the banks of the Avon. For the rules and regulations for that flagrantly inartistic piece of architecture are ordained and 'managed' by an exceedingly sage and grandmotherly Committee, and this Committee is to a great extent controlled by a 'Mrs Grundy', who is accredited with having once previously objected to Sir Henry Irving's taking any part in the Shakespeare memorial performance 'on account of his moral character'!
>
> The comic side of this objection will commend itself to everyone without criticism. It is on a par with the 'bowdlerized' edition of Shakespeare's Plays offered for sale at the self-same 'Memorial' Theatre. If we are to measure our appreciation of all our actors by their moral standard, then I fear we shall have to give up theatre-going altogether. Unless, indeed, we can persuade some of the parsons to play leading parts – though from recent disclosures as to certain little amusements of the clergy, it is to be doubted whether they are not even less immaculate than the wildest green-room motley.[9]

This last paragraph refers to the extra-marital affairs of the Revd Harvey Bloom which were becoming embarrassingly overt.

Marie was still a target for sightseers and trigger-happy photographers but had found that one way to escape was to be punted on the Avon into the more remote and inaccessible areas of the river. Annie Davis's father and brother kept a boathouse in Stratford, and Marie had made them the custodians of her boats. At the beginning of 1905 she decided that she would like something larger and more spectacular, and she imported a small Venetian gondola with all the trimmings, including a Venetian gondolier. The gondolier, in full regalia, cut quite a dash in sleepy Stratford, but ran into trouble when, after an evening of heavy drinking at the pub known as the Mucky Duck (the Black Swan), he pulled a knife on a fellow reveller. He was dismissed from his post and Marie employed her gardener, Ernest Chandler, in his place. The *Stratford-upon-Avon Herald* of 19 May commented: 'The attractions of our river have again been added to by the launching of a fully equipped gondola by Miss Marie Corelli. This lady never does anything by halves. In their plainness gondolas are not conspicuous objects. But with appropriate drapery and hangings they can be made to look very pretty and comfortable. In this instance the adornment is reported to be in exquisite taste. And that everything may be in character an Italian has been engaged as gondolier. . . . Our punts will now have to hide their diminished heads.'

Marie was always news and although she had many detractors, especially in Stratford, she also had many good and loyal friends. In January 1905, Arthur Lawrence wrote in *London Opinion*:

Life is too short to attempt the task of contradicting the many inventions concerning the charming woman which have been circulated in New York and London. . . . In the first place Miss Corelli is the best hostess I have known. . . . Of course such perfection in all that pertains to hospitality is not an acquirement. It is instinctive. It is, indeed, a rare possession, and enviable distinction. It is impossible of attainment to the non-magnetic woman. . . . The clasp of the small strong hand is magnetic, her sympathies are eager and quick. She never initiates any allusion to her own work, but is ever eager to know how you fare and what you are doing. With her the woman is not lost in the novelist. And than this, to those who have true respect for the sex, there is no higher compliment.

In the summer of 1905 Marie and Bertha were the guests of Sir Thomas Lipton on his yacht, the *Erin*, at the Cowes Regatta. On board they met their old friend Lady Byron and her future husband Robert Houston MP; an American Wilson Marshall, the owner of the yacht *Atlantic*, and Mr and Mrs Edward Morris of Chicago. Marie described to the Americans a run-down sixteenth-century house not far from Mason Croft, known as Harvard House, which had belonged to Mary Harvard, the mother of John Harvard of Harvard University fame. Marie had just purchased the old building to save it from ruin, according to Bertha, and as Marie told the Americans, 'Over and over again as I passed it, its quaint windows seemed to blink like poor tired eyes, asking "What is to become of me when I get older and still more shaky than I am?"' Marie suggested that the restoration of the house could become a sign of friendship between the two nations. They were enthusiastic about the idea; pledged their support, and asked Marie to buy the house on their behalf and arrange for its restoration at their expense. As Bertha said, the first request was easy, 'for she had already bought it'. Marie engaged a local firm, Messrs Price and Sons, builders and decorators, to do the restoration and repair work, which was to take four years to complete.

Marie was almost paranoid about being photographed or depicted in any way in papers or magazines, and those who dared to print her portrait usually did so only with a disclaimer. The *Bystander* of December 1903 had a very unflattering sketch of a short, fat Marie to illustrate an article on her, with the caption 'An un-authorised picture of Marie Corelli'. She believed that all photographers were out to humiliate her and found it hard to get away from importunate journalists. On one occasion when she and Bertha were enjoying a peaceful outing on the river they had to fling a blanket over their heads when they saw a camera lens pointing at them from a pursuing boat. The photographer decided to print the strange blanketed photograph anyway, with the caption 'Curious photograph of Miss Marie Corelli'. When some devious photographer managed to get a snapshot of Marie and actually printed it, she was beside herself with fury. Her new agent Mr Watt was commanded to retrieve it. 'I must thank you for the reports you have made on my behalf in the disagreeable matter of the libellous portrait, and I also acknowledge, with thanks, the receipt of the zinc block. There are, of course, others existent, notably one of a *much* larger size made for the *Sketch*. I cannot accept the personal assurances of such a cad as the Editor of the *Daily Mirror* who has the affrontery to tell you that he "*was assured Miss Corelli was willing it should be published*". *Who* assumed such authority to so assure him. However, I must apologise for giving you so much trouble on my account. . . . I have, I fear, placed *you* in

'Boyd made the sketch of me as repulsive as he could' (from the Birmingham Weekly Post*)*

a very awkward position . . . and I regret extremely that you should have undertaken to work for an author whose success has made her the "red rag" to jaundiced and spiteful persons who fail to see that honesty is the best policy.'[10]

Another example of the harassment Marie suffered at the hands of journalists came after she had attended a festival banquet in aid of the Newsvendors' Benevolent Fund. A large pen and ink sketch appeared in a Manchester paper of those attending the banquet and Marie was depicted sitting in the place of honour on the Lord Mayor's right hand. It is an unflattering portrait with a sour expression and heavy lines pulling down the face. The cutting had been sent to Marie with a handwritten note in heavy, black, disguised writing;

Fleet St. 26 October. 07
In the 'place of honour' were you? Oh indeed! Look at yourself! A lot of
fools called you a 'pretty woman' on Tuesday night, but we made that all
right on Wednesday morning. Lewis Coward *kissed* your hand, and we've
blacked your face! *We shall do it wherever you go* . . .
All pens and pencils sharp and ready! Tar – tar!
Yours
Press Man
(On the staff of thirty illustrated papers)

Marie immediately wrote to Mr Watt, who tracked down the culprit and
obtained an apology – of sorts. In the meantime she and Bertha went to
St Leonards-on-Sea to get away. From there she wrote to Watt.

Nov 4th 1907. – The letter of Mr Thomas is all that I could have expected
of him. But it does not alter the position. It does not change the fact that
the 'conscientious' Boyd made the sketch of me as repulsive as he could.
It is shown by the needless lines drawn all over the supposed face – lines
which I don't think I have – and which he has given to no one else, not
even to men of sixty and seventy in the same picture! . . . Plainly speaking
it amounts to this – I can never accept a public invitation without
receiving threatening letters, promising an attack or a caricature – and I
can never send a donation to any good work without a paragraph noting
it as a piece of 'self-advertisement' – Of course I can obviate the latter by
giving *privately*, but when charities ask me to 'lead off by my name' as
patron or supporter, I cannot do it. . . . What I shall one day publish will
reveal such a state of things in newspaper offices as would hardly seem
credible if it were not supported by written proof. I will be at the sea for a
few days – as all these anonymous letters made me feel quite ill.[11]

Press harassment is not just a modern curse and, as J. Cuming Walters
had written in 1902, Miss Corelli was once again the victim 'of deliberate
malevolence'.

It seems as though she could only accept herself if she believed her
image to be the fairy-like sweet young thing beloved by Mackay and
praised so fulsomely by her admirers. She was small with, from
contemporary reports, a normal body but abnormally short arms and
legs. This was less obvious when she was slim, but by 1906 she was fifty
and definitely becoming matronly. The publishers wanted a portrait, her

public wanted a portrait, but Marie rejected all the pictures she had seen. Bertha, herself a photographer, came up with a solution. She arranged a sitting with a London photographer she had heard of called Gabell, and suggested to Marie that she use the name 'Bertha Vyver' to preserve her anonymity. When Gabell sent her the proofs Marie was dismayed. Who was this short fat woman with the lined face? Refusing to accept the reality, she returned the proofs to Gabell with blue lines drawn on them to show where she wanted the changes made, and the question 'why this stoutness?' The waist was reduced, the arms made thinner, the hair was lightened, and most important of all, the lines were removed from the face. Gabell cleverly produced an idealised portrait which remained the only one used by Marie for the next nineteen years. It was not, and is not, a true portrait of Marie Corelli, but it was the only way in which she wished to be seen by her public.

The picture was first used as a frontispiece for *The Treasure of Heaven* with an author's note. 'I am not quite able to convince myself that my pictured personality can have any interest for my readers, as it has always seemed to me that an author's real being is more disclosed in his or her work than in any portrayed presentment of mere physiognomy.' Exactly so. She goes on to say that this portrait was necessitated as 'various gross and I think I may say libellous, fictional misrepresentations of me have been freely and unwarrantably circulated throughout Great Britain, the Colonies and America, by certain "lower" sections of the pictorial press'; this, she says, has been done in an attempt to alienate her readers. She wants to point out 'that no portraits resembling me in any way are published anywhere, and that invented sketches purporting to pass as true likenesses of me, are merely attempts to obtain money from the public on false pretences.'

Years later, in *The Young Diana*, published in 1918, Marie came up with a novel explanation for the misleading quality of photographs. 'Only once did an eager camera-man press the button of his "snapshot" machine face to face with Diana as she came out of a flower-show – she smiled kindly as she passed him and he thought himself in heaven. But when he came to develop his negative it was "fogged", as though it had the light in front of it instead of behind it, as photography demands. This accident was a complete mystification.' Marie implied that Diana's unearthly power wreaked this havoc on the poor photographer.

It was not only against photographers that Marie had to defend her reputation. There was a certain German professor, a Dr Reich, who spoke at Claridges Hotel on 23 February 1906 on Platonic and other Greek Philosophy, with special emphasis on the Universal and the Particular. To illustrate this he asked his audience what was the universal behind the success of Marie Corelli. 'A book by her is sold to the extent of 8,000, and 10,000. It is incredible, but it is so, and what is the reason?' Various suggestions were called out by his audience – 'vulgarity' – 'imagination' – 'a disappointed love affair'.

'But does she think?' was the unkind query by the doctor. 'Who likes her most? . . . What is the concrete something behind her success?'

'She is a disappointed woman', came a voice from the back of the hall.

'There,' cried the doctor, 'that is really what it is. Marie Corelli appeals to a class of women who don't want to marry – old maids.'

When Marie read this in greater detail in the newspaper, she was furious and asked Watt to demand an apology from Dr Reich. Watt received an ungracious answer from the doctor, with an apology and a declaration that he did not like or approve of Marie's books. He told his audience he thought that her income of £10,000 a year was undeserved earnings, and he had obtained the information from Methuen. Marie, referring to Reich as a 'German microbe' was assured by Methuen that he hadn't seen the man for five years. 'Donner and Blitzen,' Marie wrote to Watt, 'I have no wish to be either thought of or spoken of by him – and request him never to insult my name again by alluding to it.'[12]

Marie was in constant communication with Watt, who listened sympathetically to her endless demands and queries, and sorted them out. Dodd and Lippincott were her publishers and agents in America and sent her what she considered 'inadequate' cheques. She placed the matter in Watt's hands. 'I want to come to some arrangement by which this mere *waste* of my works may be stopped . . . how can it be worth Mr Lippincott's while to continue issuing books which can only bring in nineteen pounds in six months throughout the whole USA. There are mysteries in the publishing profession which I cannot fathom.'[13]

In June Marie sent the last instalment of her latest book, *The Treasure of Heaven*, to Watt and told him to 'ask Messrs Constable to tell the printers not to tear or injure the last signed page, as Bertha (Miss Vyver) keeps them all'. Marie always pasted a prayer between the final draft of the two last pages of her books. On 29 June she wrote again to Mr Watt, 'Thank you for your kind opinions of *The Treasure*, but I know it comes far short of all you would seek so kindly to express. The motive of the story is a very simple one – merely that happiness does not depend on money.'[14]

The son of her old neighbour, George Meredith, was with Constable, the publishers of the book. He was the 'happy boy' she remembered from Flint Cottage. On 25 July she wrote: 'Thank you for your kind expressions respecting the "Treasure", my object in writing it was to show that the secret of joy is not to be found in the money craze which dominates society today almost to the elimination of any other quality. It is that craze of "money" – that rouses Anarchy and Evil moods of all descriptions – while happiness is far off from realization as it can possibly be. I hope the book will take its message to both rich and poor. . . . Wishing for your firm (and myself!) a big success – in fact a treasure *with* the "Treasure".'15

The Treasure of Heaven is the story of an elderly millionaire, David Helmsley, who becomes tired of the social inanities which surround him, and disillusioned with life. 'A life of toil – a life rounding into worldly success, but blank of all love and heart's comfort – was this to be the only conclusion to his career? Of what use, then, was it to have lived at all?' Telling only his closest friend, Sir Francis Vesey, he disappears from his work and his home and becomes a vagrant, tramping through the wilds of Cornwall, relying only on the goodness and charity of those he meets on the road. All the way through this book there are undertones of the idealistic life which Marie wished was hers. Once on the road David Helmsley rescues a Yorkshire terrier and names it Charlie. The dog becomes his constant companion and friend. He discovers to his amazement the generosity of simple country folk to those they believe to be in need of help. He observes the callousness and lack of concern of the 'swagger' folk, two of whom he encounters racing through the Cornish lanes in their fast motor car. When he arrives at the Blue Anchor he finds those same two men in the bar, boasting of their speed, and laughing about some gypsy child whom they may have knocked down. 'It is really quite absurd for anyone of commonsense to argue that a motorist can, could, or should pull up every moment for the sake of a few stray animals, or even people, when they don't seem to know or care where they are going. Now think of that child today! . . . It was a mere beggar's brat anyhow – there are too many of such little wretches running loose about the roads – regular nuisances – a few might be run over with advantage.'16 At this moment the father, a gypsy, Tom o' the Gleam, comes in, bearing in his arms the dead child. He first attacks and kills the driver of the motor car, Lord Wrotham, then, broken-hearted, dies himself.

David Helmsley sees a side of life which he has never observed before and, deeply disturbed, he continues on his travels accompanied by

Charlie the dog. One night he is caught in a storm and can go no further. He is found the next morning by a kindly woman, Mary Deane, who is alerted to his plight by the frantic barking of Charlie. She takes him in and nurses him back to health, believing him to be a poor old man in need of care, and he stays on with her in the Cornish village, learning to support himself by basket making, and enjoying her simple and truthful way of living. At last David has found someone whom he wishes to make his heiress and he realises that he must return to London to make a will, astonishing his partners who had thought him dead. Having settled his affairs he returns to the safe anonymity of Mary Deane's house to die. *The Treasure of Heaven* was sentimental and immensely popular. It earned Marie over £11,000, and was published in exotic places. Marie wrote to Watt on 13 March 1908: 'By all means let the "Treasure of Heaven" be translated into Urdu! I am charmed that the "English browsing" people liked it – and pleased too that I am "Full of Morals" sufficiently to be classed along with Seneca! *This* is Fame!! –'

An American company had begun to rehearse a play based on Marie's *Barabbas*, with Tyrone Power playing the lead. Marie received urgent messages from New York asking for her approval for certain alterations and for her to sign the contract. Marie, wary since *The Sorrows of Satan*, wrote to ask Watt what was to be done. 'What cuts? At present I am being *kept in the dark*, and I will not *yield an inch*. I beg of you to be *most* precise and particular. The proposed contract is at home, *unsigned* – and I shall do *nothing* till I know exactly what is being done with my new play.' A cable arrived from New York. 'What does Corelli want? Bradon most willing to comply her wishes but fear we cannot cancel his arrangements.' Marie cabled back. 'Corelli wants *plain* dealing and answers *to her* personal letters, which she has not received.' New York panicked. 'Important star company engaged, magnificent production entirely bought, time leaving theatre contracted. Could doubtless hold us all heavy damages, answer vitally important.' On 20 September from Miss Corelli: 'I wish to make certain alterations to the play of *Barabbas myself*, which will *greatly* strengthen it, following some of the suggestions made by the actor Mr Tyrone Power.' By 25 September it seemed that matters were settled, and Marie forwarded the proposed agreement via Watt. By 9 October both play and agreements had been sent to Watt, but she asks his solicitor to be careful to check it all. 'They have been spreading reports that I am going to America, just to 'boom' the play, – I have no intention of going and I would be glad if your agent over there would contradict it *very* emphatically.'

She wrote to Watt again on 28 October. 'I'm anxiously waiting to hear about the *Play*. Is there any news? I want (of course) a lot of money – and "nothing due" comes I suppose from America.' Still nothing came from the American company but on 4 November Marie received news from a press cutting agency, which, furious, she passed on to Watt. 'I have received the enclosed cuttings from New York. Please ask your solicitors to return the play and my agreements. The dishonesty of those people is terrible – they were actually *rehearsing* my play before seeing the revised copy, *or* my signature to contract! They must be *watched most carefully*.'[17]

Copyright laws were lax in both America and the colonies. Marie with Watt's help, was able to control this particular performance of *Barabbas*, which was eventually cancelled, but she had less luck with *Thelma*. She wrote to Watt on 8 May 1907, 'You must cable your agents in New York to take decisive steps to stop the un-authorised dramatisation of my novel "Thelma" – which is being staged in New York. . . . I beg that you will cable *stringently* at once, as I have a play of my own on "Thelma" – and will not permit such impudent and wholesale *robbery* of my work.' Watt was unable to prevent the piracy. Marie also received a cutting from Cape Town in February 1907 of a 'good critique re Miss Williamson's dramatisation of Marie Corelli's *Barabbas*', and sent it to Watt with exclamation marks in the margin. Ever since she had experienced the Grosvenor Theatrical Syndicate's distortion of *The Sorrows of Satan* in 1895, she had fought fiercely to guard any of her other novels from a similar fate. In this she had the full support of Watt, but he sometimes found himself trying to tone down her fury. She wrote to him on 3 January 1907: 'I acknowledge with gratitude your most kind and sensible letter. But if these jealous and grudging souls *want* war, they *shall have it*. Fraud *can* be exposed and *should* be – and *will* be – so long as I wield a pen!'

The Sorrows of Satan returned to haunt Marie, but this time in the guise of a would-be film. The film industry, still in its infancy, was eager for sensational material for scripts, and much of Miss Corelli's work was deemed very suitable. Mr Watt was kept busy tracking down pirated stories and insisting on the payment of the appropriate rights. The complication was that Marie demanded to see the script before she would part with the rights, and as many of the early films were shot from the flimsiest of ideas, and the scripts were frequently written as scenes were shot, this posed a problem.

Elinor Glyn, the authoress, then living in America, had become the adviser on English manners and etiquette for the film company Famous

Players–Lasky. Her book, *Three Weeks*, was made into a film and another of her books was filmed, starring Clara Bow who became the original 'It' girl, an expression coined by Elinor. Not least of Elinor's achievements was to teach Rudolf Valentino how to kiss a lady's hand with panache. She wrote in her memoirs:

> The blatantly crude or utterly false psychology of the stories as finally shown upon the screen was on a par with the absurdity of the sets and clothes; but we were powerless to prevent this. All authors, living or dead, famous or obscure, shared the same fate. Their stories were rewritten and completely altered either by the stenographers and continuity girls of the scenario department, or by the Assistant Director and his lady-love, or by the leading lady, or by any one else who happened to pass throughout the studio; and even when at last, after infinite struggle, a scene was shot which bore some resemblance to the original story it was certain to be left out in the cutting room, or pared away to such an extent that all meaning which it might have once had was lost.[18]

Marie fought fiercely to prevent this happening to her novels, and with the help of Watt was largely successful during her lifetime. In 1911 the Dreadnought Film Company reluctantly agreed to show Marie their unauthorised version of *The Sorrows of Satan*, as she refused to allow it to be released without her approval. It was shown at Stratford-upon-Avon in the local cinema run by Mr Cook. On 9 March Marie wrote to Watt: 'The "film" is simply *awful!* I could *not* see it through; and the man who came with it was fully aware of its *inadequacy* and *said so!!* It is the most vulgar and commonplace travesty of my work and not for pounds would I "pass" it!' She wrote again the next day to Watt. 'I have just had the enclosed from Mr Johnston one of the curious little men who brought the "film" yesterday. I'm afraid there is something odd behind all this. They seem to have bought the rights of a *play* on my book (entirely away from my book and a travesty on it), by a man called Dacre – and they declare they are much disappointed with it and did not think for a moment I would "pass" it! What does it all mean?'[19]

What it meant was that there were several unauthorised versions of *The Sorrows of Satan* up for offer. In addition to Mr Dacre's version, the Grosvenor Theatre Syndicate, who had presented a melodramatic version of Marie's *The Sorrows of Satan* at the Shaftesbury Theatre in 1897, were now trying to sell the rights of their play to any film company willing to buy them. The Grosvenor Theatre Syndicate, as such, had been dissolved in 1902, but a certain Mr Edward Russell, a seedy retired actor, claimed to hold all the shares in the defunct company and to be the sole owner of the performing rights. The matter died down only to surface again in 1915 when Marie's solicitor wrote to Watt: 'It seems that Mr Russell (who is 70) has been hawking the rights (which he has no firm legal claim to) to film manufacturers. He is without funds or employment.' Another gentleman, C.W. Somerset, also claimed to hold the rights in the play: 'he has toured his own version of this piece for many years, but has not purchased the rights from any one'. In 1915 Somerset offered his play to the Walturdaw Company Ltd. No wonder Marie was annoyed; there were now three unauthorised people, Dacre, Somerset and Russell, offering their own versions of her novel for sale to the film companies. Marie's lawyer told Watt that Mr Russell had visited him and had demanded £1,500, 'He had no documents vesting in him the rights of the Grosvenor Syndicate. I told him this was entirely out of the question. I am afraid that it will prove quite impossible to deal with Mr Russell.'[20]

In 1915 the Society of Authors took the matter up on behalf of Marie Corelli and paid her legal costs. They had some success, for on 4 January 1916 the Dreadnought Film Company said they would be willing to make a substantial offer to Miss Corelli, but this would mean that she would have to accept the film. Marie was shown the film and disapproved, but was prepared to write a new scenario for them. On 12 April a letter was sent to Watt letting him know that the film was now to be produced by The Famous Players of America and it would be distributed in the United Kingdom by March 1917. Another note came from the lawyer to Watt on 9 May 1916: 'Mr Russell still demanding money. He is a nuisance.' A scenario arrived from the Famous Players who asked for all rights to America, South Africa and Canada. They were working in collaboration with Dreadnought and apparently problems evolved which resulted in some delay in the production of the scenario. The film was finally produced in 1926, two years after Marie's death. *The Sorrows of Satan*, made by the Famous Players/Paramount, starred Adolphe Menjou and Theda Bara, and was directed by D.W. Griffith.

There is a record of the Stratford Picture House showing a film of *Vendetta* in five parts on Monday, Tuesday and Wednesday sometime during 1915, but no record of Marie's reaction to it. Writing in the *Public Ledger* in August 1919 on the influence of films on the general public,

Marie said: *'The people do not read*; and here will come in a devastation undreamed of. The "Picture Theatre" is the delight of the staring savage to whom books are now nearly sealed – and he thinks he can understand a picture, though that is becoming difficult. . . . The "average public" is being thrust back by a greedy commerce into old savage ways of ignorance, when "signs" or "pictures" were the only way of making them understand events.'[21]

After Marie's death in 1924, it is surprising to see the number of her books under negotiation to the film companies. The list was submitted by Watt as part of Marie's estate. They included: *The Sorrows of Satan*, Famous Players; *The Treasure of Heaven*, Globe Films; *Thelma*, I.B. Davidson and R.C. Pictures Corporation; *Temporal Power*, the Marquis de Serra, which was shown at the London Alhambra; *God's Good Man*, Stoll films; *Holy Orders*, I.B. Davidson, and *Innocent*, Stoll Films. In 1943 the film rights were being sought for *Barabbas* and *The Life Everlasting*.

The persistent Mr Russell refused to relinquish his demand for his share of *The Sorrows of Satan*, and on 13 October 1924 Watt reported wearily: 'Mr Russell eventually accepted £1,500 after MUCH argument and discussion.'[22]

CHAPTER 9

The Cold Courts of Fame

Although she seldom acknowledged it, Marie was becoming increasingly isolated. 'Fame is like a great white angel, who points you up to a cold, sparkling, solitary mountain-top away from the world, and bids you stay there alone, with the chill stars shining down on you. And people look up at you and pass; you are too far off for the clasp of friendship; you are too isolated for the caress of love; and your enemies, unable to touch you, stare insolently, smile and cry aloud, "So you have climbed the summit at last! Well, much good may it do you! Stay there, live there, and die there, as you must, alone for ever!" And I think it is hard to be alone, don't you?'[1]

To read many of the contemporary newspaper reports of Marie, it is easy to see her as a difficult and cantankerous woman at odds with the world. She was, however, a highly successful and outstandingly popular bestselling novelist, who was by now a household name, invented though it was, and fierce in her defence of any possible slur on this name. As she grew older she became less tolerant and fought back savagely, threatening legal action and taking it where necessary. Her friends seldom saw this side of her character. To them she was charming, wonderful company, and generous to a fault. Her servants adored her and remained faithful until her death and beyond, and Bertha, who was no fool, was her loving loyal companion who tried to shelter her from her more intemperate actions. J. Cuming Walters, who had changed from enemy to friend upon meeting Marie in 1900, wrote an article on Marie in February 1906 for *The Boudoir, A Magazine for Gentlewomen*. 'If she has now and again pointed to some phantasmal and imaginary dangers, she has unquestionably placed her finger upon many real ones. She is by temperament ardent, and by nature she is a crusader. It cannot be charged against her that she fails to practise what she so incessantly preaches. She has been much misunderstood by those who are only half acquainted with her – that is, through her books alone. Her personality, a most remarkable personality, must be known also if the undertaking is to be complete.'[2] In a handwritten note among his papers he discussed her personality:

It was doubtless because she had a lesson to enforce, a truth to explore, or some fine daring speculation to announce that she threw herself with such ardour into her work . . . but it must often have seemed strange, almost inexplicable, to a visitor to know that the bright, girlish woman, with the merry, shining, golden hair, talking gaily as she moved about her flower-decked rooms, was she who a few hours previously had been writing burning words on Society's sordid slave market, on the horrors of the Drink traffic, on perverted Education, or misapplied Wealth and its corruptions and the Satanic influence of riches on womankind, on the barter of souls in the false name of Love and the hypocrisy of marriage, on the hollowness of religious professions unaccompanied by faith and deeds, on the tyranny of convention and the injustice of caste; – or, if these had not been her texts, that this same woman had been engaged in some bold forecasting in the region of science, or some probing into nature's deep and well-hid secrets, or some keen visionary of wonders yet to be.[3]

Marie was still busy controlling her literary empire. She was against the contentious issue of *The Times* Book Club, introduced in 1906, and she wrote in the November issue of the *Rapid Review*, 'when it is remembered that a subscription to the Times Book Club costs three pounds eighteen shillings, with the unnecessary Times forced upon the subscriber, and that a subscription to Mudie's or Smith's is only two guineas for three or four volumes, to town or country subscribers, inclusive of the appreciated privilege of doing *without* the Times altogether, the wooden-nutmeg condition of the syndicate will become apparent to the most unsophisticated lover of bargains.'

She wrote to Watt in July 1906. 'The facts are these; that the Times Book Club is a Yankee scheme for "cornering" the book-selling and publishing trade. With authors who do not "hold" the public they can succeed, – and sell books published at 6/- for 2/6*d*. But I do not want this to be done with *me*!'[4] Marie Corelli and Rudyard Kipling were against the book club and Bernard Shaw and Mrs Humphrey Ward were in favour of it. Marie was always against the issuing of cheap editions of her novels. She fought Skeffington for 'a small book of mine entitled "The Murder of Delicia" – which, according to the most unfortunate agreement he bound me to, years ago (when I needed cash), he now wishes to sell to Pearson to bring out as a 'Sixpenny' Novel. I do very vehemently *object* to *this*. I consider it to injure that particular position I hold with the public

... I wonder if you can do anything with him?' she asked Watt in March 1907. She was becoming mistrustful of Methuen, believing them to have withheld money owing to her. Again to Watt in April 1907: 'I am *flying away* at a new book – in fact *two* new books! . . . *I don't think Mr Methuen will get well until he has paid me back what he has withheld from me!* I wasn't born on the "witches holiday" (first of May) for nothing!!!!!'

In July she wrote to Watt again concerning a book issued by Methuen in the 'Red Cover Novels' series. 'My belief is that M & Co have sold a quantity of unbound sheets (quietly pocketing the proceeds) to a firm, who have bound and issued them in this way, paying M & Co a "royalty" on the sales.' When she was told the book could be bought in Boots, she wrote 'I should certainly like you to see Mr Boots, whoever he is, and point out to him the fact . . . he has *no right* to name it as one of a series or include it in the same. And that I most distinctly object to it.'⁵ Mr Watt saw Mr Boot and the matter was attended to.

In July 1907 Marie invited Mark Twain to Stratford and arranged a private train to collect him from Oxford. She had organised several events at which he was to be the guest of honour, but he pleaded to be let off, citing his age and the long journey. 'It had no effect. By God, I might as well have pleaded with Shylock himself!' The *Stratford-upon-Avon Herald* reported: 'He regretted he could not visit all the places which had been arranged for him to see and said "I'm sure if Shakespeare knew how very kind my friends are to me, and how very near I am to being killed with kindness, even he would excuse me."' He requested that his visit might be considered a personal one to Miss Corelli, and not in any way of a public nature. The boys of the boat club cheered him at the station when he arrived; the boys of the Commercial School cheered him outside the mayor's residence and, when Marie took him to the paddock to meet the boys from Trinity College, they cheered him again. He made a short speech to them before sitting down to luncheon in Mason Croft. At 3 o'clock he left, as he was to be the guest of honour at the Lord Mayor's Banquet at the Mansion House.

For many years Marie had an interest in Marie Louise de la Ramée, a novelist very much of her own persuasion who wrote under the pseudonym of Ouida. Ouida was flamboyant, extravagant and loved animals, and also, like Marie, opposed militarism and women's suffrage. She wrote forty-five novels and many short stories, but because of her extravagant lifestyle was constantly in debt. Marie had written an article in 1890 praising Ouida's work for the *Belgravia Magazine,* in the hope of getting some of Ouida's work republished. She had also, in 1894, given Ouida an introduction to her own publisher, which had proved a mixed blessing, because Ouida had then expected that Marie would become her go-between. The two women had met in Florence and enjoyed each other's company and had kept up a correspondence. At one time Ouida kept forty horses and thirty dogs, the cost of which created problems when, towards the end of her life, she was living in extreme poverty at Sant' Alessio and starving herself in order to provide food for the three remaining dogs. On 12 July 1907 the *Daily Mail* printed an appeal on Ouida's behalf, and Marie, who was deeply sympathetic, wrote a letter to the editor, praising Ouida's work and endorsing the *Daily Mail's* appeal. 'I venture to suggest that a "Fund" started by the *Daily Mail* for the purpose of placing "Ouida" above anxiety for the rest of her days, would meet with a quick and generous response, and in full anticipation that such a Fund will be started, I enclose my cheque for £25 as a first contribution.' Ouida, who was fiercely proud and wanted no charity from a daily newspaper, sent a telegram to the editor:

Massorosa, Viareggio, Friday, 12th July.
Absolutely forbid any mention of me. – De La Ramée.

She died from malnutrition in January 1908.

Marie's next book, *Holy Orders*, was published in summer 1908 and is mainly a tract against the evils of drinking, the avarice of brewers, and the laxity of the Church. In her preface she states her aims. 'The Million whose labour makes the country's position and prosperity, are awakening to the realisation of the tyrannous grip in which themselves and their earnings are held by the Drink-Trade. . . . As for the Drink-Evil, I wish that anyone into whose hands this book may fall would honestly try to realise the wide-spread misery, disease, pauperism, crime and lunacy for which that hideous vice is responsible.'[6] Methuen were so sure of Marie's popularity that they printed 120,000 copies and paid her an advance of £7,000. Their confidence was justified – in the first month the book sold 112,450 copies and earned £7,505 10*s.*

The hero, Richard Everton, is a clergyman living in a country parish in the Cotswolds and married to a beautiful, but stupid, wife. He is not happy. He lives in an intellectual wasteland, and is naively unable to cope with the problems of drunkenness and loose morals in the village. 'Religion and temperance ought to go together – and there's no getting over the fact. When men are drunkards, they have not understood the meaning of religion, or else religion has not appealed to them in the way it should do.'[7] The cause of many of the local problems is Minchin's brewery, where many of the villagers are employed. In addition to their wages they are allowed free beer, and drinking is actively encouraged. The vicar declares: 'They ought to be able to buy good, wholesome beer, not a pernicious concoction which is purposely contrived to stimulate thirst afresh and to confuse the brain as well. *Cocculus indicus* and tobacco used to be employed in the adulteration of beer, – and these deadly ingredients are forbidden now by law, but in how many instances is the law not privately set at defiance. There's never a brewery without its own "chemical shop" close by.'[8] Marie, it seems, was not against drinking in moderation, but she was against the adulteration of alcohol which was quite a common practice.

> Will your Government make it illegal to concoct poison for the national consumption? Will it insist on the making of wholesome stuff, and inflict not only heavy money fines, but prison punishment, on the rascals who sell beer which is not beer, and spirit which is a deadly mixture of chemicals? And what of the grocers? . . . It was W.E. Gladstone, I believe, and his Liberal party that gave wine and spirit licences to the grocers – licences which if the growing mania for drink among women is to be checked, ought to be at once suppressed. Who is to count the number of women that order intoxicating liquors from the grocers and have the cost put on the monthly account as so many pounds of tea or coffee. . . . Talk of 'blighted homes' and 'deserted hearths'![9]

Dan Kiernan, a labourer at the brewery, is a habitual drunkard, and, like many others in the village, is lusting after the local whore, Jacynth Millar. The beautiful Jacynth plans to escape from the village at the first opportunity, but in the meantime flirts with all and sundry, including the vicar, who is too holy to notice. Eventually Jacynth accepts a lift from a theatrical gentleman, who promises her fame and fortune in London, and escapes from the village. She achieves her ambition, marries a rich elderly Jew and becomes a society hostess. Minchin's brewery receives its just deserts and is burnt to the ground. The vicar becomes a fervent campaigner for temperance and for reform in the Church, and his sermons are so powerful that he is invited to preach in London, where he crusades against 'a craven Church and a purchased press' and the evils of Demon Drink. 'No power on earth will stop the hideous debasement of the people by drink till the people themselves realise that the brewer and distillers are coining millions of money out of the degradation, ill-health and misery of souls.' Marie spends much of the latter part of the book sermonising. 'The clergy are losing their hold on the million; the million are trying to find God for themselves – and I cannot blame them. The flocks are astray because of the sloth of their shepherds.' *Holy Orders* is overwritten, but temperance was a popular subject and the sales were huge.

Marie, as ever trying to help, wrote a letter to Mr Watt, on behalf of Fernan Gonzalez, Bertha's sister Ada's son. 'I wonder,' Marie asked, 'if in your wide experience you know anyone through whom one could get into connection with a *Gold Mining Company!* I want to do a good turn to Miss Vyver's nephew – he is a good chap – and has five years character as first class mill-man. Speaks Spanish thoroughly.'[10] Mr Watt gave her a letter of introduction to Sir Percy Fitzpatrick, who found Bertha's nephew a post in South America.

Problems remained with the Trinity School boys, now called the Army School. The main cause of friction was that the school rugger field ran across the top of Marie's garden. It was too close to Mason Croft and the boys continued to kick the ball on to the glass roof of the winter garden – often with considerable success. Some time earlier Marie had bought the rugger field from the owner John Coulson Tregarthen, but promised, as a condition of the sale, not to foreclose until the Army School ceased to require the field. It now seemed Marie's persecution might be coming to an end. The Army School had bought a new site at Maidenhead and would be moving at the end of the 1908 summer term. Marie and Bertha were delighted.

Once the school left, the rugger field was turned into a paddock for the ponies and Marie eventually obtained the houses on both sides of Mason Croft and so was able to lease them at her discretion. If she was to be at war with the town, then she would control her own lines of defence. There was an unpleasant incident in Stratford in December 1908, when a strange young man called Jarvis hid in the garden of Mason Croft. He had prowled around the garden from 6.30 to 11 o'clock waiting to get a glimpse of Marie, and then had fired his revolver towards the house hoping to bring her out to speak to him. Luckily Marie was in bed with bronchitis and so was in no danger. The young man was quickly arrested but proved to be insane and so was not charged. He was sent home to the care of his family and Marie, hearing of this, sent the mother money for his upkeep.

In April 1908 Marie was savagely attacked by the *Academy*, and, deeply hurt and annoyed, wrote to Watt: 'It is quite amazing that a professedly respectable journal should put on its front page such a falsehood as that "It is Miss Marie Corelli who, *as a rule* introduces the note of discord". Let the writer *prove* his libellous words! In my seven years residence here I have spent hundreds of pounds on *benefiting the town*, and the only "discord" ever occurring was when I *saved* for *the nation* Shakespearean property that would have been otherwise destroyed. I *most* deeply resent such an uncalled for and injurious *insult* – why I am one of the largest subscribers to the very decorations of the town. If I am a "note of discord", I only know that the people here never weary of taking my money!' Three days later she wrote again to Watt to apologise for her outburst. 'I'm sure you can understand that I sometimes get tired of personally gratuitous insults which I have not merited – especially as every unkind remark about me in the press is sent to the local paper here, and "disliked up" – by especial command and approval of the Mr Flower whose toes I trod on by defending the Shakespeare properties.'[11]

Marie and Bertha went away to Scotland for their usual holiday in August 1908, and Marie wrote to Annie Davis from The Garth, Grantown-on-Spey: 'On holiday – with "the ponies" and Miss Vyver.' Much as Marie bemoaned the constant attacks she received from the press in Stratford, she enjoyed being part of the gossip. She wrote to Annie Davis on 23 August: 'Dear Scribe – I'm *vexed* you don't write longer letters! I do not know how my little town fares at all, nor the news of its people! Mind you write *properly* next time.' Annie did write and passed on some information which delighted Marie. 'The best of news I have heard for a long day is that about Bloom! What joy! I sincerely hope that Mr Melville will soon rescind the mean tricks that have been played (by Flower as well as others) and express his opinion thereon without fear or favour. Perhaps when you are next having a chat with him, you can tell him how Bloom actually circulated a story of my having been *divorced*, and how I had to bring him to book through my lawyers!' And again on 26 October. 'Home again soon. I am very glad about Bloom!'[12]

Harvey Bloom, who from all reports was a popular clergyman, had become more blatant about his numerous and unwise flirtations. His crowning folly took place in summer 1906 when, ill from overwork, he had been sent to recuperate at St Margaret's Bay. There he had wooed a middle-aged spinster and beguiled her into believing he would marry her. The spinster, Miss Sims, discovering Bloom was already married, returned home to Bath, where her brother, the mayor, issued an ultimatum. She must give up the middle-aged married clergyman, or leave her home for ever – he gave her six weeks to decide. Miss Sims wrote to Bloom and asked if she could live at Whitchurch Rectory and make herself useful! In the row which ensued the names of some of Bloom's other ladies were revealed. For a while Bloom's long-suffering wife stayed – it must have been an impossible situation – but realising that her husband was not prepared to change his flirtatious ways, the only solution was for Mrs Bloom to leave with Ursula. She received little support from either Bloom or the community, who thought that it was a wife's duty to stay with her husband however dreadful the circumstances. Divorce was almost impossible and by choosing to leave the family home, the wife was entitled to no financial help. It was not the plight of Mrs Bloom which gave Marie pleasure, but confirmation that her old enemy was not to be trusted.

The public were beginning to change the way in which they viewed morality. In June 1907 *The Merry Widow* had opened to great acclaim in London and became an overnight success. Merry Widow dresses and hats became all the rage and everyone was humming the tunes. George Edwardes made music halls both fashionable and popular. Elinor Glyn, of impeccable morals and upbringing, wrote *Three Weeks*, a novel that was considered so shocking that the headmaster of Eton banned the book from his school, as did many of the circulating libraries. The critics declared the book to be squalid and unedifying, but the public in England, America and the colonies disagreed, and bought over two million copies. The story revolves around an exotic Russian Countess who woos and seduces a young man over a period of three weeks, much of the action taking place on a tiger-skin rug. This led to a poem which is all that most people remember of Mrs Glyn:

> Would you like to sin
> With Elinor Glyn,
> On a tiger skin?
> Or would you prefer
> To err with her,
> On some other fur?

Elinor Glyn, who was born in 1864, had several beliefs in common with Marie. She believed in reincarnation and was a follower of New Thought or the power of thought force. The followers believed the atmosphere was full of good and evil thoughts, magnetic and unmagnetic vibrations radiating like wireless waves and that the human mind could tune in and receive whatever good and bad influences were present in the surrounding atmosphere. The language of New Thought literature was quasi-Biblical with quotations from the New Testament. In an article written for *Nash's* magazine in 1912, Marie wrote 'The Churches have in great measure lost their hold upon the people, and the consolidation of family life is a thing of the past. . . . Most notable and most tremendous of all portents, however, is the earthquake tremor that is shaking the Churches to their foundations, and the growth and extension of what is called the "New Thought".' Though married, Elinor Glyn was, like Marie, sexually inexperienced and emotionally starved. In her preface to *Three Weeks* she writes 'The minds of some human beings are as moles, grubbing in the earth for worms. They have no eyes to see God's sky with the stars in it. To such "*Three Weeks*" will be but a sensual record of passion. But those who do look up beyond the material will understand the deep pure love, and the Soul in it all.' Both authors advocated romantic love above sex, both had unfulfilled love affairs (although Marie's had not yet started), and both were vilified by the critics. In 1933 in Ray Smith's Twopenny Library the three most popular women writers were Ethel M. Dell, Elinor Glyn and Marie Corelli. There is no record that they ever met.

In September 1908, Marie, who was a good friend but an unforgiving enemy, had an angry row with J. Cuming Walters over an article she had written for the *Manchester City News*. It was a furious tirade against the press, called 'The Age of Debasement'. 'The mischief done by injudicious journalism is so far-reaching that it is impossible to gauge its limits.' The remedy, she said, lay with the people who were being trapped and fooled by certain organs of the press – they must refuse to buy these papers. 'Let them also decline to fill the pockets of the literary sensualist whose "sexual problem" wares are merely the contents of his or her own moral dust-bin. The public deserves something better for their money than the rags and bones of a dirty mind.' It was a long article and all but named some of the people about whom she was the most savage. J. Cuming Walters consulted his colleagues who advised him to speak to a lawyer. It was decided it would be wise to omit certain passages. They published the cut article with an editorial by Cuming Walters. 'One of the boldest letters ever penned appears in our columns today. It is from Miss Marie Corelli, a gifted lady who has the largest following of any modern author, and who has proved over and over again that she is a publicist of the greatest courage and spirit.'

Marie was beside herself with fury, and bombarded him with telegrams. 'Please compare proof with M.S.' and again – 'You had no right to publish an altered version of my letter at all and I shall make all the facts public no one has any right to tamper with my work. The letter should not have been published at all as you make my opinions as cowardly as those of your Hysterical and nervous director.' A second telegram followed on the same day: 'The original letter in its entirety will be published and sent free to anyone applying to me for it on Wednesday.' This was followed by a four-page letter denouncing his temerity and ending with 'I call *Shame* upon you!'[13] J. Cuming Walters who had been Marie's staunch supporter and loyal friend for many years was relegated to the outer darkness. She did not correspond with him again until 1923.

In early 1909, Marie's protégé, the actor Halliwell Hobbes, was cast as Horatio opposite Matheson Lang's Hamlet, in London, and he invited Marie to the opening night. She was delighted and showered him with cheerful letters. 'Dear Horatio', she wrote. 'What a dream it seems that you and I ever went in a punt to find forget-me-nots!' Unfortunately, when the opening night came, she was suffering from a bad attack of bronchitis and couldn't go. She was deeply disappointed. She was also unable to work. She wrote a note to Annie Davis on 8 January. 'I am getting slowly better, but am not "up to much" yet. There is plenty of evidence that I have not been pursuing my usual avocations, for there is not a *pen* in the house fit to write with, and the ink appears to be thickened with the legs of defunct flies!'[14]

In 1909 the *Bookman* devoted most of the May issue to a well-written appreciation of Marie Corelli, her life and works. The cover featured a picture of her study surrounded by copies of many of her books. The author A. St John Adcock, himself a critic, wondered why 'no living author has been more persistently maligned and sneered at by certain sections of the Press – by the presumptuous and strutting academic section of it particularly – than has Miss Corelli; and none has won (by sheer force of her own merits, for the press has never helped her) a wider, more persistently increasing fame and affection among all classes of that intelligent public which reads and judges books, but does not write about them.' He writes about the influence Dr Mackay, 'the most patient, assiduous, most influential of teachers', had on his adopted daughter. He praises Marie's brilliance as a public speaker, describing how at a lecture in Leeds 'the interest and enthusiasm were so tremendous that people swarmed to shake hands with the famous novelist, women caught at her and pressed edges of her dress against their lips as she passed, and there was an attempt to take the horses from her carriage and draw her in triumph through the city'.

St John Adcock condemns the duplicity of Harvey Bloom, 'a local clergyman who was under numerous obligations to her for personal kindnesses and assistance' who 'allowed himself to be employed by a member of the Birthplace Trust ridiculing the "kindly heart" of the lady who had often been his hostess, and the house wherein he had been hospitably entertained. Moreover, he carried this insult further by going deliberately behind her seat in the Theatre at the Birthday-night performance, exhibiting to the public the "lampooned" and the "lampoonist" together.' St John Adcock also supported Marie's stand in the Henley Street matter. 'She did what an overwhelming majority of us are agreed was absolutely the right thing, at a time when nobody else would take the trouble of doing it; and the people who would have done the wrong thing if she had not stayed them have not yet forgiven her. This is the head and front of her offending. As *Punch* put it at the time, in some "Abbreviations à la mode":

> There was a fair siren of Strat.
> Who narrated the *Sorrows of Sat.*,
> She'd a gond. on the Av.,
> She was every one's fav.,
> Though she used Shake's Trustees as a mat!

and the "mat" has been nursing a feeling of resentment ever since.'[15] He went on to say that the ill-will of the official element in Stratford was more than atoned for by the affection of the townspeople as a whole. The message which comes across to the reader of the article is that Marie is a courageous woman who has been vilified and deliberately misunderstood. It must have given her some comfort.

In August 1909 she wrote a gossipy letter to Halliwell Hobbes about a marriage; the letter ended with: 'Nothing is more comic to me than to see the frantic efforts made by certain of my sex to catch that slippery fish – man! Why have *I* never tried? I never did like putting bait on a line – so I suppose that's the reason! – Forgive my nonsense! –'[16] When asked on one occasion why she did not marry, Marie is said to have replied: 'I have three pets at home which, together, answer the same purpose as a husband. I have a dog which growls all the morning, a parrot which swears all the afternoon, and a cat which comes home late at night.'

The restoration of Harvard House was completed at the end of that summer and the official opening by the American ambassador was on 6 October 1909. Marie arranged a special train to leave Marylebone station at 9.55 a.m. for Stratford and to return in the evening. The heavily embossed invitations were also the admission ticket for the train. During the ceremony the building was handed over to Harvard University in America in perpetuity, the generous gift of Marie's American friend, Edward Morris, who also paid all the expenses of the opening ceremony. The house was supplied with furniture of its own period and was to be used 'as a house of call for Americans and visitors of all nations visiting Stratford, where they may rest, or read, and write letters and postcards home'. The ambassador, Whitelaw Reid, gave a gracious tribute to Marie. 'Miss Corelli has exercised her own taste, and simply removed all modernities, and allowed the house to show itself as it is and as it was in the days when John Harvard saw it as a child.' The guests then sang 'For she's a jolly good fellow' to Marie, and trooped along the road to Mason Croft where they enjoyed a magnificent and generous feast in a palatial marquee in the garden before departing for London on the train. Marie was voted to the chair of the Harvard House Trust, and in 1913 Sir Thomas Lipton paid for a silver plate to be affixed within the house to commemorate the esteemed services of Miss Corelli and Mr Edward Morris. There were financial problems for Harvard House in the First World War, but these were solved by an endowment fund created in 1920 by Mr Morris's widow. However, once again Harvard House became too great a burden for Harvard University, and they were happy to lease it to the Shakespeare Birthplace Trust in 1991. It is still open to visitors today, and is a fitting memorial to the part Marie played not only in that restoration, but the restoration and preservation of many other old houses in Stratford.

In January 1910, Marie and Bertha's good friend, Henry Labouchere, who was now living in Florence, died at the age of eighty. In his obituary in *Truth*, the magazine he owned, he was described as 'a man of genius who never quite found himself. A man who was by nature indolent and untidy, who trifled with a variety of things, and who had a passion for intrigue.' He was also unacknowledged as the possible co-author, with Marie, of *The Silver Domino*.

CHAPTER 10

Infatuation

In summer 1906 Marie and Bertha were on holiday in the north of England. First they went to Whitby, and then to the small town of Richmond in Yorkshire. From there, by arrangement, they went to Coniston in the Lake District to visit Ruskin's House, Brantwood, where lived Mr and Mrs Arthur Severn. Severn was a man of sixty-four, an artist and Royal Academician, good-looking with a thick head of white hair, a moustache and a great deal of charm. Arthur had been successful with his first exhibition, but lacked the drive to achieve any lasting name for himself. His main claim to fame was that he was the youngest son of Joseph Severn, a close friend of John Keats, who had been nursed by Joseph during his last illness in Rome. He enjoyed the company of women, who found him amusing and attractive, and he was a known philanderer.

His wife Joan, well aware of his flirtations, tolerated them as being a necessary part of her husband's life, even joking with him about his latest conquests. He told outrageous stories about his friends in order to entertain, but there was a cruelty about some of his jokes. Joan, to whom he had been happily married for forty years, was Ruskin's cousin and was so devoted to Ruskin that, until his death in 1900, she and Arthur had spent many months of the year at his house, Brantwood, at Coniston. They still continued to visit Brantwood although their own house was in Hern Hill, London, where they lived for most of the year. They had five adult children. Marie and Bertha asked if they could visit the home of the famous artist and a boat was sent to ferry the guests across to Brantwood. It seems the first meeting was a great success. Marie was at her most charming and Bertha, as always, was the easy, appreciative companion. They all enjoyed each others' company, and the two ladies were invited back for dinner that evening. When the time came to part, the Severns were more than happy to accept an invitation to stay at Mason Croft later in the year.

It was the charming Marie who played hostess to Arthur and Joan Severn at Mason Croft in October and they declared it to be 'one of the happiest visits of our life'. Arthur was a lazy man, quite happy to use his easy-going attitude to life to gain material advantages. Marie, who was feeling battered by the unrelenting press hostility, was delighted by his overt admiration and easy manner. He made her feel attractive and womanly, and in his company she blossomed. Here was someone who needed her and whom she wanted to help. She was equally fond of Joan Severn, but Joan, busy with her family and her cousin's house, needed nothing but Marie's friendship.

Marie was defensive about her single state. 'Many women are old maids by choice as well as by necessity. Marriage isn't always bliss, you know!' But in spite of the denial, she felt that her life was unfulfilled. 'I know now what I have lost! All my love and all my joy! Gone, gone like a foolish dream, – gone for ever! Gone and nothing left but the crown of thorns called Fame!'[1]

Marie's relationships with men were generally immature. Whenever possible she reverted to the 'sweet young thing' persona which had been so successful when she was younger. Her relationship with her stepfather was questionable; he adored her when she was a child when his friends were encouraged to make much of her, but seems to have become unreasonably repressive as she grew up, protecting her from any real knowledge of the world. Her sexual knowledge was limited and distorted by fear. Her sexuality, however, was strong and pours out of the pages of her books. In one remarkable essay Marie pleads for sex education for children at school.

Any other previous close relationships with men had taken the form of an intense, and sometimes intrusive, interest in their lives and careers. With her half-brother, Eric, Marie had felt a fierce need to nurture his talents and to try and change him into someone he was not. She had allowed him to abuse her generosity in ways which seemed incomprehensible to her friends, and when the final betrayal came it destroyed her innocence. She had actively encouraged Halliwell Hobbes in his acting career, showering him with introductions and advice. Her letters to him are warm and funny, but again the relationship was based on her need to give. In early 1907 she begged him to 'let me know what you are doing from time to time – it always interests me, as I have very few friends whom I really *like* and *esteem* – and you are one of them. . . . The world is very difficult for everyone – of course I do not mean the *natural* world which is so full of beauty. I mean the world as men and women make it for each other.'[2]

At the beginning of the Severn connection there were no warning signs. Bertha was a part of the charmed circle; they were four friends who enjoyed each others' company, and Bertha was delighted to see Marie so relaxed and happy. Marie offered Severn the use of her music room as a studio to give him space to paint and develop his talent, and offered to become his 'studio boy' and supply his needs. Severn, not unnaturally, accepted Marie's generosity, and in return flirted with her in a way which meant no more to him than a pat on the arm, but which unleashed in Marie a passionate adoration which at first she managed to conceal. She reveals her unfamiliar feelings in a private journal which poignantly charts her discovery of the emotion about which she had so often written, but never truly experienced until now.

I am not unpleased with the bitter-sweet taste of this new sensation. I am conscious of joy when you are near me, and of desolation when I see you not at all – both joy and desolation are equally subtle in sweetness. . . . Nothing in the strangest fiction is stranger than I should love you, – I, who have loved no one, – or rather, to be quite truthful, I, who have had no one to love. . . . To my mind all life is rounded in the one orbed fact that YOU live; and if you live no longer I too should cease to be, for the very air bereft of your breathing would have lost its power to sustain me. But this is my secret. The flitting phantasmal forms of those around me who assume to be my friends and acquaintances know nothing of it, – if they could guess or imagine it they would be moved to inane surprise or cold scorn, while the more sedate and conventional among them would hold up their heads in pious horror and feign the usual ridiculous amazement that anyone should love where love is, by the world's estimate and law, forbidden. . . . It has come to me in its transfiguring mystery and magic when I had no thought of it coming, – when the warm firelit silence of the room in which you and I were alone for a space together gave me no hint of aught save the most ordinary peace . . . when your sudden kiss started my soul from its house of quiet, and your arm for the first time encircling me, marked the future boundary of my life. . . . You will, if you are honest with yourself and me, admit that the patient peace of my life was simple and endurable enough till your touch unfastened a locked door within my being and set loose a crowd of long-imprisoned emotions.[3]

Marie was fifty-two and had fallen in love with an uncaring roué of sixty-four. By early 1907 Marie was writing to Watt to tell him 'she would be very glad if you can get some literary folks to assist in the good cause of buying for the nation the house where Keats died in Rome, and for always keeping sacred the two graves of the poets also in Rome'. This idea was fuelled by the association between Keats and Severn's father, Joseph. For part of the year Marie worked on a joint publication with Arthur Severn, to whom she gave the nickname 'Pen', short for Pendennis. The story, *The Devil's Motor*, is an allegory of modern living and Marie wanted Pen to do the illustrations, which was one of the reasons she had installed a studio at Mason Croft so that they could work on the book together. She told Watt she had sent the text to Mr Meredith at Methuen's 'some time ago, with a view to its publication with illustrations. If they don't care to do it I mean to bring it out *somehow* and *somewhere!*' She wrote again to Watt a week later on 17 October: 'I quite agree about "The Devil's Motor" – but I know it's a good piece of writing, and it wants a *tragic* (not grotesque) artist to depict the various scenes.' Methuen were not interested; it was quite unlike any of her previous books and publication was postponed.

While in her public life Marie was overseeing her empire, writing books and suffering from unkind press attacks, her private life was a maelstrom of emotions. She wrote in her *Open Confession* of the perils of the relationship. 'For those who love as desperately as we do, without any chance or hope or even wish for marriage, the whole world is a serpent's tongue armed with a serpent's sting. As yet there is nothing said of us; we are more or less "privileged" people, both being marked out by a certain renown, – but I wonder sometimes how long we shall be considered as uninteresting as most "renowned" folk are?'[4] And a few pages further on:

> For if it is a folly to love you so much that I am not conscious of any world, any life, any time that is not possessed, endowed and illumined by you, then let the folly remain with me as the sum total and exquisite good of existence. I can dwell for hours on the merest memory of your touch – a touch that thrills me to the centre of my being; and your kiss on my lips, long and passionate, separates my soul from all common things and thrones me with angels in supernal joy. Moreover, the consciousness of your love gives me a power beyond mere mortality, – it is time I say to drop all effort at pleasing

those whose pleasure is indifferent to us, – and to take full possession of one's own identity, one's own destiny. We harm ourselves infinitely by imagining duties and ties to this or that person, when such ties and duties hamper the soul in its wider and nobler attainment . . . and those who would force us to walk in one cramped path of routine should be broken away from and left with all possible speed.'[5]

It is unexpected to read in Marie's outpourings of love such a strong plea for the breaking of marriage vows and betrayal of old friends. The book *Open Confession* was not published in her lifetime, and it is uncertain if she ever intended it to be published. It is written with impassioned sincerity by someone who was experiencing obsessive love for the first time in her life. There is nothing considered in the writing, which pours out like a river in flood. There are no messages, no sermons, nothing but a ruthless veracity. This is a love for which she would have sacrificed everything she had, until now, deemed sacred, but it was a love which was painfully imbalanced. Once again she was the giver, and Arthur Severn, like Eric before him, was the taker. When they were apart she wrote to him daily, sometimes twice daily. She developed a coy baby-talk, a secret language between them, in which she wrote sentimental rubbish. 'When is 'oo tumin? 'Oo must tum Thursday.' And again: 'Me misses 'oo.' She called herself his studio-boy. 'Would 'oo like to have 'oo studio-boy pack up 'oo drawings?' It must have been difficult for Bertha to know how to cope with this obsession, trapped in the same house as her infatuated friend. Marie wrote:

Everything in the world that was hitherto of importance pales into insignificance before the power of love. Friends, even old and tried ones, become tiresome, importunate or officious, – and one would almost shake them off if one could. . . . You should be grateful, so it appears, to these unflinching martyrs in the cause of routine – virtue, – the persistent spies on the most innocent actions, – these breakers of the most delightful peace; you have no right to be resentful of such 'true and loyal' guardians of your best interests, – no! – you ought to be thankful that they exist. Possibly it may be so – yet I am not thankful, – if these self-imposed spies on my looks and movements are blessings, they are of a kind I could very well dispense with! Alas! – how ungrateful I am to the needful things of daily use and routine![6]

It must also have been difficult for Annie Davis, whose daily task was to take dictation in the morning and answer correspondence in the afternoon. There is one undated note from Bertha to Annie which reveals a mutual awareness of the dangers. 'Mrs Severn has gone and Mr Severn is painting. The time is passing along quietly. I am resigned I suppose for the inevitable – I can but abide my time. In haste till Wednesday morning. Yrs very sincerely, Bertha Vyver.' It is also interesting that in Bertha's memoir of Marie she puts the whole relationship with the Severns into one short paragraph about the first visit to Brantwood. It was not something she wished to discuss.

The music room had now become Severn's work room, and Marie, when she was not writing, spent most of her time with him, sometimes playing the piano while he painted, sometimes just sitting and watching him work. Bertha was not welcome and felt like an intruder in her own home. Joan Severn did not seem to mind the intimacy between them; she was possibly only too glad to have him out of the way.

Marie continued with her own life, but at every possible opportunity visited Pen in London, or entertained him at Mason Croft. She suffered a very severe attack of pneumonia in early 1910, but by June she and Bertha were able to go to Scotland and join the Severns for a holiday on Arthur's yacht *Asterope*. Marie wrote to Annie Davis in July: 'I am wonderfully well, – the air is doing me the world of good. . . . I count every minute like a golden bead in the rosary of time! Never was so happy in my life before!' She signed the letter, 'Your Mason Croft scribbler! Marie Corelli.' She let Annie know when she arrived back at Mason Croft. 'August 16. I came back yesterday, after the most enjoyable time I have ever had in my whole life! . . . I am now entering on one of the hardest phases of work I have ever done! But I must not repine, now that my kind friend Mr Severn has given me *such* a holiday! *Never* have I had such a perfect rest, or such perfect enjoyment! It has been *heavenly*![7]

The 'work' which she was doing was a mystical book, *The Life Everlasting*, which was published in 1911. As she wrote in the preface, it was one of 'the chain I sought to weave between the perishable materialism of our ordinary conceptions of life, and the undying spiritual quality of life as it truly is.' The first in the chain was *A Romance of Two Worlds*, followed by *Ardath, The Soul of Lilith, Barabbas, The Sorrows of Satan* and *The Master Christian*. After the publication of *The Master Christian*, said Marie, 'I decided to change my own line of work to lighter themes, lest I should be set down as "spiritualist" or "theosophist", both of which terms have been brought into contempt by tricksters. So I played with my pen, and did my best to entertain the public with stories of every-day life and love, such as the least instructed could understand.'[8] She explains to her readers that the six spiritual novels 'are the result of a deliberately conceived plan and intention, and are all linked together by one theory. They have not been written solely as pieces of fiction for which I, the author, am paid by the publisher, or you, the reader, are content to be temporarily entertained, – they are the outcome of what I myself have learned, practised and proved in the daily experiences, both small and great, of daily life.'[9] The new book was as mystical as its predecessors, but it added a new element. Marie, just returned from her 'heavenly' sailing holiday with Arthur Severn, poured her secret passion into the love story. The unnamed heroine, and the older, good-looking Santoris are the idealised forms of Marie and Severn. Set in Scotland and particularly the Hebrides, it is the story of the heroine's search for her twin soul – a favourite theme of Marie's.

The heroine has been overworking and is invited to join some acquaintances on a luxury yachting cruise, to sail among the Western Isles, the Hebrides, and possibly on to Norway. She accepts. When they reach Mull one evening, another boat appears, as though from nowhere – 'an involuntary exclamation escaped me. There, about half a mile to our rear, floated a schooner of exquisite proportions and fairy-like grace, outlined from stem to stern by delicate borderings of electric light and making quite a glittering spectacle in the darkness of the deepening night.'[10]

She sleeps and dreams of love and destiny and twin souls. 'O Soul, wandering in the region of sleep and dreams! What is all thy searching and labour worth without Love? Why art thou lost in a Silence without Song?' So Marie begins to recreate her own experience. The mystery ship reappears one evening several days later, when they are moored at Loch Scavaig. The heroine's host, Mr Harland, sends a boat across the loch with an invitation to the owner, who when he arrives is discovered to be Rafel Santoris, an old friend of Mr Harland. The heroine finds him familiar. 'Involuntarily I raised my eyes to his, and with one glance saw in those clear blue orbs that so steadfastly met mine a world of memories – memories tender, wistful and pathetic, entangled as in tears and fire. All the inward instincts of my spirit told me that I knew him well.'[11] The heroine muses: 'Perfect happiness is the soul's acceptance of a sense of joy without question. And this is what I felt through all my being on that never-to-be forgotten night.' On board the *Dream* the next day, the visitors ask how the yacht is propelled so silently and without any obvious engine. Santoris gives a prophetic answer: 'Our yacht's motive power seems complex, but in reality it is very simple, – and the same force which propels this light vessel would propel the biggest liner afloat. Nature has given us all the materials for every kind of work and progress, physical and mental – but because we do not at once comprehend them we deny their uses. . . . A few grains in weight of hydrogen have power enough to raise a million tons to a height of more than three hundred feet. . . . And as for motive power, in a thimbleful of concentrated fuel we might take the largest ship across the widest ocean.'[12]

Santoris suggests a trip on shore to see the sunset over Loch Coruisk. Mr Harland declines, and so Santoris/Severn and the heroine/Marie set off on their own. They climb the hill overlooking the lake. 'I lifted my eyes to his. My heart beat with suffocating quickness, and thoughts were in my brain that threatened to overwhelm my small remaining stock of self-control and make of me nothing but a creature of tears and passion.' When they stop at a high point they can see over the lake and the great mountain. Santoris speaks:

Sometimes it happens, even in the world of cold and artificial convention, that a man and a woman are brought together who, to their own immediate consciousness, have had no previous acquaintance with each other, and yet with the lightest touch, the swiftest glance of an eye, a million vibrations are set quivering in them like harp-strings struck by the hand of a master and responding each to each in throbbing harmony and perfect tune. They do not know how it happens – they only feel it *is*. Then nothing – I repeat this with emphasis – nothing can keep them apart. Soul rushes to soul, – heart leaps to heart, – and all forms and ceremony, custom and usage crumble into dust before the power that overwhelms them. These sudden storms of etheric vibration occur every day among the most unlikely persons, and Society as at present constituted frowns and shakes its head, or jeers at what it cannot understand, calling such impetuosity folly, or worse, while remaining wilfully blind to the fact that in its strangest aspect it is nothing but the assertion of an Eternal law. . . . No force can turn aside one from the other, – nothing can intervene – not because it is either romance or reality, but simply because it is a law. You understand?[13]

While they sit watching the sunset, the heroine has a series of visions, in each of which she experiences a reincarnation of herself and Santoris locked in some dance of time. In each vision one of the pair is murdered by the other, only to reappear in the next scene. In the last scene the heroine sees a woman kneel alone before a great closed gateway barred across as with gold. 'So strangely desolate and solitary was her aspect in all that heavenly brilliancy that I could almost have wept for her, shut out as she seemed from some mystic unknown glory. . . . My heart ached for her – my lips moved unconsciously in prayer: "O leave her not always exiled and alone! Dear God, have pity! unbar the gate and let her in! She has waited so long!"[14]

'A choking sense of tears was in my throat as I moved on by his side. Why could I not speak frankly and tell him that I knew as well as he did that now there was no life for me where he was not? But – had it come to this? Yes, truly! – it had come to this!' They return to the boat but now the heroine is afraid of this change which has swept over her life, 'for the psychic lines of attraction between two human beings are finer than the finest gossamer and can be easily broken and scattered even though they may or must be brought together again after long lapses of time.'

At dinner with the rest of the party when Santoris is asked how he manages to look so much younger than his actual years, he replies, 'that there is no Death, only Change. That is the first part of the process. Change, or transmutation and transformation of the atoms and elements of which we are composed, is going on for ever without a second's cessation, – it began when we were born and before we were born – and the art of *living young* consists simply in using one's soul and will-power to guide this process of change towards the ends we desire, instead of leaving it to blind chance and to the association with inimical influences, which interfere with our best actions.' This was a philosophy which was very popular in America at that time, and was part of a regime which consisted, among other things, of meditation and the imbibing of a special elixir known as 'the secret of El-Zair'. Elinor Glyn was one of its adherents and she remained beautiful and youthful-looking until she died. Marie's readers were enthusiastic to read about any recipe for eternal youth.

The heroine of Marie's book realises that unless she can achieve the deeper knowledge which Santoris possesses, their love can never come to fruition. He visits her that night to say goodbye. 'Here are we two, alone with the night and each other, close to the verge of a perfect understanding

– and yet – determined *not* to understand! How often that happens! Every moment, every hour, all over the world, there are souls like ours, barred severally within their own shut gardens, refusing to open the doors! They talk over the walls, through the chinks and crannies, and peep through the keyholes – but they will not open the doors.'[15]

The heroine leaves Mr Harland's boat and sets out to discover the secret of Life. She goes to the Château d'Alselzion on the Biscayan coast three days' distance from Paris, and is permitted access to the Master. What she wants to learn, he tells her, 'is three things – the secret of life – the secret of youth – the secret of love! . . . The secret of life is a comparatively easy matter to understand – the secret of youth a little more difficult – the secret of love the most difficult of all, because out of love is generated both the perpetuity of life and of youth.'

She undergoes many ordeals to test her integrity. Tempters come and tell her lies. She has a dream when she sees Santoris with another woman. In another vision she visits the Phantom of Wealth, the Phantom of Fame and the Phantom of Pride. She is then visited in her room by the Phantom of Fear who takes her to the top of a high place and bids her throw herself from it to what seems certain death. She obeys, believing in eternal life, and when she at last wakes she finds the Master tending her. She has passed all the tests but one and he explains what she has endured. 'We took entire possession of your mentality, and made it as far as possible like a blank slate, on which we wrote what we chose. The test was to see whether your Soul, which is the actual You, could withstand and overcome our suggestions. At first hearing, this sounds as if we had played a trick on you for our own entertainment – but it is not so,– it is merely an application of the most powerful lesson in life – namely, *the resistance and conquest of the influences of others*, which are the most disturbing and weakening force we have to contend with.'[16]

The Master warns her that she will return to a world of conventions where, like Marie, she will meet 'a million influences to turn you from your chosen way. Opinion, criticism, ridicule, calumny and downright misunderstanding – these will come out against you like armed foes, bristling at every point with weapons of offence.' The heroine undertakes the final test, when, robed in white, she is escorted into the Chapel. 'I entered – then paused – the symbol of the Cross and Star flamed opposite to me – and on every side wherever I looked there were men in white robes with cowls thrown back on their shoulders, all standing in silent rows, watching me as I came. My heart beat quickly, – my nerves thrilled – I trembled as I walked, thankful for the veil that partly protected me from that multitude of eyes! – eyes that looked at me in wonder, but not unkindly, – eyes that said as plainly as though in actual speech – "Why are you among us? – you, a woman? Why should you have conquered difficulties which we have still to overcome? Is it pride, defiance, or ambition with you? – or is it all love?"'

She undertakes the last test and walks fearlessly into the inferno, only to find the flames do not burn her but change to beautiful patterns of light. She walks on until she hears a beloved voice and is clasped tenderly in the arms of Rafel Santoris. She has found her love, she has won all she wants in this world and the next, and nothing can ever separate their Souls again.

Fifty-five years after this book was first printed in 1911, it was still being praised and read by those who were looking for meaning and guidance in their lives. The following piece came from a new edition of the book published in California in 1966:

In the great outpouring of spiritual inspiration which formed the career of Marie Corelli, *The Life Everlasting* stands out as an undying masterpiece. It is a vital book. Marie Corelli was one of the most brilliant women of her time as well as a literary figure of lasting significance. Her importance lies in two factors: the transcendental vision which made her religious and spiritual research illuminate the human soul like a searchlight of truth; and her courage.

It took great courage to write *The Life Everlasting.* It is a challenging book. It dares to ride roughshod over human dogma and spiritual apathy and timidity. Its psychical exploration is direct and forceful. Its ideals soar irresistibly to levels that defy our conventions. Its inspiration is like a clear, cold wind sweeping away petty doubts and fears. But more than this, *The Life Everlasting* is one of the greatest love stories of all time. Its hold upon the heart is complete.

All through this book Marie is putting her own love for Severn into the heroine's experiences, and the book is almost as revealing as her secret journal. But by now, in spite of the declarations in *The Life Everlasting*, Marie's relationship with Severn was deteriorating. They had just completed their joint venture *The Devil's Motor*, a strange book, written by Marie and illustrated by Severn. It purports to be an allegory; the text is declamatory and the illustrations nightmarish. In 1911 the book was published by Hodder and Stoughton in a lavish edition with six illustrations by Pen. It did not sell well. Perhaps influenced by *The Devil's Motor*, Marie finally overcame her prejudice against motor cars in April 1911, and bought one of the new Daimlers, into which she had a special little seat built for her Yorkshire terrier, Czar, so that he could look out of the window. She wrote to the motor shop; 'May I trouble you so far as to tell me how to Insure my Car? – and also, if possible, my Chauffeur as well?'

She was still enjoying her public life and in June 1911, she was invited to the coronation of George V, and wrote a glowing account for the front page of the *Daily Mail*. Unlike her modest outfit for the coronation of Edward VII, this time she shone in her full glory. In October, instead of going to Braemar, Marie and Bertha motored in their new car to Rohnmere, Mullion, in Cornwall for their holiday, from where she wrote to Annie: 'I am enjoying the great solitude and silence of this place very much. Stratford will seem quite wildly hilarious and gay after it. . . . Nobody pays me any visits but the seagulls. . . . I rest a great deal, and think a great deal, and write a *little*. Do send me a wild long letter full of news, please – for I am a sort of Robinson Crusoe on a desert island, and Miss Vyver says she is my "man Friday"!'[17]

Marie was losing her looks and growing increasingly stout, although that didn't stop her dressing as though she was ten years younger. As she grew wider, her lack of inches made her look more dwarf-like, and it was harder for her to pretend she was young and beautiful. A description of Marie comes from Ada Augusta Holman, the wife of an Australian politician, who visited her during a tour of Europe in 1912. 'I made a further pilgrimage to the house of one whose works are certainly more widely read than Shakespeare's – in Australia, at least, and probably in the land of his origin. . . . Even those readers of fiction who are not among her admirers are profoundly interested in her extraordinary vogue, asking themselves in what lies the secret of her popularity. I confess that a long interview with the lady has not granted me a great deal of light on the question, although it has convinced me that she is a decidedly piquant study in personality at the present moment, when almost every woman in England who is "doing things", is numbered amongst the revolutionaries. Marie Corelli, on the other hand, may be decidedly classed as a reactionary.'

Ada Holman wrote of Mason Croft: 'It is an immense chateau for two maiden ladies, Miss Corelli and her companion for twenty years, Miss Bertha Vyver, and a perfect setting, one would say, for romance and inspiration.' She described the vast music room, 'with panelled walls, panelled ceilings and polished floors and a big open fireplace the size one sometimes sees in bush huts'. She then went on to say of Marie: 'She is a very short woman, with a habit of standing on tip-toe to address those of greater height, and quite comfortably plump. She holds herself very well, and has an air of dignity rather unusual in little people. She might be given rather less than the forty-two years she claims [Marie was fifty-seven], having a good fresh colour and a lot of very light brown, frizzy hair. Her eyes are blue, and her expression very smiling and pleasant. Her dress, when I saw her, was of peacock blue chiffon velvet, with a long train, and cut low enough in front to show a plump neck. Into her corsage was tucked a bunch of white violets, and across her chest was a large "MARIE" in diamonds. In her hair were two large rosettes of peacock blue satin, and on her pretty hands were several uncommon rings. She talks freely and eagerly, if not with a London cachet, yet with nothing to betray either her Scotch or Italian parentage.'

Mrs Holman observed a spinning wheel in one of the nooks and was told by Marie that she used it to spin wool, 'with which to knit socks and vests for her men friends, among whom, she assured me, she is very popular, chiefly because she does not want a vote, and is content to be adored. She is quite honestly convinced that all women desiring political equality or working for social reform are despised and hated by men. . . . At the mere suggestion that the opinion of the other sex is not necessarily the rule of conduct for an individual, she was horrified, and by answering, "Well, I, for one, believe that a woman's place is in her home," was convinced that she had clinched the argument. She had certainly silenced me. . . . Few novelists have been more parodied than Marie Corelli. Few, perhaps, are easier to parody. She exasperates the critics and delights the multitude.'[18]

Marie's love for Severn was possessive and sometimes embarrassing, but she was so obsessed that she no longer cared. She made a scene at an exhibition of Severn's watercolours in London, when a picture which she particularly wanted was bought by the Dowager Countess of Birkenhead, Severn's niece, who at a private viewing on the morning of the exhibition had asked for a red seal to be put on a picture on behalf of her husband. She went back to the gallery in the afternoon and Marie, who had just arrived, noticed the 'sold' sticker on the picture. She found Lady Birkenhead and, deeply upset, seized her by the arm. 'Oh, you've taken my picture!' she cried out, 'Pendennis said I could have it. He *promised* it to me. You *must* let me have it!' Lady Birkenhead was taken aback, but explained that it had been bought at the request of her husband who particularly liked it. Marie burst into tears, flung her arms around Lady Birkenhead's neck and said that it was her picture. Pendennis had painted it especially for her, and it was her 'most favourite of all'. The situation was embarrassing for Lady Birkenhead, who extricated herself and left the gallery telling Marie to 'have the wretched picture!'

It seems that the publication of *The Life Everlasting*, which could be seen as an overt, and very public, declaration of love, had not improved the relationship between Marie and Severn. He became openly scornful of Marie. He humiliated her and argued with her in public; he mocked her writing and left her intimate letters to him lying around so that his family or any stranger could read them. Yet he still took advantage of her generosity, he still went for holidays with Marie and Bertha, and still visited her in Stratford. Marie may have been behaving foolishly, but Severn's behaviour was cruel and insensitive. In *Open Confession* Marie reveals her disillusionment.

> Nothing was or is in you, save the ideal shape of such virtues as I foolishly endowed you with, and your very personality is only my thought and my creation. You are a mere shred of man, out of which my imagination wove a divinity! But it is your own hand that has struck the destroying blow at the stately image of yourself – it is your rough voice and boorish manner which has clashed the music of love into discord, – how much better and nobler it would have been had you gone suddenly away from me and never returned, leaving me to dwell on a vanished dream rather than on a degraded Reality! For I never judged you capable of stabbing the heart of a woman you professed to adore, nor could I have believed you would develop an ungratefulness of which a dog might be ashamed![19]

Her relationship with Severn was by now disintegrating into quarrels and rejection. In *Open Confession* she asks the question:

> There are millions of women who deliberately deceive themselves as I have done, – and why? Because the first joy of love – love which seems given to them to sanctify life, – possesses them with so much unreasoning rapture that they are unable to foresee any end to its glad and inspiring influence. And so they go on believing, trusting

and idealising. Then the veil is either rudely torn asunder or gradually lifted, and the ugly Real shows itself, – a Real which is sometimes so vile and appalling in base selfishness, cruelty, vulgarity and harshness, that it drives some women to madness – or badness – most frequently the latter. What shall it do to *me*? I confront your 'real' self, and quite calmly, quite dispassionately I say now – I who loved you – that I find no words strong enough to express my utter contempt of you![20]

Marie tries to analyse her sudden and unexpected passion.

I can only imagine that the strange and sudden 'love' with which you inspired me, was the result of my own loneliness in this world, – my own long-stifled longing for some scrap of tenderness. For I have been lonely all my life, – as a child I was one of the most solitary ever born. I was not allowed to play with other children; and I had no games, no diversions of any kind. I lived with elderly folk, and my only companions were books – fine books certainly, – written by the fine-brained authors of a bygone era; nevertheless hard reading for a child, especially a girl-child. . . . I was considered a 'strange' child, 'old- fashioned' and a 'dreamer'. You came in as part of the constant 'dream', – but, like a rough wind which breaks the smooth edge of a sunset cloud into jagged fire and swift dispersal, you destroyed its former placid beauty.[21]

When the clouds hang low, and the cold autumnal wind blows thousands of dry fallen leaves along the ground, then perhaps a new sense of solitude makes my heart ache and brings tears to my eyes – a new sense that is an old sense – the old, old dreariness of my solitary and unloved childhood, returning to me now in my solitary and unloved womanhood, rendered doubly difficult to endure because of the ephemeral delight of the brief love-story I have known.[22]

However, despite Marie's feelings, she collaborated with Severn on an illustrated book on Shakespeare, and Hodder & Stoughton agreed to print it on the understanding the illustrations should be paid for from the author's royalties. It was first commissioned for 1912, then 1914, but Severn was slow with the illustrations which meant the date of publication was postponed. In 1914 Severn was paid £500 for his nearly completed work, but by 1915 the book was abandoned. Marie wrote to Joan Severn on 9 September 1915, it seems in response to a letter from Pen. She explained that Pen had already received £500 of the £1,000 he had been promised, which was to be paid to him 'on the understanding that I should do without payment for my work, till the book paid its own expenses. I never "included his share in the work as an injustice to me" – that is indeed an amazing misunderstanding of my last letter, as no one could be more proud of his work, or more anxious for its advantage than I. But I consider, and still maintain, that his roughness and rudeness to me are grossly unjust and wholly undeserved, and no one knows it better than himself.'[23] She finishes by declaring that she will not now be writing the 'Literary part' of the book, which 'may be preferable to Pen as he has been told that I am not in literature'. No evidence has been found of this work, apart from a few letters, and none of Severn's illustrations.

Extracts from some of Marie's letters over the last two years of the relationship make one wonder why she failed to end it sooner. '"Twaddle" is the word *you* adopt towards *me* on *every* occasion that I venture to utter an opinion. . . . I was proud and happy when I thought you cared for me . . . but *now!* I wonder *why* you ever disturbed my peace? I was *quite* happy *before I ever knew you – and did not want you. Why did you not let me alone?*' She learned that Severn had taken up with a certain Miss Walsh, which sent Marie into a jealous fury, but she still continued to bombard him with letters, and he continued to reply.

Marie and Bertha escaped to the Princes Hotel in Brighton in February 1916, where Severn joined them. Marie wrote in desperation to Joan: 'I am quite at a loss to understand *why he has come here*, it can't be for *my* company – as he *does nothing but find fault with me!* Last night I fairly lost my temper, for he *goaded me on*, nearly to madness, being so very *rude* to both *Bertha* and me – mocking her expressions and *sneering* at every word *I* said – and it really is *not* cheerful to have to sit quite silent for fear of saying something he flies at! . . . It makes me quite ill.' Severn stayed on in Brighton and continued to abuse Marie. Again she wrote to Joan. 'You've *no idea of the misery we're having!* Pen is really *too* rude, even *before the waiters!* – and *now* he says he may not go till *Tuesday!!!* I do wish you could wire to him or something to hurry his return! I don't want to complain, but our 'change' to Brighton has been *completely spoilt* by him; it's positive *wretchedness*. . . . Never again! – never again will I endure it!'

All through 1916 she continued with this strange dance of attraction and repulsion. She pleaded and raged, and loved and hated, but by 1917 the affair was over. By September she was writing to demand that he return all her letters. 'I will do the same loyally with yours, keeping nothing back.' Severn ignored her demands. Her letters are now in the University of Detroit, Mercy, Michigan. The fate of Severn's letters to Marie is unknown. She wrote: 'I have never desired anything in life save love, and this, though I thought it had been given to me, was nothing but a cheat.'[24]

Shuddering I rose and left that fateful strand,
Crushing my sorrow in my bosom deep,
Freezing my tear-drops with the ice of pride.

Look I not fair and mirthful as of old?
Lo! I can bear life bravely! though that life
Be but despair and heartache unto death!

Yet if I weakly weep and wail sometimes,
Bear with my folly – though I know full well
That tears will ne'er revive the faded Past.

Wouldst thou not grieve for loss of Happiness?
Wouldst thou not sigh above a ruined Heart?
And weep in silence for a shipwrecked Love?[25]

CHAPTER 11

Lonely Woman

Marie, exhausted by the writing of *The Life Everlasting* and her difficult relationship with Severn, now directed her energies towards an unceasing string of articles for various magazines and papers. She was eagerly sought after as a contributor, for her name on the cover of a magazine always ensured good sales. She was not to publish a new book for three years. Her public life continued unchecked. Ella Wheeler Wilcox, the American poet, visited Mason Croft with her husband and, according to Bertha, 'knelt at Marie's feet, in a way that only Americans and the Latin races can with dignity and homage'. Another visitor was the popular authoress, Florence Barclay, whose book, *The Rosary*, Marie had read and much enjoyed. Mrs Barclay returned the compliment and wrote to Marie, 'the only book I have brought away with me is *The Life Everlasting*. The theory of Eternal Youth is a wonderful idea and a great gift to this worn-out generation, if only people can be made to grasp it. It would be a secret of power to so many if a vital force within could keep their spirit, soul, and body young and vigorous. The sheer beauty of it all, of course, carries its own appeal, which none can miss. "The sinking moon – *like a white face in sorrow.*" Perfect! it puts all the emotions of moonlight into six words.'[1]

A strange incident, reported by Bertha, involved W.T. Stead, the critic who had made some scathing attacks on Marie's work. He called on Marie before sailing to America on the *Titanic*, to ask her, on bended knee, if she would forgive him for the savage criticism he had bestowed on her work. They parted good friends, but never met again. He was one of the passengers who went down with the ship.

The global unrest in 1914 was reflected in Stratford-upon-Avon in an event which led to the loss of Marie's 'Dear Scribe', Annie Davis. Annie was the unmarried second daughter in a close-knit family of four daughters and one son, and she was the one who remained at home to care for her parents. They lived in Nos 58 and 59 Waterside Cottages, near the Memorial Theatre and right beside the Avon where her father and brother, Vincent, ran a thriving boat business from the family boatsheds situated in front of the cottage. They looked after all Marie's skiffs and punts, including the gondola, and in the early days Vincent occasionally acted as gondolier after the imported Italian was dismissed for drunkenness. The gondola was too cumbersome to moor opposite Waterside, and so was kept under some old arches further upstream near Trinity Church. Marie's one-time gardener, Ernest Chandler, took over the role of gondolier, and in late May 1914 she handed over to him the sole care and maintenance of the gondola. She then wrote to Mr Davis to tell him of this, asked him to continue to care for her other boats, and went away to Land's End for a holiday with Bertha. Mr Davis, who was seventy-two and proud of his skills as a boatman, was deeply hurt and told Annie that as Miss Corelli no longer trusted him with her gondola, he could not care for any of her boats. This news was conveyed to Marie at Land's End, who dashed off a hurried reply to Annie.

Dear 'Scribe' – I am *very much* surprised at the way your father takes my entirely well meant action of handing over the gondola to Ernest's care. . . . The idea that your father will actually give up the care of my punts and boats *because* I give the gondola over to Ernest, is *absurd* and small! and *so* 'petty' – that I can hardly believe it for I have always liked your father, and always been kind to him. I always wished to have the gondola managed away from the punts etc, as I thought it would be a favour to *both* sides, and prevent friction – and I do hope that you will persuade your father to see that matter in its *true* light, and keep on our always friendly relations. Why should he *not* keep my punts and boats as usual? The gondola is quite a thing *apart*, and I rather owe it to Ernest to give him sole charge, for Ernest has been a good and honest servant, and has *never* disobeyed me or been uncivil. If he was 'disrespectful' *I* am not aware of it – but there is far *too much* 'talk' and spiteful back-biting of each other in Stratford for me to believe a *word* against *anyone* till I can *prove* it. For 11 years Ernest has been *constantly* in my sight, – and I can find no *real* fault with him. I wish to retain his 'spare time' – and therefore give him a chance to make it worth his while. If your father is so 'small' and unkind as to give up the care of my punts and boats for such a very simple cause, he is injuring *his own interests* and putting himself *in the wrong*. . . . I think it quite unfair and cruel to worry me over such a small and simple matter, and I hope you will ask your father to see it in the *right light*. Yours affectionately, Marie Corelli.

Marie had no conception of the hurt caused by her actions and how Annie, who loved her parents dearly, was torn in two by her loyalties. She had become Marie's confidante and friend, and had lived with Marie's infatuation with Severn for the last eight years, but now she did the only thing she felt she could do in the circumstances. She resigned from her position as Marie's 'dear scribe'. Her final letter to Marie no longer exists, but the roughly worked and re-worked notes show how deeply upset she was.

Dear Miss Corelli, I left everything in order last week at Mason Croft because in your sudden distrust of the Davis family in general it did not seem reasonable that you would wish me to remain with you. Nor do I wish it for myself for the heart has been taken out of me by the wretchedness of the last three weeks. Do you think it means nothing to me to see my old father insulted and worried and upset for no real reason. You yourself would resent it if you were in my place.

You write to him and of him as if he were a contemptible back biter and jealous of a young man's success. You know it is not true. He has never harmed anyone in his life. You say it is 'petty' he should give up the care of your boats etc. in the circumstances, it is the only thing he could do, for either you have the full confidence you once had in him, or you have none at all. You say that in giving up your boats etc he is injuring his own interests, that may or may not be, but when a man reaches the age of 72 'interests' are of small importance compared with peace of mind. . . . I had no intention of writing to you. I wanted to see you but I am not able to call for I have not been well for over a week. . . . Even if you would see me I could not talk to you. Dr Ross will bear out my statement.[2]

Marie's reaction to Annie's resignation is not recorded, but it must have been a bitter blow. She had lost a loyal and efficient secretary and friend who had stood by her through all the damaging years of Henley Street and its aftermath. Ernest Chandler, the unwitting cause of the rift, enlisted in the army at the outbreak of the war and was killed in action. The gondola was never taken out on the river again.

After leaving Marie's employ Annie continued to teach shorthand. In 1936 she bought a large wooden hut from the rebuilding of the burnt-out Memorial Theatre, had it erected in the garden of 58 Waterside, and turned it into the Stratford-upon-Avon Shorthand School. Years later, long after Marie's death, Annie was asked to give a talk about her famous employer, to the London Incorporated Phonographic Society. She told them she would like to talk about the golden hours with Marie Corelli: 'The last book I typed was *Innocent* and it was then, in the middle of that book, after 13 years of work with the Author, that the grey days came of which I shall not speak.' She seldom talked of her time with Marie and always remained loyal, but her memory of their first meeting is echoed in a poem she wrote when in her seventies.

'Go on with a brave heart!' the message said
'You're sure to succeed.' That was all.
Yet to one who sometimes felt hope had fled
It sounded a clarion call.

The words were from one who had reached the heights
Of imagination so bold,
That the venom of critics had lost its bite
As success grew a thousand-fold.

And often these words have returned again
When health failed, or courage seemed wan.
Then once again comes the hopeful refrain:
Go on with a brave heart, go on!'[3]

Annie died in 1951 aged eighty. The book Marie was writing when Annie left is the revealing and highly personal account of an illegitimate child, Innocent, left in the care of an elderly farmer, one dark and rainy night, by a stranger on horseback. Innocent grows up, believing herself to be the legitimate daughter of Farmer Jocelyn, until one day knowing himself to be dying, he tells her the truth. 'YOU were the babe that was left with me that stormy night, and you've been with me ever since. But you're not *my* child. I don't know whose child you are.' Innocent's world is shattered: 'I'm not yours – and you don't know – you don't know who I belong to! Oh, it hurts me! It hurts me, Dad! I can't realise it! I thought you were my own dear father! and I loved you! – Oh, how much I loved you! – yet you deceived me all along. . . . I'm nothing! I'm nobody! I have not even a name!'

The cry is bitter and the pain tangible. Innocent was to marry her cousin but this changes everything. She tells him: 'Even if I loved you with all my heart, I would not marry you. How could I? I am nothing – I have no name – no family – and can you think that I would bring shame upon you? No, Robin! – never!'[4] It is then that Innocent decides, as Marie did, that if she is to survive she must make a new name for herself and find a way to earn a living. 'She would have to earn her bread; and the only way to do that would be to go out to service. . . . She pictured herself going into service – as what? Kitchen-maid probably, – she was not tall enough for a house-parlourmaid. . . . With a deepening sense of humiliation, Innocent felt that her very limitation of inches was against her. . . . One other accomplishment she had, – one that she hardly whispered to herself – she could write, – write what she herself called "nonsense". Scores of little poems and essays and stories were locked away in a small old bureau in a corner of the room, – confessions and expressions of pent-up feeling which, but for this outlet, would have troubled her brain and hindered her rest.'[5]

Innocent runs away to London, and finds herself a lodging with an elderly lady, Miss Leigh, where she settles down to write a book, which is published anonymously and becomes a bestseller. Miss Leigh chaperones her to parties and one day, at an 'At Home' given by a famous artist, Innocent meets her nemesis, Amadis de Jocelyn; 'a rather handsome man of middle age, who gazed at her observantly and critically with a frank openness which, though bold, was scarcely rude. She caught the straight light of his keen blue eyes – and a thrill ran through her whole being, as though she had been suddenly influenced by a magnetic current – then she flushed deeply as she fancied she saw him smile.'[6] Innocent soon learns 'that he was a somewhat famous personage, – famous for his genius, his scorn of accepted rules, as well as for his *brusquerie* in society and carelessness of conventions.' It seems the character of Amadis de Jocelyn owes much to that of Arthur Severn. He confesses that he is essentially a selfish man. Notwithstanding, 'the impression he had made on Innocent's guileless and romantic nature was beyond analysis, – she did not try to understand it herself. . . . Whereby it will be seen that the poor child, endowed with a singular genius as she was, knew nothing of men and their never-failing contempt for the achievements of gifted women . . . she was the very last sort of creature to realise the ugly truth that men, taken *en masse*, consider women in one only way – that of sex, – as the lower half of man, necessary to man's continuance, but always the mere vessel of his pleasure.'[7]

Innocent reveals that she is the author of the books, and when her publisher tells her she must be happy to be so suddenly famous Innocent/Marie replies: 'Are famous persons happy? I don't think they are! To be stared at and whispered about and criticised – that's not happiness! And men never like you!'[8] Her fame grows, but Amadis refuses to take her seriously as an artist. '"She's a nice little thing with baby eyes," he was reported to have said, "but she couldn't write a clever book! She may have got some man to write it for her!" Innocent gave a little cry of pain. "Oh! – did he say that?" "Of course he did! All men say that sort of thing! They can't bear a woman to do more than marry and have children."'

Some weeks later on, when the London season was at its height, Innocent begins to consider her own invidious position.

> Up to the present no one had asked who she was, or where she came from – she was understood to be an orphan, left alone in the world, who by her own genius and unaided effort had lifted herself into the front rank among the 'shining lights' of the day. This, so far, had been sufficient information for all with whom she had come in contact – but as time went on, would not people ask more about her? who were her father and mother? – where she was born? – how she had been educated? These inquisitorial demands were surely among the penalties of fame! And if she told the truth, would she not, despite the renown she had won, be lightly, even scornfully esteemed by conventional society as a 'bastard' and interloper, though the manner of her birth was no fault of her own, and she was unjustly punishable for the sins of her parents, such being the wicked law![9]

Marie wrote this book when for nearly sixty years she had been fiercely trying to conceal her past and her dubious parentage. Although written as fiction, *Innocent* is almost as revealing as her posthumously published *Open Confession*. She had a driving need to explain to her readers what it was like to be scorned for being illegitimate. Hurt by Severn's indifference to her work, Marie comes back again and again to a familiar theme. 'Few men are proud of any woman's success, especially in the arts. Their attitude is one of amused tolerance when it is not of actual sex-jealousy or contempt. Least of all can any man endure that the woman for whom he has a short spell of passionate fancy should be considered notable, or in an intellectual sense superior to himself.'[10] Amadis/Severn tells Innocent/Marie: 'Your ideas of love and mine are totally different. You want to live in a paradise of romance and tenderness – I want nothing of the sort. Of course with a sweet caressable creature like you it's very pleasant to indulge in a little folly for a time. . . . You have – yes! – you have amused me! and I've made you happy – given you something to think about beside scribbling and publishing – yes – and what is much more to my credit – I have taken care of you and left you unharmed.'[11]

191

This somewhat melodramatic tragedy of love and betrayal becomes far more interesting when taken in conjunction with Marie's own love story, and it was one of her most popular books.

As early as 1901 Marie had proposed that a guild should be formed in Stratford, to deal with matters pertaining to the preservation of historic buildings. The idea aroused no interest at the time and was allowed to drop. The subject was raised again in 1913, and this time received general approval. The first public meeting of the Guild of Stratford was held at the Town Hall on 9 May 1913. The committee included Miss Corelli, Mr Severn, the mayor, Mr Ballance, and Marie's friend, Mr Frank Benson. There were other members from the town and Council and most of the guild business dealt with matters of conservation.

Marie saw her role as instigator and chief motivator, a role not always welcomed by other committee members. In a letter to the secretary, Mr Wellstood, dated 25 August 1913, she protested, 'I hear there is to be a meeting of the "Guild" tomorrow at Hall's Croft. *I have not been asked –* and I should like to know if I am to be deliberately left out of these things? – if so, I shall withdraw my name entirely.' She did not withdraw her name and continued to chivvy her fellow members. In January 1914: 'Miss Corelli draws attention to the large number of trees being sold at Loxley and Welford – will the Guild do something about it.' And again in February 1914 she was worried about the wanton defacement of the Waterside Cottages – 'Anything I *can* do I *will.* Do you think the efforts of the Committee in this direction are likely to meet with success? – Stratford folk seem to wish to "cut off their noses to spite their faces".'

Later she was pleased to hear that the trees had been saved and thought that the owner ought to be thanked and invited to become a member of the guild. She was surprised about Waterside and couldn't think what the authorities were doing. 'Those Waterside Cottages must be saved.' In April 1915 she stirred the guild again. 'What has the guild been about to permit the horrible, *desecration and mutilation* of the "lime-tree avenue" – leading to the church by Mr Melville [the vicar] – it is a ruffianly deed on the part of a temporary cleric who has no more *soul* for the sacred things he has in his charge than a bat or a weasel. . . . It is *too* disgraceful.'[12] Mr Melville had replaced the Revd George Arbuthnot, who was appointed Archdeacon of Coventry in 1913.

With the outbreak of the First World War in 1914 the mutilation of trees became of secondary importance. Just before the war, Marie wrote 'The Savage Glory', an impassioned anti-war tract, first printed in *Nash's Magazine* in 1913.

Civilisation is a great Word. It reads well – it is used everywhere – it bears itself proudly in the language. It is a big mouthful of arrogance and self-sufficiency. Yet it is all the veriest game of make-believe, for we are mere Savages still. . . . WAR is unquestionably the thrust and blow of untamed Savagery in the face of untamed Civilisation. No special pleading can make it anything else. We may if we like call it 'Patriotism' in our perpetual life comedy or tragedy of feigning, but in sane moments we must surely realise that we are wilfully deceiving ourselves. Patriotism is understood to be that virtue which consists in serving one's country; but in what way is this 'Patria' or country served by slaying its able-bodied men in thousands? – the very men whose peaceful and progressive toil makes the country worth living in? . . . The 'civilised' State protests against the murder of one individual, but looks upon the ghastly holocaust of slaughtered lives in battle as something almost noble and inspiring! Is this reasonable? Is it reconcilable with sane judgement? Is it any proof that our 'Education' is of real worth? – or does it not rather testify to the amazing fact that in our greed of possession, our thirst of conquest, and our curious conceptions of religion and humanity, we have progressed scarcely a step ahead of our 'barbarian' ancestors and their 'savage' customs![13]

Her sentiments were out of step with the jingoism of the time and *Nash's Magazine* published the article with a disclaimer to the effect that the author's opinions were not necessarily those of the magazine. Once war had been declared, Marie became vehemently patriotic and pro-fighting. In the *Sunday Pictorial* of March 1915 she urged women to send their men into battle. 'But have I, as a woman, nothing to say of the war? Oh, yes! I, as a woman, could say much in a woman's way. Of the agony of parting from men dearer to us than life, and seeing them vanish behind a veil of impenetrable silence for weeks or months, their fate or fortune all unknown! . . . I long to speak words of consolation and hope to the dear women who wait in strained suspense for news of their husbands, fathers, lovers, and sons! I know all they feel; and the aching throb of their unuttered misery strikes on my own heart with keenest pain! But with all the sorrow and all the suffering, I would not, if I could, hold back one man from taking his share in the noble struggle for the betterment and future peace of the world! One can die but once; and "Greater love hath no man more than this – that a man lay down his life for his friends!"'[14]

Marie had written no books for four years, and now threw all her energies into war work, writing innumerable articles exhorting, condemning and cajoling. She took no payment, considering this was her contribution to the war effort. Fifty of the articles, written between 1914 and 1918, were gathered together in a volume, *My Little Bit*, published in 1919. Many of the articles berate the bureaucrats for their impossible rationing restrictions. 'Complaints are rife and bitter concerning the tough, indigestible, and injurious, mixture permitted to the tax paying public as "war bread"! which is condemned by bakers and shows up the ineptitude of the Ministry of Food.' Marie was equally scathing about a plan to dig up the public parks to plant potatoes. 'Pessimist Bathurst states "gravely" that "there will be no potatoes for any one in about six weeks". Well, all who have vegetable gardens know that there is always a scarcity of potatoes every year, when the old ones are practically finished and we are waiting for the new; and owing to the general "sensationalism" the scarcity this year is likely to be more pronounced. But it need not disturb any one's equanimity.'[15]

Her own war efforts were generous. In December 1917 Marie wrote an appeal on behalf of Queen Mary's Hospital in London which was read by Mrs Patrick Campbell at a fund-raising at the Alhambra Theatre in Leicester Square. George Robey then auctioned the manuscript for 100 guineas. Marie offered Mason Croft for use as a hospital, and when it was rejected because the rooms were too small she offered the old Trinity School building, now in her possession, as a convalescent home for wounded American soldiers and paid all the expenses. She gave £100 to Sir Arthur Yapp for YWCA huts, and corresponded with him about the injustice of forcing poor women to queue for their rations in the cold.

Because of food shortages and restrictions during the war, the Food Controller introduced a Hoarding Act. Marie wrote: 'It opened the door to all petty spies and scandal-mongers of every neighbourhood, especially to the provincial types of these gentry. . . . The "Hoarding" order suited them down to the ground and set them all on the alert, peering into windows and peeping through open doors – following their "dear friends" into shops and taking eager notes of their purchases.'

Bertha recorded that 1917 was a marvellous year for fruit, and the gardens and orchards of Mason Croft produced nearly 1,000 lb of plums and apples. The Hoarding Act stated clearly that the sugar restrictions did not apply to sugar obtained for preserving home-grown fruit, and as the local grocer did not have enough supplies, Marie telephoned her old friend, Sir Thomas Lipton, for help. He replied 'Ye'll never want for sugar so long as Tom Lipton's on the phone.' Supplies were sent from London in crates clearly marked as sugar, and delivered to Mason Croft. There the surplus fruit was turned into jam, 'for the public good', as Bertha said, 'jam of which Marie would probably have given away the greater amount, or would have sold as and where the authorities instructed'. Certain people in Stratford could not forgive her for her past meddling and the authorities, alerted by local tradesmen angry that she had gone above their heads, decided to have Mason Croft searched for any evidence of the heinous crime of 'food hoarding'. The policeman found some empty crates in the outhouses, containing nothing but electrical fittings – but no hidden caches of sugar.

In spite of this Marie was summoned to attend the local magistrate's court on 2 January 1918. The charge was ludicrous; Marie had no need to hoard sugar. She appealed to Arthur Yapp, the Director of Food Economy, who said he would get in touch with Charles Bathurst, the Chairman of the Sugar Commission. Bathurst, whom Marie had attacked in her article 'The Potato Scream', professed ignorance of the affair – and the case proceeded to court. The local magistrates before whom she was summoned included Fred Winter and some of her other enemies from the Henley Street controversy. As Bertha reported: 'The Bench, though there were dissentients, refused – by, I understand, a majority of one – to believe that we had not used any of the sugar in our tea. Though our servants were present to answer questions on oath, they were not called, and my own replies to questions in the witness box were not believed. Marie was convicted. Next day the Press blazoned abroad through the country the statement that Marie Corelli was a hoarder of food.' She was fined £50 and ordered to pay costs of 20 guineas. As Marie wrote, 'of course press-reporters rushed down like hounds in full cry directly they scented possible injury to me. . . . As they never saw me, and I made no appearance in court these poor untidy pressmen were reduced to their usual fictions, and wired all over the world that I had "made a scene in court", "attacked Lloyd George", etc. etc! They had no idea that I count the Lloyd George family among my personal friends.'

She had been convicted on a red-tape clause which said that the sugar for jam making must be obtained from local suppliers through a ration card. By going straight to Sir Thomas Lipton because the local shops were unable to supply her, she had technically broken the law. This unwitting crime did not merit the banner headlines 'MARIE CORELLI CONVICTED OF FOOD HOARDING!' and she was deeply hurt. She was inundated with letters accusing her of being a hypocrite and a hoarder, but also many letters backing her. The pettiness of the conviction aroused a storm of protest from Marie's supporters.

The relationship between Marie Corelli and the Stratford-upon-Avon authorities had the hallmarks of guerrilla warfare for most of her twenty-five years' residency and it is interesting to link this conviction with an earlier event. Because of her keen conservationism, in July 1916 Marie had urged the guild to pay for the uncovering and preservation of the old timbers on no. 30 High Street, owned by her old enemy Fred Winter. She offered to make up the guild's subscription and in August 1917 she again offered to pay the bulk of the money needed, which was estimated as £75. She would contribute £60 and the guild £15 towards the costs, but 'only if Mr Winter will publicly admit that she is paying the lion's share'.

In November 1917 she wrote to Mr Wellstood 'I have *not* made "a bountiful grant to the funds" of a Society which at present is not *vital* enough to please any lover of Stratford – I have simply consented *to help* Mr Winter. I shall expect *you* to *insist* on the thing being properly worded, considering the *very exceptional circumstances under which I am doing the town this service,* after the libellous concoctions of Sidney Lee, Flower, Boyden *and* Winter in connection with my saving the Shakespeare property on Henley Street!' The guild accepted her offer and the work was carried out. Then came the 'food hoarding' accusation. After that episode she was angered when Fred Winter still refused to sign the receipt for which she had asked. The matter dragged on for another year. Marie's solicitors were demanding 'a properly worded receipt' for the £60 she had paid, signed by the President, Secretary and Treasurer of the Guild. Winter was evasive and refused to sign; no doubt he realised that to acknowledge a gift of money from a woman whom he had just fined could be misconstrued. Maffey & Brenthall, Marie's solicitors, asked repeatedly for a receipt, in September and October 1918 and again in March 1919. Mr Fincher the builder pleaded for his money: 'I am unable to allow any longer credit, eighteen months one would have thought quite sufficient for all reasonable purposes.' The matter was finally resolved at a guild meeting on 31 March 1919 when, after a long discussion, the builder was paid and Fred Winter extricated himself from an embarrassing situation by giving a donation of £50 to the guild.[16]

We have three descriptions of Corelli at this time. One comes from Marguerite Steen's autobiography, *Looking Glass.* The writer encountered Marie and Bertha when she was a 24-year-old dancing student in Stratford-upon-Avon. She saw Marie, 'the Stratford showpiece', making her royal progress along Chapel Street, 'attended by her lady-in-waiting, Miss Bertha Vyver, currently known as Fat Bertha'. She goes on to describe Marie as 'A fat little dwarf. . . . Her enormous torso, which was that of a normal adult, only looked enormous because of her dwarfed arms and legs, which would have fitted a child of ten. Her face was a ball of pink putty into which were pushed the dark beads of her eyes, and trimmed with yellowish curls.' In spite of her dislike of the spectacle, Marguerite Steen tried to take a snap of Marie, but was, deservedly, 'swooped upon by Fat Bertha, mountainous in rusty black'.

Marie was also interviewed by Sir Landon Ronald, for his 'My Portrait Gallery' article in the *Strand Magazine*, published after her death. 'I knew she would never allow her portrait to be published or permit any representative of the Press to interview her. I had been told she was beautiful – golden hair, blue eyes and a *petite* figure. As a matter of fact the portrait which is reproduced here [the Gabell portrait] will give you but a small idea of her actual appearance, because, to be honest, it is absurdly flattering. Perhaps I should add that it might have been like her when she was many years younger than when I first met her, but I can trace but little resemblance to her as I knew her in 1918. She proved to be a hospitable and delightful hostess, and was aided and abetted in her schemes to make you thoroughly at home and comfortable by her lifelong companion, Miss Vyver.'[17]

One more description of Marie is given by the Revd Stuart Scott, a long-time admirer of Marie's books, who met her for the first time in 1919. He was invited to Mason Croft and taken by Bridges, the butler, into the famous Presence. He had listened to the sound of a distant piano since his arrival, which grew louder as he approached the large music room into which he was ushered. 'An enormous fireplace surmounted by a great stone mantelpiece was the dominant feature of the wall nearest to me; easels, busts, pictures, tables, chairs and occasional carpets, furnished the room. On the far side from where I stood, with a floor about two feet higher than the floor of the hall, was a platform, on which stood a grand piano and a harp. And there, seated on this raised dais, extemporising at the piano, was the lady I had come to see.' As he entered she stopped playing and stood up as he approached the dais. She was wearing a greenish-brown velvet frock with lace trimmings and a train. 'This she swept forward – so that it hung down the step of the dais, thus giving her an impression of height. She first met me, therefore, by looking down on me. That was cleverly done. As she reached my side, shook hands, and motioned me towards a chair near the fire, I was truly astonished to begin with by her diminutive stature. She was such a little lady; she did not at all reach my shoulder. I feel positive that she looked upon this dwarfishness as a defect; her long train dresses were part of her apparatus for overcoming it.' He said that this lack of inches was not apparent when she was seated when she appeared the same height as others round the table – 'I conclude, therefore, that she was exceptionally short-legged.'

Stuart Scott added: 'if in 1906 she was fifty-one and looked like forty, in 1919 she was sixty-four and looked like eighty. The Marie Corelli who greeted me was, indeed, disillusioning; her little figure bulged at every seam of her frock, her face and hands were an unhealthy red, her mouth slightly twisted, her hair colourless, and her eyes revealing the faint suspicion of a squint, added up to nothing like – either the beautiful heroines of her books, which she was reported to resemble, or even the authentic photographs which had appeared. It was obvious that if at fifty she had looked so charming, the past decade had dealt hardly with her.' William Stuart Scott then went on to say that the moment you talked to Marie, all your reservations disappeared. She was full of vitality with a ready smile and twinkling eyes. She showed interest in everything you were doing and entertained you with reminiscences of her own life, and had an engaging habit of laying her hand on your arm when she was talking to you. As Stuart Scott left she said to him 'Now, I hope you won't tell people that I am an ugly old woman!' He didn't, not until long after her death. As he said 'Your critical faculties simply refused to function – when you remembered that this little person of unknown parentage had invented a name for herself and splashed it across the world. . . . Let criticism be dumb.'[18]

William Stuart Scott and his wife, Enid, were invited to a Daffodil Dance at Mason Croft in March 1919. Enid Scott remembered. 'Our hostess and Miss Vyver stood side by side receiving their guests. Marie was in a tight fitting gown of gold lamé with a train, and held a large bouquet of daffodils. In spite of the warning given to me by my husband I was yet surprised at her tiny stature. . . . Miss Vyver, kindly and stately, remained guardian-like at her side, and unlike the majority of the lady guests, was dressed with no concession to the daffodil colour scheme. She wore a very dark, very décolleté trained gown, – a foil to her friend's golden outfit.'[19] Stuart Scott added: 'neither lady found her train any sort of encumbrance, since they did not dance but spent most of the evening with their arms around each other looking on at the rest'.

Marie's book, *The Young Diana*, released in 1918, was her first novel since Annie Davis had left in 1914 and since her break with Severn in

1917. There is a bitterness about the writing which is not found in her earlier works. The heroine, Diana, has been betrayed by a man to whom she had been betrothed for seven years: 'I asked for love – now I ask for vengeance! I gave all my heart and soul to a man whose only god was Self, and I got nothing back for my faith and truth. So I have a long score to settle, and I shall try to have some of my spent joys returned to me – with heavy interest!' Diana goes to Geneva in answer to an advertisement by a Dr Feodor Dimitrius, a scientist looking for a suitable collaborator to help him in his search to find an elixir for eternal life. He requires a human subject for his experiments and Diana signs a Faustian agreement to be the guinea-pig. He explains: 'For my purpose you are not a woman, you are simply an electric battery. . . . It is what we all are, men and women alike. Our being is composed of millions of cells, charged with an electric current which emanates from purely material sources. We make electricity to light our houses with, and when the battery is dry we say the cells need recharging – a simple matter. Youth was the light of your house of clay, but the cells of the battery are dry, they must be recharged!'[20]

The dangerous experiment is a success and Diana, who becomes young and beautiful, acquires a power she has never before experienced: a power over men given to her not only by her appearance, but also because she no longer cares. She explains that although she is outwardly young, she is in truth old. 'Deep in my brain the marks of lonely years and griefs are imprinted – of disappointed hopes, and cruelties inflicted on me for no other cause than too much love and constancy – those marks are ineffaceable! . . . A woman seldom loves deeply and truly more than once in her life – she stakes her all on the one chance and hope of happiness, and the man who takes advantage of that love and ruthlessly betrays it may well beware. For there is no destructive power more active and intense than love transformed to hate through falsehood and injustice.'[21] The aftermath of Marie's affair with Severn had left a bitter legacy.

Marie wrote one last major novel, *The Secret Power*, in 1921, which is partly science fiction. Much of the book is fragmented and confusing, but it is of interest because of her prophetic description of germ warfare and the atom bomb. A beautiful golden-haired woman, Morgana, has invented an airship, driven by small circular plates of some shining substance which line the cabin. When two tubes of gold are inserted into two small boxes, one at either end of the hull, the airship becomes mysteriously powered, and flies without an engine. A scientific friend of Morgana's, Roger Seaton, is looking for other inventions. He has discovered how to harness radioactivity to create a massive force of destruction as well as how to annihilate the world with a holocaust of deadly microbes concealed in small phials. Seaton proposes to sell his secret to the United States of America in order to give them the bargaining power to prevent any further wars. His friend smiles when told of this plan: 'these days governments break promises as easily as eggshells. . . . War makes money for certain sections of the community, – you must think of that! Money! – money! Stores – food, clothing – transport – all these things in war mean fortunes to the contractors – while the wiping out of a nation in *your* way would mean loss of money. Loss of life wouldn't matter, – it never does really matter – not to governments! – but loss of money – ah well! – that's a very different and much more serious affair! . . . War is an inhuman act, but it brings considerable gain to those who engineer it, – this makes all the difference between humanity and *in*humanity!'[22]

The story itself is slight and rather disjointed, but some of the concepts were prophetic. Marie talked of communication through sound rays which transmitted voice without wires and light rays which beamed pictures through vast distances; she also described the defensive use of force-fields and the use of the sun's energy for power. She continued to be interested in the new discoveries of science and foretold the possible effects of some of these inventions on global pollution. In October 1923 she wrote to the *Manchester City News*:

Many of the wonders of creation are the result of the 'Law of Vibration' – a law which works its way through everything – through which we enjoy the glory of vision, the sense of sound, the ability of speech. Each word we utter, each action we perform, 'vibrates' – that is, sets in motion a million responsive tremors, which, like the ripples made in water by a beating oar, spread themselves far and wide and are never lost. Man is at the moment playing with these vibrations – he has set up his 'wireless' and, what is more dangerous, his 'broadcasting' apparatus for his own convenience and amusement, utterly forgetful of the fact that he is toying with powers of which he is as ignorant as a new-born child is of the alphabet. The enormous 'pull' on the vibrations of light and air surrounding this tiny terrestrial globe of ours, caused by the incessant strain of 'wireless broadcasting', and also by the constant traffic across the sea, of aeroplanes whose movements disturb the atmosphere and charge it with petrol effluvia, cannot fail of disastrous effect in the long run if continued.

CHAPTER 12

Bertha's Legacy

Marie's last few years were calmer. She divided her time between Stratford-upon-Avon and London with frequent holidays to the coast with Bertha. She began to reconsider many of her entrenched beliefs. In the early days she had crossed swords with suffragettes, denouncing them as 'ladies who scream'. But in a tract entitled *Is All Well with England?* written in 1919, she confessed:

> Some years ago I was one of the many who were strongly opposed to the 'Votes for Women' movement judging it to be totally unnecessary. I had been brought up on the chivalric view of man as taken by Sir Walter Scott in his immortal romances. . . . But when it was forced on me that man was more ready to deride rather than worship woman, and that as a matter of fact men denied to women such lawful honours as they may win through intellectual achievement, and that in certain forms of their legal procedure women were classed with 'children, criminals, and lunatics', I began to change my mind. In the war women worked instead of men without demur or hesitation, and taking their full share of the hardest and most menial labour . . . it *was* and *is* no longer possible to deny them equal rights with men in every relation of life and every phase of work. By every law of justice they should have the vote – and I who, as a woman, was once against it, now most ardently support the cause.[1]

In 1920 a collection of unremarkable short stories by Marie was published by Methuen called *The Love of Long Ago*. The most interesting part of the work is the advertisements at the back for Marie's previous books, which disclose the immense appeal she still had for the public: *The Mighty Atom* is in its thirty-sixth edition, *God's Good Man* has reached 160,000 copies, *The Master Christian*, 184,000 copies, *Thelma* is in its fifty-first edition, as is *Barabbas* and *The Sorrows of Satan* has achieved 202,000 copies. All the other books listed are in double figure editions. Even in 1920, twenty-five years after her peak, Marie Corelli was still a household name.

On New Year's Eve, 1921, Marie wrote a letter of appreciation to Mr Watt.

No doubt you are familiar with the eloquence of the elder d'Israeli in his sympathetic discourse on 'The Miseries of Authors'. You and your firm were not existent then; if you had been, that famous essay would scarcely have been written! For, whatever were the miseries of authors in the past, you do your best to alleviate them in the present. During the years you have acted as my sole business agent I have had as complete an immunity from 'miseries' and worry as is possible to the worker in the thorny ways of literature. Such thorns as have crossed my path your dextrous hand has turned aside or changed into roses: and I thank you with all my heart for the energy and kindliness which has made all business with you a pleasure, giving me not only financial advantage, but also the benefit of a warmly appreciated friendship which I hope may long endure!

By 1921 Marie was busy healing long-standing rifts. She presented a special medal to the Grammar School to be awarded annually for the best essay on Shakespeare. In July she wrote a warm letter to Sir Sidney Lee, thanking him for agreeing to judge these essays. 'I cannot thank you enough for your great kindness. It *is* good of you to be so helpful to the boys, who, I think, are really keen. Before the "Medal" was offered these youngsters knew nothing of the "so far known" life of their great schoolmate.' She would send him the first batch selected by the headmaster, and 'I do earnestly hope that they will not give you too much trouble'. She had forgiven him for his part in the Henley Street controversy and they continued to correspond and exchange visits.

Another admirer from her past who was reinstated into her favour was John Cuming Walters. After a frosty silence of fifteen years, Marie wrote in reply to a letter from him in October 1923: 'Your letter comes upon me like "a bolt from the blue"! – I *assure* you I have *no* recollection of the nature of any "difference" between us, if difference occurred! *What was it all about?* I, myself, cannot recall anything. When I no more heard of you, I concluded that you, like so many busy journalists who crossed my path, had "dropped" me for "fresh fields and pastures new"! . . . Now do please believe me that I have *utterly forgotten* any sort of difference in opinion between us, what ever it was; it must have been trivial.'

She wrote to him again on 6 December 1923, just four months before she died. 'The point that moves me to some surprise in your letter is that *you seem to have forgotten* all about *my* views of "spiritualism"! . . . It grieves me to think that you – a clever man – should even in half theory accept "Mediums" – as between living and dead. There is no need of them. A great man departed has no use for an illiterate vulgar person to convey messages from *his* state to ours. I do really feel a tiny bit *hurt* that you should forget that *all my life* I have been and am a "spiritualist in the *highest sense of the word*".'[2]

For the last two years of her life Marie kept up a friendly correspondence with a Mrs Greenwood, an admirer who had sent her a pair of hand-knitted blue shoes for a Christmas present. It shows a vulnerable side to Marie's character not seen in most of her letters, and illustrates perhaps why she was loved by ordinary people: '22 January 1922. Dear dear Lady, how good and kind of you to think of me! and here I have been crowded with guests – very tiresome most of them! and then laid up with cold and dreadful sort of depression called 'neurasthenia' – which has made me feel so dispirited; and then a cold settled in my right eye which made it semi blind for a time! and all a blur! – though it is slowly getting better. . . . I will write again as soon as the silly eye gets better.' In November Marie and Bertha went for a holiday to Hindhead, and Marie returned to find a distressed letter from Mrs Greenwood. She replied at once. 'My dearest Lady! I would not worry at all over the "Boots" young person – *my* experience of "Boots" is such that I never deal there! "A Woman of No Importance", is, I believe by that pestiferous creature Oscar Wilde – fortunately no longer living. Of *course* you are clear. I wish the people at "Boots" were as clear. And *never* talk of old age! Only the heart gets "old" and yours is ever young!'

Again, on 5 August 1923:

My very dear friend
You seem to be quite an example of the 'live and grow young' theory which some of our scientists preach and teach – But really I think the world is getting wiser on the subject of *age*! as for example, there is no *real* age in music, in mathematics, or in science – so there should not be in *Life* which gives us all these wonders.

I am writing this to you at six o'clock (Sun time – *not* Govt time!) in the morning; it is glorious to look out upon the blue sky and the rich green foliage of the garden burnished with the gold of the sunshine, and I love the quiet of this hour when the maids are still asleep! . . . I am writing in my study, clad in a little white dressing gown – so pleased to be talking to you at leisure. A new book of mine is to be published in September – not an 'important' novel! – but just the simplest of stories, which tells of a very grumpy and cross philosopher – and of a gentle little English maiden whom he *loves*! – though you will doubt if he could love anybody but himself! . . . You know there *have been* and *are* such *horrid* books written about 'love' – which is not real *clean* love at all! – and I thought I would like to set forward a story that should be *simple* and straight, without 'sex' problems. So there it is – fit to be given to the 'Young Person'!

And on 8 October 1923: 'You must be "in the blues" to talk of "senile decay" – there is no such thing! – and as our most advanced scientists tell us there is no "natural" death! We all get some ailment which carries us off, but it is not "natural". . . . I have been very depressed lately – it must be the weather I suppose – but people seem so callous and apathetic to everything but themselves; and here in Stratford everything is so slow and stagnant!'[3]

Marie was out of tune with the permissiveness of the flapper age in which she now found herself. Her book sales were falling off and her writing no longer reflected the world in which she lived. She had been warned by her doctors that her heart was not strong and in January 1924 she had a serious heart attack. She was too ill to leave her room, and, unable to breathe properly while lying down, for three months had to spend her days and nights sitting half upright in a chair. She could just manage to walk about in her bedroom. She did not want to be looked after by a stranger and refused to have a trained nurse, but was cared for devotedly by Bertha and her maid, Augusta Threadgold. When she developed congestion of the lungs at the end of April, Dr Murray, her physician, decided she must have more professional care. Bertha wrote: 'On Sunday, 20th April, a hospital nurse took my place. Marie would not be consoled. Sitting upright in her chair all night, she implored, with tears in her eyes, that I might be sent for; but the nurse, not realising how close was our sympathy, would not humour her. Next morning she passed away without again seeing me or feeling the touch of my hand.' Marie, so lonely throughout her life, was without her dearest friend even at her dying.

The news of Marie's death on 21 April competed with the death of Eleanor Duse who had died in Pittsburgh, and full-page articles on the opening of the huge Wembley Empire Exhibition in London. In Stratford it was the day before Shakespeare's birthday and the *Stratford-upon-Avon Herald* recorded, 'the atmosphere of the celebration has been somewhat overcast by the death of Miss Marie Corelli, who has been a prominent figure in the town of Stratford and at the birthday festival. The weather however has been brilliant.' The brilliance faded and Marie's funeral took place in pouring rain on Saturday 26 April. Crowds of mourners gathered outside Mason Croft some hours before the start of the funeral procession. The service was held in Holy Trinity Church which was packed with people, and muffled peals were rung on the church bells. There were crowds waiting outside in the rain to follow the procession to the churchyard. The coffin, carried on a hand bier, bore the inscription 'And though through the valley of death I walk, I shall not be afraid.' It was preceded by twenty girls carrying sprigs of rosemary and two large carloads of wreaths. The pit of the grave was walled with white bricks, the sides were lined with narcissi, snow of the mountain and ivy, and after the coffin had been lowered, the girls threw in their sprigs of rosemary for remembrance. The mourners included Lord Dundonald, Sir Algernon and Lady Methuen, Mr A.S. Watt, Mr Brenthall, Joan and Arthur Severn, Sir Brumwall Thomas, Sir Sidney Lee, Dr Murray, Fred Winter and the mayor and corporation of Stratford. Bertha was too ill and upset to attend. She sent a wreath with the words: 'To the best and purest soul I have met on earth, whose ideals were always of the highest, from her devoted and loving friend, Bertha.' Above the inscription were the words *Amor Vincit.*

Marie's former adversary, Sir Sidney Lee, paid her a tribute in *The Times.*

However one accounts for Miss Marie Corelli's literary fame, no one who knew her can fail to recognize that her death removes from social life an outstanding personality, in which independence of mind, strength of will, and combativeness of spirit mingled with a genuine zeal for good causes.

At Stratford-on-Avon, where she resided for the past quarter of a century, or in the neighbourhood, she had a number of devoted friends. But with most of her near neighbours, especially those in positions of local authority; she carried on a constant feud, and she often spoke and wrote of them with a biting scorn. . . . By her influence or at her own cost many old houses in the town were preserved when they were threatened with rebuilding on modern lines. She was keen to protect from the invasion of the builder picturesque open spaces on the boundaries of the town. She constantly protested with her wonted vehemence against innovations which seemed to her to be out of harmony with worthy sentiment. Her standard of the theatrical interpretation of Shakespeare was high, and she freely denounced what she regarded as histrionic deficiencies on the local stage . . . her courage was always equal at need to fighting her battles single-handed. . . . As a trustee of Shakespeare's birthplace, I, in my colleagues behalf, crossed swords with her on points of inaccuracy in her indictment, and thereby I incurred for an extended period her displeasure. But looking back from this distance of time on the old polemic, I acknowledge that, in spite of, or perhaps because of, her strong language, her intervention had the effect of modifying at a crucial point the original plan of demolition in a manner which has proved of real benefit to the Shakespeare Birthplace Trust.

In course of time the breach between us healed . . . of late she often wrote to me in her old vein about the fears which proposals to modernise Stratford excited in her. Her last letter was an appeal to me to oppose the local scheme for widening Clopton Bridge. At a meeting with the Prince of Wales last year I was impressed by her charming frankness of manner and her ease of conversation, which bore witness to her social aptitude.[4]

Marie was laid to rest, and might have been soon forgotten if the newspapers hadn't tried to discover the mystery of her birth. There was little factual evidence of her origins, for Marie Corelli had no history. The newspapers began to invent their own stories which ranged from the improbable to the impossible.

Marie had been abandoned in a snowstorm by a stranger and adopted by Charles Mackay, said one paper. Another declared she was the daughter of a mysterious Italian lady, Signora Marie Coralie Gonzalez, whom Charles Mackay had chanced upon at Shakespeare's tomb in Trinity Church, on a visit to Stratford-upon-Avon. The *Sphere*, rather strangely, thought Marie was the daughter of a labourer Thomas Cody, and had been christened Caroline. A birth certificate to prove this was printed by the paper on 10 May 1924, showing that this child was born on 1 May 1855, and a member of the Cody family talked to the press about 'Aunt Marie'; but the reasoning which turned Caroline Cody into Marie Corelli remained suspect. The majority thought her to be the illegitimate daughter of Charles Mackay and Mrs Mills, but were uncertain as to her claims for Italian or Scottish parentage. As the *Evening Standard* conceded: 'the truth will probably never be known, for Miss Bertha Vyver, the novelist's lifelong friend, is said to have declared: "What Marie left sealed shall remain sealed." Miss Vyver is probably the only person living who knows who Marie Corelli really was.'

There was some speculation as to Bertha's role in Marie's life and the *Shields Daily Gazette* of 28 April, talking of the 'Romance of Two Women', confided that 'nobody at Stratford was surprised that Miss Vyver did not attend Miss Corelli's funeral on Saturday. So intimate was the bond between them that the authoress's death has left her companion stricken with grief. Youthful and vigorous to the end, Miss Corelli was in practical matters still something of a child, and to her occasional eccentricities the watchful guardianship of Miss Vyver provided an effective contrast. Miss Vyver was indeed Miss Corelli's guardian angel. In a word, Miss Vyver "mothered" Miss Corelli from the days of their earliest association; when both were without a friend in the world, right through to later life. They were never seen in public out of each other's company. Although Miss Vyver has only been known as Miss Corelli's companion, she is herself a clever woman. Widely read, a capable business woman, her favourite hobby is colour photography, in which she has achieved considerable success.'

The *Evening Standard*, discussing Marie and Bertha's 'Friendship Romance', thought that 'Miss Marie Corelli in leaving her entire estate to Miss Bertha Vyver, her devoted companion, has set a posthumous seal on one of the most romantic friendships ever formed between two women.' Explaining that the friendship was formed when Miss Vyver came to help Marie care for her sick father 'from then Miss Vyver never left the novelist. . . . Miss Vyver watched over the writer's career from its start encouraging her through preliminary trials and much adverse criticism. "Try again, Marie," she would say when disappointment followed disappointment. When fame came, and Miss Corelli retired to the peaceful seclusion of Stratford, the association continued, and Miss Vyver still made herself responsible for all practical details of the household.'

Details of Marie's will were released in July when probate was granted, and it was noted that Marie had left her whole estate unconditionally for her lifetime to her 'dear and lifelong friend' Bertha Vyver. This was subject to terms mutually arrived at and agreed by them both, that no relative of Bertha's should benefit from this arrangement. The gross value of the estate was £24,076 out of which the net personality was £8,914. The *Daily Express* was surprised that 'the sum left by Miss Corelli is not so great as might have been supposed considering her large earnings. She gave lavishly to charities during her life time.' In her will, made in June 1922, Marie asked that the land surrounding Mason Croft be preserved as 'a breathing space and air zone for the health of the town of Stratford-upon-Avon now endangered by the overcrowding of buildings entirely disadvantageous to the well being of the population'. She also specified that after Bertha's death, Mason Croft was to become a trust, 'to be incorporated upon the lines of those of The Leighton House Association London, for the promotion of Science, Literature and Music among the people of Stratford upon Avon'. The estate was to be preserved in perpetuity for the benefit of those visiting Stratford from far countries, selected and recommended by the Council for the Society of Authors, to be used as a meeting place or at the service of any 'selected or distinguished persons visiting the town of Stratford upon Avon who would otherwise seek their quarters in a hotel, only out of this provision absolutely excluding actors, actresses and all persons connected with the stage'. Neither were any officials from Stratford permitted to have any part in the carrying out of this trust.

Marie left her servants with legacies to be effective on the death of Bertha. Alfred Bridges was given two houses in Church Street, a quantity of furniture and pictures, £100 and the Silver Knight Mascot from the car. She also asked him to remain as the paid custodian of Mason Croft 'so that he and his wife may always have a house there'. To her maid, Augusta Threadgold, Marie gave the Croft Cottage in the paddock for her lifetime, £100 and a diamond brooch. To her second maid, Bella Barber, Marie gave £100 and the choice of her jewelled ornaments, and the right to remain in Mason Croft as her home. Marie also decreed that her personal effects should be shared by the two maids. The cook, Anne Dance, was given £100 and the right to live at Mason Croft. The gardener, F. Prior, was given 'the cottage he now lives in and the ground pertaining'. The chauffeur, H. Moore, was given the motor car and asked to care for the ponies 'till the natural end of their lives', and the assistant gardener, O. Court, half the kitchen garden and £50.

The trustees of the will were named as Bertha Vyver; Alexander Strachan Watt and his successors in his firm; Percy Smith Brentnall of the firm of Maffey and Brentnall, Solicitors; the secretary for the time being of the Society of Authors; and C.D. Medley of the firm of Messrs Field & Roscoe & Co., Solicitors. Into their care Marie placed her estate and her effects 'upon trust that nothing whatsoever be sold or disposed of out of Mason Croft, and that all books, pictures, furniture, curios, and household goods shall be kept intact and carefully preserved as they now are'. She asked A.P. Watt & Son to continue to deal with all her copyrights, and to guard and hinder from any sale or publication all correspondence between herself and others. It all seemed reasonably straightforward.

Marie, as the adopted daughter of the late Charles Mackay LLD, FSA, had no natural heirs. She declared: 'I have no living person who has any claim upon me or my estate, the terms of my adoption having been of complete surrender.' She wished, following the death of her dearest friend, Bertha, to leave her house, Mason Croft, fully furnished and with its contents intact, as a memorial for the benefit of distinguished visitors to Stratford-upon-Avon, either as a place for them to stay, or as a centre for conferences and meetings.

The first question was that of Bertha's income. Was the trust fund set up by Marie's will, for the benefit of the house only, or could it be used by Bertha for her own living expenses as well as the preservation of Mason Croft? On 8 August 1924, Mr Medley, the solicitor for Field Roscoe & Co., wrote to Watt, 'The Master today made an Order, the Attorney General not objecting, for payment of £3,800 to Miss Vyver which will at any rate put her in funds for some time.' As the will was not clear about the distribution of funds, Watt was advised to clarify it in law. In the High Court of Justice Chancery Division, the case was before Mr Justice Eve on 23 April 1925. Miss Vyver, the claimant, versus Mr Watt, as representing the trustees, won the case. As 'the tenant for life' Bertha was entitled to the money paid into the deposit account including the royalties. They were both pleased and Bertha wrote to Cuming Walters on 17 May 1925: 'I thank you for your last letter and your congratulations on winning my case. It is really what Marie wished for & I will do my best to carry out her wishes – Now I hope to start on my memoir . . . . "Open Confession" is in its 20th thousand.'

Marie's *Open Confession* was published posthumously in 1924 and had been serialised. Bertha was concerned that the *Express* was 'overbooming it, and may do more harm than good to the book' – but it seemed that there was no cause for worry for the book was selling well. There are many letters between Watt and Mr Medley and Watt and Mr Brentnall about the distribution of money and the payment of taxes and legal costs. The Trinity College building was sold, and from the proceeds Bertha paid for the kitchen garden. The servants stayed on at Mason Croft, and the house was run as though Marie was still alive.

In July 1924 the marble angel Bertha had ordered for Marie's grave arrived by cargo ship from Italy, and was put in place. It is easily visible when passing by the cemetery, with one hand upraised, pointing the way to heaven. After Marie's death, Ellen Terry had asked Bertha to take her to the grave where, placing a wreath of lilies at the feet of the angel, Ellen Terry fell to her knees and said 'God bless the darling.'

Bertha was working hard on her *Memoir of Marie Corelli*, and consulted with Cuming Walters, seeking his professional advice. In June 1926 she wrote: 'I want to avoid the mistake of the Coates and Bell life of her. It has 300 pages on the Books and neither man had a subtle or imaginative use of the pen. – It was badly done. Such books as The Romance, Ardath, Soul of Lilith, The Life Everlasting, Secret Power would blend together. The religious Power of the Pen – Barabbas, Sorrows, Master Christian etc. Then the human – Vendetta, Thelma, God's Good Man, Treasure of Heaven etc. When we meet I could better explain.'[5]

In July 1927 Bertha organised a memorial party and invited many of Marie's friends. Some of Marie's poems were specially set to music by Amy Hare and sung by the Dutch singer, Tilly Koenan. 'The singing was sublime. It was a sad but lovely Day to Marie's memory & her vital spirit was not far away. I felt her with me, we all did – over 100 guests from all parts.'[6] Bertha's *Memoirs* were published in 1930, six years after Marie's death, and she wrote: 'The house remains as she left it. Her own bedroom and study are kept daily aired and decked with flowers as when she lived. On a chair in the Winter Garden is her garden hat, to which her dove flies when its cage is opened, and perches as it did before it lost her.'[7] Marie's bedroom clock was stopped at 7.15 a.m. 'God's time', the time of her death; Marie had refused to accept the new Summer Time. Flowers were put in all the vases in the house, as always, and in her study pens and paper were laid out as though she might return, though the ink was allowed to dry in the inkwell. Her books remained where she had left them. It was as if Bertha and the faithful servants were in a time-warp waiting for Marie's reincarnation.

Bertha was having financial problems. Marie's last book, *Poems*, was also published posthumously in 1924 and most of the huge royalties for her earlier successes had been paid in advance and were already spent. The income needed to keep Mason Croft going was considerable, for in addition to the daily running costs there was a full staff to be maintained. Marie had been lavish in her lifetime, but had made little provision for the future, believing that her books would continue to earn good money. By 1925, a year after her death, the annual income had dropped to less than £5,000 and continued to fall at an alarming rate. In 1930 Bertha received an offer for the annex and the garden on the other side of the road and Mr Brentnall advised her to accept it. This brought in a welcome £2,500, and this was also the year in which her *Memoirs of Marie Corelli* was published.

A visitor who called one evening in 1934 was shocked at the changes. He found that the garden was neglected and overgrown and the paddock had become a hayfield. There was no electric light, the house was dark and shuttered and Bertha showed him around by candlelight. Much of the furniture was shrouded in dustsheets. The music room was cluttered with mementos, with Marie's manuscripts displayed in glass cases. The bird cages in the winter garden were empty. Mason Croft was becoming a place of memories.

By 1938, 84-year-old Bertha was finding it hard to make ends meet. All the extra staff had been allowed to go, leaving only Bridges, Mrs Threadgold and Bella Barbour, all devoted to the memory of Marie and all determined to carry out her wishes at whatever cost to themselves. When George Bullock visited Mason Croft that year, he found that everything was done as though the little lady was still alive. Bertha showed him Marie's bedroom which he found quiet and almost eerie, 'with its massive white bedroom suite and thick red carpet; the dressing table with the impressive silver candlesticks. The large empty bed covered with a heavy white quilt. Let posterity do with her as it may. If Mason Croft remain intact as it stands today Marie will be sacred from oblivion. It seems that she lives there even now, with all the background of the romantic tradition she created for herself.'[8]

On 16 October Bertha wrote to Watt: 'I feel I must write and explain that I must have some money advanced to me on the estate – I have overdrawn my account at my bank to the tune of £200. Will you kindly let me know by return what can be done.' Watt consulted Medley, the solicitor, who sent the following answer: 'If the expense of Mason Croft and residence there is permanently in excess of the income available, so that not only is there an existing overdraft, but that overdraft must go on increasing, then it may be that the proper remedy would be to sell Mason Croft and invest the money.' Watt added a note for Bertha, 'At first sight it seems to me that, looking at the matter from your point of view, the most satisfactory course to take would be to sell the estate, to invest the proceeds, and to give you income arising therefrom.' Bertha replied at once on 22 October 1938, 'Thanks for your letter and copy of Mr Medley's letter. I wish *now* nothing further to be done.' On 14 December she wrote again: 'I would like as you suggested to me, that I should be provided with sufficient income to keep Mason Croft & not be under the anxieties I have to undergo. Awaiting your reply.' On 21 December 1938 Medley replied via Watt. 'There is no means of providing Miss Vyver with a sufficient income from Miss Corelli's estate to keep Mason Croft. If the income from the rest of the estate is not sufficient for her to live in the house, then I am afraid that the house must either be let or sold.'

For Bertha, Marie's last wishes were a sacred trust. She replied on 29 December: 'Very many thanks for your kind advice. I must consider that dear little Marie never realized that I should live 15 years after her and that her royalties would fall to under a hundred a year. I will explain one day when we meet, it is very interesting and incredible. Anyhow I shall manage on my capital with good management. Now I must thank you for the magnificent box of chocolates. I spent Xmas alone, influenza and the weather prevented my niece & [her] mother keeping their promised visit. With kindest regards.'[9]

Both Watt and Brentnall were becoming concerned with Bertha's well-being. She was fighting a losing financial battle with courage and determination, but with no money. Brentnall wrote to Watt in May 1939, 'You will know with regret that Miss Vyver has suffered a good deal over the last winter and that she has come out of it with health, if not impaired, at any rate with less reserve of strength than heretofore . . . and above all she is more a victim of worry than formerly. She has written to me upon several occasions lately upon the subject of her growing inability to bear the burden of the maintenance and upkeep of Mason Croft in keeping with the wishes of the late Miss Marie Corelli who never contemplated that her royalties would in a few brief years be practically eliminated. . . . Miss Vyver has for years been encroaching on her own diminishing private resources until it is safe to say that they will not last out the next year or so.' He suggested the only solution was to let Mason Croft, 'but I also feel that to suggest such a course to Miss Vyver in her present state of health might be tantamount to signing her death warrant.' Watt was so concerned that he paid a visit to Mason Croft and though he saw that Bertha was much reduced in strength, he found her determined to follow Marie's wishes and remain in Mason Croft 'while she has a bean'.[10]

Brentnall, still worried, wrote to Watt on 14 October 1940: 'I know you feel with me that anything we can do to avoid hurting Miss Vyver's feelings should be done, and I do think that whilst she does not perhaps appreciate things as she did, she would not like to be ignored in these Trusts.' These were trusts Bertha had taken over after Marie's death. They asked Dr Murray for his professional opinion on Bertha's health and he replied that her heart was weak and she could not get about much. 'Since Bridges' illness, Bella and Mrs Threadgold have helped and guided her in her business affairs. Mentally she is getting very childish, she is slightly deaf and apt to take things up wrongly. She has developed a craze for going out for motor car drives, she says she must have "fresh air". She also visits an antique shop where she occasionally buys trivial articles e.g. a brooch, ring etc., of which she has plenty. . . . Neither you nor I would willingly hurt her feelings but I certainly consider that she should be relieved of the responsibility for these trusts both for her own sake and for others. Bridges will not be able to do any more work at Mason Croft as his health is broken down and he is quite an invalid, however, as you know she has two devoted people, Bella and Mrs Threadgold, who are doing all they can for Miss Vyver's comfort.'[11]

In May 1941 the financial position became serious. Methuen's royalty cheque had just come in for only £26 16*s* 10*d* and that from Constable for £2 2*s* 2*d*. The trustees could no longer afford to pay the insurance costs, which were compulsory, and schedule A of properties, collected by the Inspector of Taxes. 'Again there is very considerable demand and no money to meet it.' Brentnall wrote to Medley, Bertha's lawyer, to ask him if they could delay taking action as Bertha was so ill they did not wish her to be troubled. 'Sentimentally as distinguished from legally, he [Mr Watt] would like, as I would like, the position to be left where it is for a few months pending developments.'

On 1 September 1939 Europe had been plunged into chaos; Germany invaded Poland and on 3 September Britain and France declared war on Germany. Now in 1941, Mason Croft was being assailed from all sides. The music room was requisitioned by the WAAF and they wanted permission to use the paddock for PT and recreation. Fortunately Bertha was no longer aware of very much going on about her and on 6 November 1941 Mrs Threadgold reported that she was happy, but very frail. Bertha died aged eighty-seven on 20 November 1941.

With immense sacrifices she, and the three old servants, who had worked without pay for some time, had honoured Marie's last wish to preserve Mason Croft for posterity. In this they had been aided by Messrs Watt, Brentnall and Medley. Bertha was buried beside Marie, as they had both requested, under the watchful care of the marble angel from Italy. Watt wrote to Brentnall. 'In the circumstances, I am glad to think that our old friend Miss Vyver is now at rest in a place where she would have wished to be, beside Miss Corelli.'

The lawyers now had the mammoth task of sorting out the muddled estate. From mid-1940 London had been suffering from night bombing raids. The Blitz took a severe toll of both people and buildings and there was a feeling of national emergency. By 1941 many cities were seriously bomb-damaged, with London the worst hit. Mr Brentnall wrote to Medley of Field & Roscoe: 'You, like my firm, lost no doubt most of your papers, and we only had the contents, badly damaged – of two safes out of four, others being broken up and useless, including the muniments of title of the late Miss Marie Corelli as well as, of course, the immense amount of paper referring to her matters which were not sheltered by the safes. It is very difficult for the moment to arrive at any conclusions until Miss Vyver's affairs are in some order.' Brentnall recommends paying Bella Barbour £1 a week and her keep, to preserve intact the contents of Mason Croft. 'She is being assisted by both Bridges the old butler and Mrs Threadgold, the old ladies' maid, gratuitously as she has been for the last 12 months or so, and so the place remains a perfect example of what it should be in the views of the late Miss Marie Corelli.'

Hugh Walpole and his brother visited Mason Croft after Bertha's death.

An old servant showed us round. Small, white haired, bespectacled, in a black silk dress and apron. 'I hope you were a friend of Miss Corelli's and never spoke or wrote harm of her,' she said, her eyes flashing. . . . 'She was a sweet little lady,' she repeated many times, and had obviously adored her, as had all her servants.

She took us over everything – all as it had been in Marie Corelli's lifetime. All dead or dying. The harp, the faded photographs, paper roses, cracked looking glasses, a spinning wheel from which a moth flew out, faded books. . . . Above all the famous gondola and the Christmas card her gondolier had sent her just before he was killed in France. The ink she had used corroded in the ink bottle. Rows of hideous china ornaments in her bedroom. The paddock thick with grass and her pony over forty! The garden with no flowers, only weeds. Death and decay over everything. . . . I left feeling very sorry that I had ever laughed at her. She seemed to be there, alive and affectionate among all the decayed material things.

Brentnall thought that though the assets were small they would be sufficient to survive the war, and then funds could be collected for the trust, with the consent of the court, by perhaps selling the paddock as a building site. However, the war made this impossible. Six months after Bertha's death the Air Ministry demanded the use of Mason Croft. They would either requisition it, or if this was refused, they would take it for nothing. They had already requisitioned the music room for the WAAFs. Brentnall wrote to Watt, 'personally I do not see why they should not pay for what at present is a burden upon the Executors, namely the maintenance and management of the Estate of the late Miss Marie Corelli until after the War, for really little or nothing can be done with regard to it during these times.'

The bills kept coming in and there was not enough money to pay them. Brentnall wrote to Watt in late 1942: 'To be candid the income of the Corelli Trust will not meet outgoings for rates, taxes, War Damage Contribution, maintenance charges and custodian, and I think it would be madness in the circumstances to resist the inevitable in circumstances the Will never contemplated.' It was becoming obvious to all the trustees that the demands of Marie's will were no longer possible to meet. In January 1943 the estate agents Hutchings and Deer wrote to Brentnall. They had heard that the Air Ministry would be requisitioning Mason Croft and the National Fire Service the paddock: 'should the Air Ministry not take Mason Croft all would be well as it would sell readily, as would also the furniture and effects on your obtaining the sanction of Chancery Division to sell.'[12]

The trustees were in a difficult position. The war was at its peak, the Air Ministry was clamouring for the property. No decision to sell Mason Croft could be made without application to the courts for a ruling, and there was no income coming in to pay outstanding bills. In a memorandum Watt noted, 'we shall have to apply to the court or charity commissioners, or what ever it is, for direction as to what we are to do. Obviously it is impossible now to carry out Miss Corelli's wishes as expressed in her Will.' The only way they could buy time was to allow the Air Ministry to take over the property and in order to do this all the contents of the house would have to be sold. 'If the Air Ministry take Mason Croft we must ask them to post-date the Requisition so as to enable a sale of the furniture to be held on the premises', wrote Brentnall. 'We quite agree with you that it is advisable to hasten the application to the court. If Mason Croft can be sold it is much more attractive when furnished, on the other hand the sooner the furniture is disposed of the better.'[13]

On 29 July 1943 Mr Justice Cohen delivered a reserve judgment dealing with questions arising under the will of Miss Marie Corelli. *The Times* reported the outcome: 'The testatrix directed her freehold land to be used as a breathing space and air zone for the health of the town, and her house to be kept up in perpetuity for the benefit of distinguished visitors from overseas to be selected by the Society of Authors, but all actors and actresses and all persons connected with the stage to be excluded. HIS LORDSHIP declared that the establishment of a hotel for the entertainment of distinguished foreigners was not a valid charitable bequest, and that this was the dominant motive of the trust the testatrix intended to create, other objects being subservient. The trusts not being charitable were void for remoteness and there must be an enquiry whether the testatrix left any heir or next-of-kin.' The will was declared null and void.

The judgment left the trustees with no choice. The intention of Marie's will, to leave Mason Croft as a gift for the nation, had been overthrown. The Treasury Solicitor established that there was insufficient income for the maintenance of the house and recommended that the contents be sold. The nineteen years of struggle and sacrifice by Bertha and the loyal and loving servants had been for nothing. Marie's plea 'that nothing whatsoever be sold or disposed of out of Mason Croft, and that all books, pictures, furniture, curios, and household goods, shall be kept intact and carefully preserved as they are now', was as though it had never been. It was a heartbreaking decision.

Over three days, on 28, 29 and 30 October 1943, starting at 10.30 a.m. precisely, the entire contents of Mason Croft went under the hammer. In those three days Marie's whole life was paraded before the public gaze, and disposed of as though it was so much trivia. There was very little warning of the sale, travelling in wartime was almost impossible, and friends who might have been able to save some of her cherished possessions learned about the sale too late, through newspaper reports. William Stuart Scott wrote: 'I cannot describe the pain with which my wife and I read this news. The tolerant amusement with which we had come to regard Marie Corelli changed to emotions of deep anger and pity. Anger that loopholes of law could exactly reverse all one's intentions and desires so clearly set forth in a "will" and cause to happen the very thing one had willed with all one's heart should not happen.

And pity, – pity that a wonderful and entirely worthy life should be treated so disdainfully and callously, that in the town to which she had given such generous and devoted service for nearly a quarter of a century, the very memory of Marie Corelli should be wiped out, as off the slate.'[14]

The press thought it a great joke and reported how as the items were sold, usually for far less than their value, there was laughter and comments from the crowd. One Stratford-upon-Avon alderman bought for 2 guineas the huge oil painting by Arthur Severn, *The Angry Sea*, for which Marie had given 500 guineas. He thought he was buying the easel on which the painting rested. Lot 444 was a complete set of the novels of Marie Corelli in rich blue leather with gilt tooling, M.C. monogram, presented to Miss Vyver by the author, the first copy inscribed: 'With the devoted and grateful love of her "wee" author, Marie Corelli.' The large portrait of Marie by Helen Donald Smith, which had hung on the stairs, was offered to the National Portrait Gallery, but they declined it. It was eventually given a home by Dr Murray and when it did at last find its way back to the National Portrait Gallery it had deteriorated so badly that only the top part could be salvaged; it is at present being housed in one of their stores.

The Elizabethan Tower in the Mason Croft garden, where Marie wrote many of her books, was furnished with the small furniture Marie had had as a child. Lot 96 consisted of: 'Miniature couch, tub chair, and cane seated occasional chairs and arm chair. Panther skin rug.' It, too, was sold. Piece by piece Marie's life was carried out of Mason Croft. The more spectacular items were bought for theatrical props. Lot 897 was a 'Useful pony chaise, rubber tyred, rear coachman's seat, in good condition.' Marie's famous carriage was bought by Mr Emile Littler, the theatrical manager, for 32 guineas. That Christmas it carried the two comedians, Nervo and Knox, in the London Coliseum pantomime, *Humpty Dumpty*. It was later destroyed in a fire. Lot 896: 'Very fine Italian gondola, 26 ft long, having cabin 5 ft by 3 ft and finely ornamented.' The gondola is now at Kingston upon Thames and is hired out for commercials.

A week after the sale the Ministry of Works was given the keys to the empty house. Now that the will had been declared invalid, the judgment required that enquiries should be made for possible heirs, and until this enquiry had been completed Watt, Medley and Brentnall continued to administer what was left of the estate. Medley wrote to Watt on 16

October 1944: 'We placed on deposit £4,500 out of the sale of furniture retaining the balance to pay debts and refunds to the executors of the late Miss B. Vyver for financing the Corelli liabilities, rates, taxes and the like until the order of Mr Justice Cohen, including the maintenance of Mason Croft until requisition and sale of furniture. With regard to the balance of the accounting we are before Master Holloway on the 17th instant on the enquiry as to heirs.'

The situation was still confused in January 1945. Medley to Watt: 'I have been looking further today into the position created by the judgement of Mr Justice Cohen. It is to my mind not at all clear what the true position is; that is to say what is the true construction of Miss Corelli's Will, and secondly what is the effect of the judgement of Mr Justice Cohen upon that Will, the Will, as you know, is a rather odd document. . . . I think under the circumstances the opinion of Mr Waite must be accepted and the Trustees must therefore act, although personally I am not at all disposed to do this if it can be helped.'

When the solicitors advertised for claimants to Marie's estate it is recorded there were nineteen applicants. The Treasury Solicitor refused all the claims. Brentnall wrote to Watt on 18 January 1945: 'I proceeded to Master's Chambers where all the remaining claimants were represented. The Master finally declared his decision at the end of the afternoon to make a certificate to the effect that of all the claimants none could prove sufficiently to displace the claim of the Crown. Messrs Barfield & Messrs Joynson-Hicks both indicated that they might, following filing of Certificate, apply to vary as is their right in Chancery Chambers if they wish to appeal against the Master's decision.' On 16 February Marie's estate came under the jurisdiction of the Crown. Brentnall wrote: 'Just a line to inform you that yesterday the Masters Certificate was filed in favour of the Crown, and disallowing other claims.'[15]

What of the three faithful servants who were caught in the machinations of the law? Mrs Threadgold was given permission to remain in the Croft Cottage in the paddock for the remainder of her life, but Bella Barbour and Alfred Bridges had to wait until January 1948, twenty-four years after Marie's death and seven years after the death of Bertha Vyver, to receive an ex gratia payment of £450 each from the Treasury Solicitor. One can only imagine their feelings as they watched all that they had painstakingly cherished for their beloved 'little lady' being sold off piece by piece to a crowd of strangers.

A.P. Watt & Son still held the copyright of Marie's novels, which had become more popular during the war, but in 1953 reluctantly relinquished it to Methuen for the sum of only £750. Many of Marie's mystical books were reprinted well into the 1960s, when they achieved quite a following among the New Age generation, especially in America. The end of the matter for Watt, Medley, and Brentnall came in 1955 when the residuary estate escheated. The realty passed to the Crown; the trustees converted it into cash and the net balance was paid by the Treasury Solicitor into the coffers of the Commissioners for Crown Lands. The amount was £10,579 15s 2d.

It is very difficult to get a complete picture of the events after Bertha's death. It was the height of the war, communications were poor and many documents had been destroyed in the savage bombing of London, or mislaid, as temporary offices had to be found. We have records of the small number of the letters which survived, but there still appear to be many unanswered questions. It seems incomprehensible that Marie's clearly stated last wishes were so completely ignored. It would appear from reading her will today that her main intention was to preserve Mason Croft as a place for visiting celebrities to stay without charge, and as a memorial to herself. There is no mention of Mason Croft being used for a hotel, and yet it was on those grounds that the will was declared invalid.

Once the contents were so callously and hurriedly sold, the spirit left the house. After the war Mason Croft became the home of the British Council who stayed there for six years; following their departure, the house was taken over by the University of Birmingham to be used for the Shakespeare Institute. This is the function it serves today and perhaps, in some part, Marie's wishes are being met. The house is a study centre for many overseas students completing postgraduate work on her beloved Shakespeare. The paddock has at last been reclaimed from the Fire Station and is now leased to Warwickshire County Council for a playing field. The Elizabethan Tower still stands in the garden watching over the old archway which once supported a sundial, and the glassed-in winter garden is warmed by the winter sun.

The front of the house has been stripped of the festoons of greenery which made it so attractive and is now bare and functional brick, and the only record for the visitor that this was, for a quarter of a century, the home of the bestselling author in Britain, is a small plaque by the front door bearing Marie Corelli's name.

Inside, the house, denuded of all its knick-knacks, is plain and practical, a place of study, but in the large music room, where Marie once greeted her guests from a raised platform to give her the authority of height, is a poignant reminder. The room is now a bare hall with rows of chairs stacked along the panelled walls, but carved on the centre stone above the huge boarded-up fireplace remains the laurel wreath enclosing for all time the initials M.C. and B.V. *Amor Vincit.*

Afterword

After Marie's death in April 1924, she rapidly faded from public memory. Her books were deemed old-fashioned and too moralistic for the 1920s. When Bertha died in 1941 the world was embroiled in a savage war for survival. There was blackout and censorship and a tangle of rules and regulations, and the disappearance of Mason Croft was of less importance than the endless destructive bombing raids. By the time the war ended many people had forgotten about Marie Corelli. There is no monument to her in Stratford-upon-Avon, and only the angel on the grave to mark where she lies. One can only remember with affection what this small, contentious and fiercely brave woman did to save Stratford from 'the vandals'. 'Marie Corelli' may not have existed, but whoever that woman was – Mary Mills, Minnie Mackay, Vivian Erle Clifford, Rose Trevor or Marie – she was entirely successful in her fight to 'be somebody'.

Her concerns were very much the concerns of today. She was worried about the lack of moral leadership among clergy and politicians and the bad example their laxity gave to the people. 'There is no real government in England at present, just as there is no real church. The government is made up of directly self-interested speculators and financiers rather than diplomatists, – the Church, for which our fore fathers fought, is yielding to the bribery of Rome. It is a time of Sham, – sham politics, and sham religion![1]

She was worried about the power of addiction, and the way in which this was encouraged by the addition of chemical substances to alcohol. 'If you feed a man on absinthe, he ends in a lunatic asylum; in the same way if you feed a man on doctored beer and adulterated whisky, you make him a criminal and the father of criminals.'[2] She abhorred smoking, especially among women, not because she thought it unhealthy but because she thought it unwomanly. 'The act of smoking in itself is not wrong – but the associations of the habit are unfit for womanhood.'[3] She deplored the way in which the press harassed her in their need to get a good story, and even more did she object to being chased for her photograph. She wrote to Watt on 8 October 1910: 'Please do not think me cowardly – but I have not the physical *strength* to stand the mean and despicable way these curs of the press are all again yapping at my heels. I am *so tired of it* – I really long to die and be out of it. Not even the commonest justice is accorded to me.'

In *The Silver Domino*, she had nothing good to say about 'Critics [who] have no time to read any finished and careful work – they seldom can do more than scan the first page and the last. I know this, being a critic myself, and I think it is a thousand pities authors should take any trouble to write a middle part to their stories.'[4] She believed society to be shallow and amoral, and tried to depict the perils of a decadent, money-driven world. 'The thoughts that are spreading in our nation today are not the thoughts that build up national welfare. They are thoughts of personal greed, personal amusement, personal advantage, sensuality and sin. . . . A great thought sows other great thoughts, – and evil thought sows a spreading crop of evil.'[5]

Marie was a strong, and often unacknowledged, feminist. 'Through all the ages, so far as the keenest explorer or historical student can discover, [man's] highest ideals of life have been depicted in the feminine form. Fortune, Fame, Justice, the Arts and Sciences, are all represented by female figures lovingly designed by male hands. . . . Faith, Hope and Charity, are represented as female spirits, as are the Three Graces. The Muses are women; so are the Fates. Hence, as all the virtues, morals, arts and sciences are shown by the highest masculine skill as wearing woman's form and possessing woman's attributes, it is easy to see that man has always been perfectly aware in his inward intelligence of woman's true worth and right place in creation, though, . . . he has put up whatever barriers he can in the way of the too swift advancement of so superior and victorious a creature. . . . Stop, oh Man! You have had a very long, long innings, remember! . . . It is now woman's turn to taste the sweets of freedom.'[6]

Some of her books, with their interminable sermons, are long-winded. They were written for a time when the pace of life was much slower and for a generation avid for inspirational works. But buried in the wordiness are many messages which are still very relevant today:

> The ponderous Law and the stolid Police hem us in on each side, as though the nation were a helpless infant toddling between two portly nurses, – we dare not denounce a scoundrel and a liar, but must needs put up with him lest we should be involved in an action for

libel; and we dare not knock down a vulgar bully, lest we should be given in charge for assault. . . . Society sits smirking foolishly on the top of a smouldering volcano, – and the chief Symbols of greatness among us, Religion, Poesy, Art, – are burning feebly as tapers in the catacombs, – the Church resembles a drudge, who tired of routine is gradually sinking into laziness and inertia, – and the Press! – ye gods! – the Press! . . . It is the veriest bound slave that was ever hampered by the chains of party prejudice, – and the only attempt at freedom it ever makes in its lower grades is an occasional outbreak into scurrility! And yet think what a majestic power for good the true, real Liberty of the Press might wield over the destinies of nations! Broadly viewed, the Press should be the strong, practical, helping right hand of civilization, dealing out equal justice, equal sympathy, equal instruction, – it should be fosterer of the arts and sciences, – the everyday guide of the morals and culture of the people. . . . It should be, – but what is it? Look round and judge for yourself.'[7]

She was a fearless fighter, who sometimes mistook her targets, but who fought with a passion which swept all before her. She came from nothing, and against huge odds became a superstar and one of the most famous women of her time. She lived in Victorian England and yet there is something very modern in the way in which she carefully created her image through selective publicity and so created her own legend. Numerous children were called after her heroine, Thelma, whose name she is said to have invented, and many of her mystical novels are very much in tune with today's interest in reincarnation and astral travelling.

She is an example of amazing courage and tenacity, and lived such an extraordinary life that not only does she command affectionate respect, but her work may now be reassessed in the context of the fast-changing Victorian and Edwardian world. The impetus of her writing carried all before it, and to use Wilde's phrase, she 'wrote at the top of her voice'. It may be a different voice for us today, but as a mirror of her time, she reflects the concerns of the generation for whom she wrote.

The Mystery of Marie Corelli's Birth

The mystery of Marie Corelli's birth remains, as she wished, unsolved, although by carefully following a trail of clues, some new facts have emerged. Marie said she was born on 1 May 1855, and though there is no reason to disbelieve her, there seems to be no record of this. There is a birth certificate for Isabella Mary, born on 27 April 1855, and registered in Turnham Green. The mother's name is Mary Mills and the father is unnamed. In 1945 this certificate, always thought to be genuine by Marie's lawyers, was rejected by the courts. There was no compulsion to record a birth, and strong reasons for not doing so if the child was illegitimate. Or if she was born overseas.

Marie Corelli's origins are so clouded by myths and lies that it would be helpful to take a brief look at Charles Mackay, who is generally thought to have adopted her at the age of three months, but who may have been her natural father. By the time Marie, then known as Mary or Minnie, became part of his household, he was a 41-year-old embittered and failing journalist. Mackay was born in Perth, Scotland, in 1814, the year before Waterloo, was first sent to school in London and then, when he was fourteen, went to school in Brussels, where his father now lived. When he was sixteen he became secretary to an old English gentleman, William Cockerill, to keep his accounts, answer his letters, and read French and English newspapers to him. Mr Cockerill lapsed into senility and Mackay, finding that there was little for him to do, began to write occasional verse for the *Brussels Telegraph*.

He returned to England in 1832 aged eighteen, determined to 'make his way in Literature and Journalism'. He spoke fluent French and German and could read Italian and Spanish. Some of these skills he passed on to Marie. That same year Charles Mackay met and married his first wife, Rosa Henrietta Vale. In 1833 Mackay began work for the *Sun*, a Liberal evening paper. A four-page newspaper was then 7*d* a copy; news was not for the poor. In 1835 Mackay and Thackeray competed for the position of sub-editor on the *Morning Chronicle* which specialised in publishing parliamentary business. Mackay was chosen and his duties consisted of collecting all the reports on Free Trade meetings. Also on the parliamentary staff of the newspaper was the young Charles Dickens. Mackay and Rosa had three sons and a daughter: Charles Bruce, born in 1833, George Eric born in 1835, Robert born in 1837, and Rosa born in 1838. By the time Mary/Minnie appeared in 1855, Charles and Robert were in Canada, Rosa was dead, and George Eric was in Italy.

In 1840 the Mackay family were living in London at 30 Burton Street, Burton Crescent, close to St Pancras Church and Tavistock Square. The census of 1841 shows that Charles Mackay, and his wife Rosa, were sharing the house with Charles's father, George; his stepmother, Susan; Robert, his son, who was four, and a Jane Mackay. Because of both his Scottish background and his London connections, Mackay acted as London agent to raise funds for the Scott Memorial in Edinburgh and was given the office of Honorary Secretary in February 1844. On 9 October of that year he wrote to tell Sir Thomas Lauder that he had left London and the *Morning Chronicle* and was now living in Glasgow, employed by the *Glasgow Argus*.[1]

In 1847 Charles Mackay, with his family, returned to London after working for only three years on the *Glasgow Argus*. It was the time of the Highland clearances and Mackay was dismissed from the newspaper after the *Argus* became involved in political controversy. In December 1847 he was invited to join the new *Daily Telegraph* which was established by Mr Herbert Ingram, proprietor of the *Illustrated London News*. That same year, in London, Jenny Lind, 'the Swedish Nightingale', created a sensation at Her Majesty's Theatre where a young Italian, Signor Corelli, was the second tenor. The theatre was manged by Benjamin Lumley, an old friend of Charles Mackay.

The *Daily Telegraph* folded, but the *Illustrated London News*, the first newspaper to consist mainly of pictures, appointed Charles Mackay in 1848 as political and literary editor. Mackay travelled much between 1851 and 1853, and it is during these years that he and Henry Russell wrote and presented an epic entertainment, *The Way West*, at Her Majesty's Theatre. The sets were painted by a young artist, Mr Mills. About this time Mackay was said to have met 'an imperfectly educated young person' by name of Kirtland, or Elizabeth Mary Mills, with whom it is alleged he had an affair. It is now that the mystery of Marie Corelli begins.

According to the 1851 census, 39-year-old Mackay was living at 21 Brecknock Crescent, Camden Town, with his wife Rosa, his fourteen-year-old son Robert and his daughter Rosa Jane, aged twelve. The two eldest boys were at school in Inverness. There were also two servants, Caroline Channing and Ellen Carpenter. Close by in Camden Town at 37 Gloucester Street (now the northern part of Albert Street) lived Mrs John Kirtland, aged sixty-five, with a married daughter, 32-year-old Mary Walker, and Mary's younger husband, 24-year-old Mathew Walker. There was an elderly general servant, Mary Jones, who had been the children's nurse. There is no mention of the other daughter, 22-year-old Elizabeth Mary Mills, who Mackay is said to have met in about 1852.

Mackay and his wife Rosa Henrietta separated in 1853 for reasons unknown, but it was alleged that Mackay was having an affair with Elizabeth Mary Mills. Some confusion comes from Elizabeth Mary Mills's real name. In the *Post Office Directories* she is called Ellen; Mackay addresses her as Nellie in a poem he wrote to her in 1858; on a marriage certificate she is Elizabeth Mary, and on her death certificate she is called Ellen which is then crossed out and Elizabeth Mary written in below. Having wondered if she was two people, this late double entry makes it seem as though Elizabeth Mary and Ellen were one and the same. Later gossip from Stratford-upon-Avon suggested that two men had been involved with this flirtatious lady and when she was discovered to be pregnant, drew lots to see who would pay the expenses of the confinement. Mackay lost; which may have been the reason why he then left the family home in 1854 and moved to a handsome house at 40 Camden Square, considerably closer to Mrs Mills.

A girl was born on 1 May 1855. She was named Mary, and later became Marie Corelli. Her mother is unknown, but was possibly Elizabeth Mary/Ellen Mills. By 1856 Ellen was installed at 24 Gloucester Crescent, almost next door to her mother, Mrs Kirtland, who was still at 37 Gloucester Street on the north-east corner of Regents Park.

Having settled Ellen and the child, Mackay continued to travel – first with Mr Ingram to Scotland in 1856 to collect material for his songs, and again to America for eighteen months in October 1857, 'to narrate his impressions in a series of letters to the *Illustrated London News,* and to deliver a series of lectures on poetry and song'. He was given letters of introduction by Mr Thackeray, and later published his experiences in a book, *Life and Liberty in America.*[2] In February 1858 Charles Mackay, still married to Rosa, wrote a Valentine poem to Ellen/Nellie from New Orleans:

All these I miss this pleasant day;
All these and something more divine –
Thy smile, dear Nellie, far away,
Thy hand, sweetheart, to clasp in mine;
The voice oft heard from lips of thine,
That breathes the words 'tis joy to hear
Even in remembrance – Wanting these
I bless the skies so balmy clear,
The heath, and gladness on the breeze;
But miss my joy beyond the sea,
And pine for England and for thee.[3]

On 25 February the same year Mackay wrote another poem from America for three-year-old Mary, entitled 'The Wayside Spring in Alabama' which he sent to a Mr Henry, with a note in the corner saying 'please to read and punctuate carefully. Mr Henry to preserve the copy and return to C.M.' It was published in its corrected form in 1859 in *Life and Liberty in America*, the account of his American tour, but in the original handwritten copy, kept by Bertha, there is one very important line which was changed before publication:

To what shall I compare thee
For the love I bear thee
On this sunny day,
Bonnie little burnie
Gushing by the way?

Like the heart's romances,
Like a poet's fancies,
Like a lover's visions
Of the bliss to be,
Like a little daughter's daughter,
[changed to] –
Like a little maiden,
Crowned with summers three
Romping in the sunshine
Beautiful to see –[4]

The changed line for his 'daughter's daughter' is heavily scored out, but the poem was carefully stuck into Bertha's scrapbook which shows that some pains had been taken to preserve it. Could this mean that Marie Corelli was Charles Mackay's granddaughter rather than his natural daughter?

From this fascinating, but otherwise uncorroborated, evidence comes another possible solution to Mary/Minnie's origins. Mackay in his recollections says his daughter, Rosa, died in Italy from a fever at the age of seventeen. This would have been in 1855, the year of Mary/Minnie's birth. There is no record of where Rosa's mother, Rosa Henrietta, lived after her separation from Mackay and it is possible that she went to Italy with Eric and her daughter. If Rosa became pregnant and died from fever after childbirth, then Marie's claim to have an Italian father and a Scottish mother is acceptable. It is possible that Mrs Ellen Mills, née Kirtland, was engaged to care for the baby in a separate establishment provided by Mackay. It was common practice in France for a baby to be reared by a foster mother for the first four years of its life, away from its natural parents. There is no evidence, apart from the poem, to support this theory.

What happened to the little girl from the time of her birth in 1855 until 1871? From Mackay's own autobiography some new facts have emerged: some small pieces to help with the jigsaw of Marie Corelli's childhood.

Mackay returned from his tour of America in June 1858 to his home at 40 Camden Square, but by 1859 had moved temporarily to 64 Lincoln's Inn Fields. Ellen Mills had moved from 24 Gloucester Crescent to Avenue Road, just north of Regents Park. The little girl would have been four. On 28 November 1859, Mackay's estranged wife Rosa, aged forty-three, died from 'a head affection following Scarlet Fever' at 10 Cecil Street, off St Martin's Lane in the Strand.

Mackay left the *Illustrated London News* in 1859 when it was about to be sold, and made plans to set up his own weekly paper, the *London Review*. On 20 July 1860 this new paper was inaugurated at a dinner at the Reform Club. It was advertised as 'The London Review and weekly journal of Politics, Literature, Art and Society. Conducted by Charles Mackay LLD. A thoroughly original journal and complete record of the events and opinions of the day with first class literature adapted for the homes of the empire.'[5] The paper was founded with five partners, and it was not a happy collaboration. Against Mackay's advice, three-fifths of the capital was spent on advertising, and without sufficient funds to support it the paper collapsed within six months. Mackay then went on to found a fiction magazine *Robin Goodfellow* with John Maxwell. They were desperate for a serial for the first issue and Mary Elizabeth Bradden, who though unmarried was living with Maxwell and was about to bear his child, wrote throughout the night to produce the first instalment of *Lady Audley's Secret*. After only twelve issues, *Robin Goodfellow* failed in September 1861. *Lady Audley's Secret* was completed for another magazine and was so popular that it was printed by the Tinsley Brothers in the three-volume format.

With his wife now dead, and having observed the customary year of mourning, Mackay could marry Mrs Mills and provide a proper home for the little girl. The wedding took place on 27 February 1861 at the Register Office in Marylebone where Charles Mackay, forty-eight, son of George Mackay (deceased), Officer Royal Artillery, married Mary Elizabeth Mills, thirty, widow and daughter of John Kirtland (deceased), gentleman. 'It is a small and humble marriage, plain and unpretentious in all its incidents and accessories, and takes place in a Registry Office, before an attorney-like functionary and his clerk. The two witnesses are all but unknown to the bridegroom and the bride, casual acquaintances, in fact, who take the slightest and most perfunctory interest in the shabby ceremonial. . . . The Marriage is intended to be private, if not secret, and is quite as secret as the law allows it to be.'[6]

Charles Mackay's address is now given as 18 Avenue Road, Regents Park, and Elizabeth Mary/Ellen's address on the marriage certificate, as Croydon, Surrey, which is not far from Box Hill. This is where, according to Mackay's poem, 'The Swing on the Apple Tree at Fern Dell', he first met her in 1853. It is interesting to note that the Croydon Directories, of both 1850 and 1855, list an Elizabeth Mills, laundress, married to Nathaniel Mills, labourer, living at 58 Mitcham Road, Croydon. It is now that the trail goes cold. Strangely, the three vital entries in the census taken in April 1861, which should reveal where, and with whom, young Mary Mills was living, are all missing from the census records.

In 1861 Charles Mackay is recorded as living at 18 Avenue Road, Regents Park, with two nineteen-year-old servants. He has been married for two months but there is no mention of Elizabeth Mary or of young Mary/Minnie. His other given address, at 64 Lincoln's Inn Fields, is noted as missing from the census records. For the same census Mrs Kirtland is living at 8 Gloucester Place, Camden Town. There are records for nos 1–5 and 31–38 Gloucester Place, but the other house numbers, including no. 8, are listed as missing. Ellen Mills was living at 24

Gloucester Crescent in 1856 and 1857 and thereafter a Mrs Mills is listed at 19 Avenue Road, Regents Park. In the 1861 census the records for both these addresses are missing. Elizabeth Mary/Ellen Mills and six-year-old Mary/Minnie, unbelievably, have not been found on any census for 1861. The first verifiable record of Marie's existence is in the 1871 census, by which time she was sixteen years old.

Some tantalising leads have been uncovered, many of which seem to point to a possible solution to Mary/Minnie's identity, but which are insufficient as evidence without further corroboration.

What we do know is that the child was brought up by Charles Mackay as his adopted daughter, and that Elizabeth Mary/Ellen became Mackay's wife in 1861. Who was Elizabeth Mary/Ellen Mills, with whom Mackay had an affair at Fern Dell? Was she the laundress from Croydon, or, as seems more likely, was she the wife of his colleague, the scenic artist, Mr Mills? Was Marie the result of this liaison?

If not, was there a connection between the tenor, Signor Corelli, and Mackay's daughter, Rosa Jane? Her Majesty's Theatre closed from 1852 to 1856 largely due to financial problems caused by competition from the new Italian Opera Theatre at Covent Garden, and Corelli may have returned to Italy. Rosa Jane, according to Mackay, died there from a fever in 1855, the year of Marie's birth, and there is that revealing line in his poem to 'a little daughter's daughter'.

Marie always maintained that she had an Italian father. She sent Bentley a copy of a letter from the Queen of Italy, written in 1886, which mentioned an Italian godmother. Marie herself talked of an Italian godfather, and an old uncle in Italy who supplied her with money. In Marie's Stratford-upon-Avon house there was a signed portrait from the Queen of Italy. Was this part of Marie's invented past, or was she descended from Italian nobility? Was Marie Mackay's adopted daughter, illegitimate daughter, or granddaughter? Did Mackay marry Elizabeth Mary/Ellen to give Marie a stable home, or because he was the father of her child? Or was Marie, in truth, left on his doorstep one snowy winter's night?

Marie's possible origins are as fanciful as any of her romances, and all remains speculation. It seems that until some further evidence can be uncovered, the mystery of her birth will remain unsolved. As Bertha said – 'What Marie left sealed, shall remain sealed.'

Notes

INTRODUCTION

1 Marie Corelli, *Free Opinions*, Constable, London, 1905, pp. 235, 237
2 Ibid., pp. 176, 178
3 Anon. (Marie Corelli), *The Silver Domino*, Lamley, 1892, p. 100
4 Ibid., p. 97
5 Marie Corelli, *Free Opinions*, p. 136
6 Ibid., p. 119
7 Ibid., pp. 303, 309

CHAPTER 1

1 Shakespeare Birthplace Trust, Records Office (SBTRO), Marie Corelli Papers, n.d.
2 UCLA, Papers of Marie Corelli, Collection 748, Box 2
3 Ibid.
4 Marie Corelli, *Innocent*, Hodder & Stoughton, 1914, p. 60
5 Charles Mackay, *Forty Years Recollections of Life, Literature and Public Affairs from 1830–1870*, Chapman & Hall, London, 1877, vol. 2, p. 303
6 Ibid., vol. 2, p. 216
7 Ibid., vol. 2, p. 314
8 *Daily Mail*, 26 July 1924
9 Charles Mackay, *Gossamer and Snowdrift*, 1890, p. 39
10 Bertha Vyver, *Memoirs of Marie Corelli*, Alston Rivers, London, 1930, extracts pp. 29, 31

11 Marie Corelli, *The Sorrows of Satan*, OUP, 1996, p. 320
12 UCLA, Letters to Herbert Halliwell Hobbes, Collection 748, Box 2
13 SBTRO, Marie Corelli Papers, Scrapbook
14 Kent Carr, *Marie Corelli*, Henry Drane, London, 1901, p. 14
15 Bertha Vyver, *Memoirs*, p. 15
16 Ibid., pp. 34, 35, 36
17 Ibid., p. 19
18 Ibid., p. 11
19 SBTRO, DR904/1
20 Marie Corelli, *The Young Diana*, Hutchinson, 7th edn, 1953, p. 255
21 Marie Corelli, unpublished MS written at Fern Dell, n.d.
22 *Daily Mail*, 28 April 1926
23 National Library of Scotland, Blackwood Papers, MS 4322
24 Ibid.
25 Ibid.
26 MS 4335
27 Ibid.
28 Ibid.
29 Ibid.
30 National Library of Scotland, Blackwood Papers, MS 4422
31 Kent Carr, *Marie Corelli*, pp. 16, 17
32 Bertha Vyver, *Memoirs*, p. 146
33 Kent Carr, *Marie Corelli*, p. 21
34 Ibid., p. 23
35 T.P. O'Connor, *Daily Telegraph*, 22 April 1924
36 National Library of Scotland, Blackwood Papers, MS 4422

37 UCLA, Clement Scott, Collection 737

38 *Manchester City News*, 3 May 1924

39 'A Londoner's Diary', *Evening Standard*, 22 April 1924

40 Marie Corelli, *A Romance of Two Worlds*, Bentley & Son, 14th edn, 1896, p. 84

41 Bertha Vyver, *Memoirs*, p. 50

42 Marie Corelli, *A Romance of Two Worlds*, p. 268

43 UCLA, Papers of Marie Corelli, Collection 748, Box 2

44 *Manchester City News*, 3 May 1924

45 Marie Corelli, *Innocent*, Hodder & Stoughton, London, 1914, p. 213

46 Ibid., p. 186

CHAPTER 2

1 T.E.G. Coates and R.S. Warren-Bell, *Marie Corelli*, Hutchinson, London, 1903, p. 38

2 Marie Corelli, *The Sorrows of Satan*, p. 28

3 Marie Corelli, *A Romance of Two Worlds*, p. 113

4 Bertha Vyver, *Memoirs*, p. 58

5 Marie Corelli, *A Romance of Two Worlds*, Introduction

6 Ibid., p. 3

7 Ibid., p. 163

8 Ibid., p. 174

9 Ibid., p. 192

10 Ibid., pp. 232, 235

11 Ibid., p. 132

12 Ibid., p. 195

13 Ibid., p. 323

14 Charles Mackay, *Forty Years Recollections . . .*, 1877, vol. 1, pp. 313, 318.

15 Bertha Vyver, *Memoirs*, p. 56

16 Coates and Warren-Bell, *Marie Corelli*, Hutchinson, 1903, p. 41

17 Marie Corelli, *Vendetta*, Methuen, 8th edn, 1893, p. 1

18 Ibid., p. 2

19 Ibid., p. 206

20 Marie Corelli, *A Romance of Two Worlds*, p. 126

21 Bertha Vyver, *Memoirs*, p. 66

22 Ibid., p. 74

23 Marie Corelli, *A Romance of Two Worlds*, pp. 94, 121

24 Frances Power Cobbe, 'The Little Health of Ladies', *Contemporary Review*, 1878

25 Marie Corelli, *Thelma*, Methuen, London, 17th edn, 1897, p. 284

26 Ibid., p. 286

27 Ibid., p. 356

28 Marie Corelli, *Ardath*, Methuen, London, 29th edn, 1953, p. 208

29 Ibid., p. 242

30 Ibid., p. 448

31 Ibid., p. 477

32 Ibid., p. 488

33 Marie Corelli, *The Life Everlasting*, Methuen, London, 1911, p. 270

CHAPTER 3

1 Bertha Vyver, *Memoirs*, p. 96

2 UCLA, Papers of Marie Corelli, Box 1

3 SBTRO, Marie Corelli Letters

4 Bertha Vyver, *Memoirs*, p. 90

5 Ibid., p. 88

6 Marie Corelli, *The Sorrows of Satan*, p. 56

7 British Library, Manuscript Department, Gladstone Papers, 44507, ff. 3

8 Bertha Vyver, *Memoirs*, 1930, pp. 106, 107

9 Anon (Marie Corelli), *The Silver Domino*, 1893, pp. 109, 123

10 Bertha Vyver, *Memoirs*, pp. 104, 105

11 Marie Corelli, *The Sorrows of Satan*, p. 66

12 Marie Corelli, *My Wonderful Wife. A Study in Smoke*, F.V. White & Co., 1889, p. 53

13 Ibid., pp. 107, 111

14 Marie Corelli, *Free Opinions*, p. 169

15 Bertha Vyver, *Memoirs*, p. 110

16 Michael Sadleir, *The Camel's Back*, *XIX Essays*, OUP

17 British Library, Manuscript Department, Gladstone Papers 44507

18 National Library of Scotland, Blackwood Papers, MS 4322

19 SBTRO, Bertha's Letter Book

20 Marie Corelli, *The Master Christian*, Methuen, London, 1900, p. 89

21 Marie Corelli, *Wormwood*, Bentley & Son, London, 1891, p. 472

22 Bertha Vyver, *Memoirs*, p. 377

23 Marie Corelli, *The Soul of Lilith*, Methuen, 25th edn, 1952, p. 318

24 Marie Corelli, *A Romance of Two Worlds*, p. 136

25 Marie Corelli, *The Soul of Lilith*, p. 319

26 George Bullock, *The Life and Death of a Best-Seller*, 1940, p. 114

27 *Strand Magazine*, pp. 34–43

28 UCLA, Papers of Marie Corelli, Collection 748, Box 2

CHAPTER 4

1 Bertha Vyver, *Memoirs*, p. 120

2 Ibid., p. 122

3 Ibid., p. 124

4 Ibid., pp. 120–6

5 Marie Corelli, *Temporal Power*, Methuen, 9th edn, 1964, pp. 4, 5

6 Ibid., p. 13

7 Ibid., p. 60

8 Ibid., p. 386

9 Ibid., p. 541

10 Ibid., p. 479

11 Bertha Vyver, *Memoirs*, p. 118

12 Anon. (M.C.), *The Silver Domino*, p. 345

13 William Rothenstein, *Men and Memoirs*, London, Faber & Faber, 1931

14 Anon. (M.C.), *The Silver Domino*, p. 18

15 Ibid., p. 56

16 Ibid., p. 215

17 Ibid., p. 362

18 Marie Corelli, *Barabbas*, Methuen, London, 41st edn, 1906, pp 189, 216

19 Ibid., p. 20

20 Bertha Vyver, *Memoirs*, p. 128

21 Ibid., p. 130

22 Ibid., pp. 131, 132

23 Marie Corelli, *The Sorrows of Satan*, p. 261

24 British Library, Bentley Papers, 46646/225, 226, 238

25 Ibid., 46646/299

CHAPTER 5

1 Marie Corelli, *The Sorrows of Satan*, p. 3

2 Ibid., p. 54

3 Ibid., p. 139

4 Ibid., pp. 352, 253

5 Bertha Vyver, *Memoirs*, pp. 139, 140

6 New York Public Library(NYPL), Berg Collection.

7 Ibid.

8 Marie Corelli, *Delicia*, Constable, London, 1907, Introduction, p. viii

9 Ibid., p. ix

10 Ibid., p. 144

11 UCLA, Letters, Collection 748, Box 2

12 *Daily Mail*, 18 March 1898

13 UCLA, Letters to Marie Corelli, Collection 748

14 Ibid.

15 Ibid.

16 Arthur Lawrence, 'Illustrated Interviews LIX, Marie Corelli', *Strand Magazine*, 1898, pp. 17–26

17 UCLA, Letters to Coulson Kernahan, Collection 748, Box 2

CHAPTER 6

1 UCLA, Letters, Collection 748

2 Ruth Ellis, *The Shakespeare Memorial Theatre*, London, 1949

3 UCLA, Letters to Herbert Halliwell Hobbes, Collection 748, Box 2

4 Bertha Vyver, *Memoirs*, pp. 167, 168

5 Marie Corelli, *Boy*, Hutchinson, London, 1900, p. 303

6 Ibid., pp. 337, 338

7 Bertha Vyver, *Memoirs*, p. 149

8 Marie Corelli, *The Master Christian*, p. 10

9 Ibid., p. 134

10 Ibid., p. 395

11 Ibid., p. 622

12 Bertha Vyver, *Memoirs*, p. 154

13 UCLA, Marie Corelli Letters to Cuming Walters, Collection 748, Box 1

14 *Daily Mail*, 5 November 1900, letter from Marie Corelli

15 SBTRO, Mary Hutchings' Scrapbook

16 UCLA, Letters to Herbert Halliwell Hobbes, Collection 748, Box 2

17 Marie Corelli, 'The Vanishing Gift', *Free Opinions*, pp. 275, 288

18 UCLA, Letters to Cuming Walters, Collection 748, Box 1

19 M.E. Sadler, *A Memoir*, London, Constable, 1949

20 Ursula Bloom, *Rosemary for Stratford-on-Avon*, Robert Hale, 1966, pp. 61–4

21 Marie Corelli, *God's Good Man*, Methuen, London, 1904, p. 269

22 Marie Corelli, *The Passing of the Great Queen*, Methuen, 1901, p. 5

23 Ibid., p. 33

24 *The Gentlewoman*, October 1902

25 UCLA, Letters to J. Cuming Walters, Collection 748, Box 1

26 UCLA, Letters to Herbert Halliwell Hobbes, Collection 748, Box 2

27 *Stratford-upon-Avon Herald*, 23 January 1903

CHAPTER 7

1 Marie Corelli, *The Plain Truth*, Methuen, London, 1903, p. 4

2 Marie Corelli, *The Avon Star*, A.J. Stanley, 1903, p. 70

3 Ibid., p 81

4 Ibid.

5 SBTRO, Mary Hutchings' Scrapbook

6 Marie Corelli, *The Plain Truth*, p. 23
7 Ibid., p. 17
8 Bertha Vyver, *Memoirs*, p. 192
9 Marie Corelli, *The Plain Truth*, p. 28
10 Ibid., p. 41
11 Ibid.
12 SBTRO, ER 85/1/1/1
13 Marie Corelli, *The Plain Truth*, p. 46
14 SBTRO, Marie Corelli Papers
15 UCLA, Letters to Cuming Walters, Collection 748, Box 1
16 Ibid.
17 SBTRO, Annie Davis, court transcript of evidence
18 Ibid.
19 *Stratford-upon-Avon Herald*, 18 December 1903

11 Ibid., 4 November 1907
12 Ibid., 1906
13 Ibid., February 1905
14 Ibid., 29 June 1906
15 SBTRO, DR 904/2
16 Marie Corelli, *Treasure of Heaven*, Constable, London, 1906, p. 195
17 NYPL, Berg Collection, Letters to A.P. Watt & Son
18 Elinor Glyn, *Memoirs*
19 NYPL, Berg Collection, Letters to A.P. Watt & Son
20 NYPL, Berg Collection, Field Roscoe & Co. Ltd to A.P. Watt & Son
21 SBTRO, *Corelli Papers*, ed. James Knowles
22 NYPL, Berg Collection, A.P. Watt & Son to Field Roscoe & Co.

CHAPTER 8

1 Marie Corelli, *A Romance of Two Worlds*, p. 86
2 Marie Corelli, *Pagan London*, 22 June 1904, p. 133
3 Marie Corelli, *God's Good Man*, Methuen, London, 12th edn, 1907, p. 135
4 Ibid., p. 476
5 Ibid., p. 501
6 Marie Corelli, *Free Opinions*, p. 320
7 W. Stuart Scott, *Marie Corelli, The Story of a Friendship*, Hutchinson, 1955, p. 173
8 Marie Corelli, 'The Happy Life', *Strand Magazine*, July 1904, p. 75
9 W. Stuart Scott, *Marie Corelli*, pp 111, 112
10 NYPL, Berg Collection, Letters to A.P. Watt & Son

CHAPTER 9

1 Marie Corelli, *Delicia*, p. 150
2 UCLA, Marie Corelli Letters, Box 1
3 Ibid.
4 NYPL, Berg Collection, Letters to A.P. Watt & Son
5 Ibid.
6 Marie Corelli, *Holy Orders*, Methuen, London, 1908, Preface pp. vii, viii
7 Ibid., p. 15
8 Ibid., p. 80
9 Ibid., p. 337
10 NYPL, Berg Collection, Letters to A.P. Watt & Son
11 Ibid.
12 SBTRO, Annie Davis Papers
13 UCLA, Marie Corelli to J.C. Walters, Collection 748, Box 1

14 SBTRO, Annie Davis Papers
15 *The Bookman*, May 1909, pp. 59–75
16 UCLA, Marie Corelli Letters, Collection 748, Box 2

CHAPTER 10

1 Marie Corelli, *Delicia*, p. 129
2 UCLA, Letters to Halliwell Hobbes, Collection 748, Box 2
3 Marie Corelli, *Open Confession*, Hutchinson, London, 1925, pp. 2, 3, 8, 9
4 Ibid., p. 26
5 Ibid., pp. 31, 32
6 Ibid., p. 28
7 SBTRO, Annie Davis Papers
8 Marie Corelli, *The Life Everlasting*, Methuen, London, 17th edn, 1954, Prologue, p. 25
9 Ibid., p. 26
10 Ibid., p. 65
11 Ibid., p. 121
12 Ibid., p. 150
13 Ibid., p. 168
14 Ibid., p. 194
15 Ibid., p. 271
16 Ibid., p. 408
17 SBTRO, Annie Davis Papers
18 Ada Holman, *My Wander Year*, Sydney, 1914, pp. 100–6
19 Marie Corelli, *Open Confession*, p. 95
20 Ibid., pp. 107, 108
21 Ibid., pp. 154, 155
22 Ibid., p. 161
23 SBTRO, *Corelli Papers*, ed. James Knowles, April 1994
24 Marie Corelli, *Open Confession*, p. 181
25 Marie Corelli, *Poems*, Hutchinson, 1925, p. 67

CHAPTER 11

1 Bertha Vyver, *Memoirs*, pp. 215, 216
2 SBTRO, Annie Davis Papers
3 Annie E. Davis, *Avon Arrows*, Fortune Press, 1950, p. 32
4 Marie Corelli, *Innocent*, 1914, pp. 51, 107
5 Ibid., pp. 73, 74, 75
6 Ibid., p. 254
7 Ibid., p. 265
8 Ibid., p. 270
9 Ibid., p. 282
10 Ibid., p. 355
11 Ibid., p. 396
12 SBTRO, Marie Corelli Letters
13 Marie Corelli, 'The Savage Glory', *My Little Bit*, Collins, 1919, pp. 3, 4
14 Ibid., p. 52
15 Ibid., p. 244
16 SBTRO, Marie Corelli Letters
17 *Strand Magazine*, June 1925
18 W. Stuart Scott, *Marie Corelli*, 1955, pp. 72, 75, 76
19 SBTRO, *Corelli Papers*, ed. James Knowles
20 Marie Corelli, *The Young Diana*, Hutchinson, 1918, pp. 151, 152
21 Ibid., pp. 203, 208
22 Marie Corelli, *The Secret Power*, Methuen, London, 1921, pp. 131, 132

CHAPTER 12

1 Marie Corelli, *Is All Well with England?*, Jarrolds, London, 1919, pp. 25, 25
2 UCLA, Letters from J.Cuming Walters, Collection 748, Box 1
3 SBTRO, Letters, DR627/1–16

4 *The Times*, 23 April 1924

5 UCLA, Letters to Cuming Walters,
Collection 748, Box 1

6 Ibid.

7 Bertha Vyver, *Memoirs*, p. 241

8 George Bullock, *The Life and
Death of a Best-Seller*, Constable,
1940, p. 262

9 NYPL, Berg Collection, Letters
between Brentnall and Watt

10 Ibid.

11 Ibid.

12 Ibid.

13 Ibid.

14 W. Stuart Scott, *Marie Corelli*, p.
217

15 NYPL, Berg Collection, Letters
from Brentnall, Watt & Medley,
Folders 1–6

AFTERWORD

1 Marie Corelli, *Temporal Power*,
p. 151

2 Marie Corelli, *Holy Orders*, p. 457

3 Marie Corelli, *God's Good Man*,
p. 438

4 Anon, (M.C.), *The Silver Domino*,
p. 190

5 Marie Corelli, *Holy Orders*, pp. 515,
516

6 Marie Corelli, *Free Opinions*,
pp. 172, 174

7 Marie Corelli, *Ardath*, p. 493

APPENDIX

1 Scottish National Library,
Advocates MSS, Letters, 15974,
ff. 136

2 Charles Mackay, *Forty Years
Recollections . . .*, 1877, vol. 2, p.
376.

3 Charles Mackay, *Interludes and
Undertones*, London, 1884, p. 22

4 SBTRO, Bertha's Letter Book

5 *Illustrated London News*, 1860

6 Charles Mackay, *The Twin Soul*,
London, 1887, vol. 2,
p. 167

Bibliography

Bigland, Eileen, *Marie Corelli, the Woman and the Legend: A Biography*, Jarrolds, 1953

Bloom, J. Harvey, *The Errors of the Avon Star*, 1903

Bloom, Ursula, *The Elegant Edwardians*, Hutchinson, 1957

——, *Parson Extraordinary*, Robert Hale, 1963

——, *Rosemary for Stratford-on-Avon*, Robert Hale, 1966

——, *Life Is No Fairy Tale*, Robert Hale, 1976

Briggs, Asa, *A Social History of England*, BCA, 1994

Bullock, George, *Marie Corelli, The Life and Death of a Best-Seller*, London, Constable & Co. Ltd, 1940

Carr, Kent, *Miss Marie Corelli*, Henry J. Drane, 1901

Caine, Barbara, *Victorian Feminists*, Oxford University Press, 1992

Carruthers, Robert, LLD, *The Highland Notebook* 1843, new edn 1887, printed at the Courier office, Inverness.

Coates, Thomas F.G. Bell, R.S.W., *Marie Corelli, The Writer and the Woman*, Hutchinson, 1903

Ellis, Ruth, *The Stratford Memorial Theatre*, London, Winchester Publications Ltd, 1949

Forster, Margaret, *Significant Sisters*, London, Secker & Warburg, 1984

Giffin, Michael, *The Greater Tradition, Literature, Religion and the Western Eye*, unpublished ms

Grierson, Edward, *Storm Bird, the Strange Life of G. Weldon*, Chatto & Windus, 1959

Glyn, Anthony, *Elinor Glyn*, London, Hutchinson

Glyn, Elinor, *Three Weeks*, Virago, 1996

John, Alun, *The Corelli Comeback. A Turbulent Tale of Literary Revival*, radio play, broadcast on the Midland Home Service, 1 December 1955

Kernahan, Coulson, *Celebrities, Little Stories about Famous Folk*, 1936

Lumley, Benjamin, *Reminiscences of the Opera*, London, Hurst & Blackett, 1864

Mackay, Charles, *Voices from the Crowd and Other Poems*, London, 1846

——, *Memoirs of Extraordinary Popular Delusions and the Madness of Crowds*, London, 1852

——, *The Lump of Gold and Other Poems*, London, 1856

——, *Life & Liberty in America*, Smith, Elder & Co, 1859

——, *The Far West, or the Emigrants Progress, a Vocal and Pictorial Entertainment*, John R. Chapman & Company, 185-?

——, *Under Green Leaves*, London, Routledge & Co., 1857

——, *Voices from the Crowd*, London, Routledge & Co., 1857

——, *A Man's Heart*, London, Smith & Elder, 1860

——, *Under the Blue Sky*, London, Low & Searl, 1871

——, *Forty Years Recollections of Life, Literature and Public Affairs from 1830–1870*, London, Chapman & Hall, 1877

——, *Interludes and Undertones*, London, Chatto & Windus, 1884

——, *The Twin Soul, The Strange Experiences of Mr Rameses* (2 vols), London, 1887

——, *Through the Long Day*, London, W.H. Allen & Co., 1887

——, *Gossamer and Snowdrift*, London, George Allen, 1890

Masters, Brian, *Now Barabbas was a Rotter*, Hamish Hamilton, 1978

Mitchell, Virginia, *Thelma*, dramatised from the novel by Marie Corelli, a comedy-drama, in three acts, London, Samuel French, 1941

Pearson, Hesketh, *The Life of Henry Labouchere*, London, Hamish Hamilton, 1936

Russell, Henry, *Cheer! Boys, Cheer!*, John Macqueen, Strand, 1895

Scharlieb, Mary Ann Dacomb, *Reminiscences, 1845–1930*, London, Williams & Norgate, 1924

Scott, William Stuart, *Marie Corelli, The Story of a Friendship*, Hutchinson, 1955

Steen, Marguerite, *Looking Glass*, London, Longmans, 1966

Trehearne, Philip, *A Plaintiff in Person. Life of Mrs Weldon*, London, William Heinemann, 1923

Van der Vyver, P.F.A., *Henrietta's Promise*, London, Simpkin, Marshall & Co., 1882

Vyver, Bertha, *Memoirs of Marie Corelli*, Alston Rivers, 1930

Weldon, Georgina, *Musical Reform*, 1875

——, *The History of my Orphanage, Or, The Outpourings of an Alleged Lunatic: A Pamphlet*, 1878

Other Sources

British Library, Manuscripts Department

New York Public Library

Berg Collection of English and American Literature, Astor, Lenox and Tilden Foundations

National Library of Scotland, Manuscripts Department

Shakespeare Birthplace Trust Record Office, Stratford-on-Avon

University of California, Los Angeles, Department of Special Collections, Charles E. Young Research Library

The Bookman, 1909

The Bystander, 1904

Ladies Realm, 1897

London Opinion, 1906

Bibliography

Longman's Magazine, 1904
Printers Pie, 1906
The Rapid Review, 1904, 1906
The Times, various
Truth, 1912
The Strand Magazine, 1898
The Writer, 1901

Marie Corelli's books dated in chronological order, with the edition and date referred to in the text

1886 *The Romance of Two Worlds*, 2 vols, London, Richard Bentley & Son
1886 *Vendetta*, London, Richard Bentley & Son, 8th edn, 1893
1887 *Thelma*, London, Richard Bentley & Son, 42nd edn, Methuen's Colonial Library, 1911
1889 *Ardath*, 1896, London, Bentley & Son, 29th edn, 1953, Methuen
1890 *Wormwood*, London, Richard Bentley & Son, 27th edn, Methuen, 1962
1892 *The Soul of Lilith*, London, Richard Bentley & Son, 24th edn, Methuen, 1930
1892 *The Silver Domino*, London, Lamley and Co.
1893 *Barabbas*, Sydney & Brisbane, Australasian edn, Edwards Dunlop, 1894
1895 *The Sorrows of Satan*, Oxford University Press, 1996
1896 *The Mighty Atom*, London, Hutchinson & Co, 48th edn, London, Methuen, 1960
1896 *Cameos*, Hutchinson & Co., 17th edn, London, Methuen, 1919
1897 *Ziska, The Problem of a Wicked Soul*, Bristol, Arrowsmith, London, Methuen, 1960
1900 *Boy*, London, Hutchinson
1900 *Jane*, London, Hutchinson
1900 *Delicia*, London, Constable, 1907 edn
1900 *The Master Christian*, London, Methuen, 24th edn, 1954
1902 *Temporal Power*, London, Methuen, 9th edn, 1954
1904 *God's Good Man*, London, Methuen, 28th edn, 1953
1905 *Free Opinions Freely Expressed*, London, Constable
1906 *Treasure of Heaven*, London, Constable, 1939
1908 *Holy Orders*, London, Methuen's Colonial Library
1910 *The Devil's Motor*, illustrated by Arthur Severn, London, Hodder & Stoughton
1911 *The Life Everlasting*, Alhambra, California, Bordern Publishing Co., 1966
1914 *Innocent*, London, Hodder & Stoughton
1918 *The Young Diana*, London, Hutchinson, 7th edn, 1953
1919 *My Little Bit*, London, W. Collins & Sons
1920 *The Love of Long Ago*, London, Methuen

1921 *The Secret Power*, London, Methuen
1923 *Love and the Philosopher*, London, Methuen
1925 *Poems*, London, Hutchinson
1925 *Open Confession, to a Man from a Woman*, London, Hutchinson

Articles and pamphlets by Marie Corelli

1889 *My Wonderful Wife. A Study in Smoke*, London, F.V. White & Co
1896 *The Modern Marriage Market*
1903 *The Avon Star*, Stratford-on-Avon, Stanley
1903 *The Plain Truth of the Stratford-on-Avon Controversy*, with illustrations, London, Methuen & Co.
1907 *Woman, or – Suffragette? A Question of National Choice*, London
1913 *The Marie Corelli Calendar. Quotation for Every Day*, selected by E.M. Evans, London, Frank Palmer
1919 *Is All Well With England? A Question*, London, Jarrolds

Index